Advance Praise

Based on a rigorous research, this book offers a credible explanation of the way job search and hiring practices work in India's urban labour market for formal employment, which may be a small one but it is where people seeking jobs aspire to be. It is also an arena where discrimination is a fact of life often camouflaged in the name of merit, resulting in inequality of not only wages but also employment and finally of opportunities. I recommend the book not only to students of labour economics but also to a wider audience of informed citizens, given the political importance of the findings contained in this book.

—K.P. Kannan,
Former Director and Honorary Fellow,
Centre for Development Studies, Thiruvananthapuram

This is a highly insightful book examining the way in which generations-old inequalities by caste, ethnicity and religion interact with modern labour markets to reshape the opportunity structures in contemporary India. Its primary strength lies in its careful examination of job search strategies and the processes through which employers choose to interview and hire some candidates while excluding others.

—Sonalde Desai,
Professor of Sociology, University of Maryland,
Senior Fellow, National Council of Applied Economic Research,
New Delhi

Professor Mamgain meticulously combines what we know from large-scale surveys with the findings of his sample survey of the urban labour market. He focuses on issues relating to access and inclusion in the context of interactions between job seekers and job providers. He convincingly shows that the socially marginalised do not get a fair deal, particularly from the private sector. This book should be of interest to labour economists, sociologists and others interested in development issues.

—J. Krishnamurty,
Former Senior Employment Specialist,
International Labour Organization, Geneva

Employment is at the heart of debates on economics and politics in contemporary India. This engaging book, based on a large sample survey, provides a systematic analysis of job search and hiring practices in the formal sector, characterised by asymmetric information, where unequal opportunities combined with discriminatory practices accentuate inequalities and reinforce exclusion. In doing so, it makes a valuable contribution to our understanding of a relatively unexplored domain while making important suggestions about how to improve the quality of employment in a rapidly changing, yet imperfect, labour market. The book will be a valuable reading for teachers, students and researchers in economics, as well as for policymakers and practitioners in labour studies.

—Deepak Nayyar,
Emeritus Professor of Economics, Jawaharlal Nehru University,
Former Vice Chancellor, University of Delhi

FORMAL
LABOUR MARKET
IN URBAN INDIA

FORMAL LABOUR MARKET IN URBAN INDIA

JOB SEARCH, HIRING PRACTICES AND DISCRIMINATION

RAJENDRA P. MAMGAIN

Los Angeles | London | New Delhi
Singapore | Washington DC | Melbourne

First published in 2019 by

SAGE Publications India Pvt Ltd
B1/I-1 Mohan Cooperative Industrial Area
Mathura Road, New Delhi 110 044, India
www.sagepub.in

SAGE Publications Inc
2455 Teller Road
Thousand Oaks, California 91320, USA

SAGE Publications Ltd
1 Oliver's Yard, 55 City Road
London EC1Y 1SP, United Kingdom

SAGE Publications Asia-Pacific Pte Ltd
18 Cross Street #10-10/11/12
China Square Central
Singapore 048423

Published by Vivek Mehra for SAGE Publications India Pvt Ltd. Typeset in 10.5/13 pt Adobe Caslon Pro by Zaza Eunice, Hosur, Tamil Nadu, India.

Library of Congress Cataloging-in-Publication Data Available

ISBN: 978-93-532-8322-3 (HB)

SAGE Team: Rajesh Dey, Guneet Kaur, Arshita Saxena and Rajinder Kaur

*Dedicated to my dear parents Gyan Dev and
Sateshwari Mamgain, wife Dhanpati, sons
Vivek and Anoop and my teachers
for their affection and great support as ever.*

Thank you for choosing a SAGE product!
If you have any comment, observation or feedback,
I would like to personally hear from you.

Please write to me at **contactceo@sagepub.in**

Vivek Mehra, Managing Director and CEO, SAGE India.

Contents

List of Figures

List of Tables

List of Annexures

List of Abbreviations

AA	affirmative action
AAP	Affirmative Action Policy
ASI	Annual Survey of Industries
ASSOCHAM	Associated Chambers of Commerce and Industry
BAY	Bring Another You
BBC	British Broadcasting Corporation
BPO	business process outsourcing
CAGR	compound annual growth rate
CDRI	Central Drug Research Institute
CEB	census enumeration blocks
CII	Confederation of Indian Industry
CIMAP	Central Institute of Medicinal and Aromatic Plants
CODISSIA	Coimbatore District Small Industries Association
COINDIA	Coimbatore Industrial Infrastructure Association
DI	Dissimilarity Index
DICCI	Dalit Indian Chambers of Commerce and Industry
DM	diversity management
EEOL	Equal Employment Opportunity Laws
EPF	employees' provident fund
EUS	Employment–Unemployment Surveys

FCs	Forward Castes
FICCI	Federation of Indian Chambers of Commerce and Industry
GDP	gross domestic product
GIDS	Giri Institute of Development Studies
HR	human resources
HRM	human resource management
HSBC	Hongkong and Shanghai Banking Corporation
ICCI	Indian Chamber of Commerce and Industry
ICSSR	Indian Council of Social Science Research
ICT	information and communications technology
IIDS	Indian Institute of Dalit Studies
IT	information technology
ITeS	information technology-enabled services
ITI	industrial training institutes
ITRC	Industrial Toxicology Research Centre
LFPRs	labour force participation rates
LUA	Lucknow Urban Agglomeration
MIDC	Maharashtra Industrial Development Corporation
MNCs	multinational companies/corporations
MSMEs	micro, small and medium enterprises
NASSCOM	National Association of Software and Services Companies
NBRI	National Botanical Research Institute
NCO	National Classification of Occupations
NCR	national capital region
NCS	National Career Service
NCT	National Capital Territory

NDDB	National Dairy Development Board
NEET	Neither in Employment, Nor in Education and Training
NHDC	National Handloom Development Corporation
NIC	National Industrial Classification
NSC	non-schedule caste
NSDM	National Skill Development Mission
NSSO	National Sample Survey Organisation
OBCs	Other Backward Classes
OLS	ordinary least squares
ORMs	other religious minorities
OCs	other castes
PCDF	Pradeshik Cooperative Dairy Federation
PPS	probability proportional to size
RDSO	Research Design and Standards Organisation
RPO	recruitment process outsourcing
SCs	scheduled castes
SCSP	Scheduled Caste Sub-Plan
SITRA	South India Textile Research Association
SMEs	small and medium enterprises
SRF	Shri Ram Fibres
SSIs	small-scale industries
SSS	second-stage strata
STs	scheduled tribes
TCS	Tata Consultancy Services
UNSDGs	UN Sustainable Development Goals

Foreword

Late Professor T. S. Papola observed, 'In order that the best applicants have the opportunity to be hired, all potential candidates must have equal access to the information about the job opportunities, and equal access to the channels, and process of hiring.' He further added, 'It is precisely the absence of these conditions in the labour markets which led to the discrimination and exclusion of certain socio-economic groups in the labour markets.' Studies show that in the past, information on jobs opportunities has been inaccessible to workers in general, remaining the privilege of a few insiders. The recruitment processes have been far from transparent in Indian industries, which have been highly informal and personalised. Various studies conducted from the late 1950s to the late 1980s show how a large majority of workers used informal channels for job information from personal contacts or sources. The account of various modes and mechanisms practised by the private sector indicates how social exclusion and discrimination have been a common feature throughout the period of modern industrial development in India.

Urban labour markets have undergone a tremendous change since the late 1980s. The use of more formal channels like the National Employment Service has declined to the minimum. New forms and institutions which engage not only in job recruitment and supply of job information but also in supply of human resources have emerged. These include third-party manpower services such as private placement agencies, educational institutions (through on-campus recruitment) and IT-enabled platforms, among others. The obvious questions are as follows: Do these new institutional mechanisms make job search more transparent with easy access to job information? Are these new institutional mechanisms egalitarian in servicing the weaker sections and marginalised social groups, and those with relatively better socio-economic background? This book provides fresh insights into and understanding on unequal access to employment opportunities to various socio-religious groups, especially SCs/STs and Muslims, in the private sector in a broad framework of demand and supply in labour market. Little is known about the job search methods and processes of hiring by employers, particularly in the formal sector in the urban labour market from the perspective of marginalised groups.

The book is based on a comprehensive primary survey of house-holds, enterprises and labour market intermediaries in four Indian cities with different socio-economic characteristics along with an intensive analysis of the latest secondary data from NSSO and Population Census. The four sample cities include Delhi, a global city; Lucknow, the capital of India's most populated state Uttar Pradesh; Pune, a hub of industry and services; and Coimbatore, a hub of small and medium enterprises. Given the wide yet complex set of research questions, information for both demand and supply side actors has been collected for the study. For understanding the supply side characteristics such as participation in labour market, job search strategies, household members' experiences of participation in hiring by employers, job mobility, nature and quality of employment, and income, an intensive sample survey of about 3,200 urban households is undertaken through systematic random sampling without replace-ment with a larger share of marginalised social groups in the sample cities. Another sample of 1,650 final-year graduates/postgraduates from select higher educational institutions (new entrants to labour market) is also used to explore their job search methods including their experiences of participation in campus placement drives, success rate of getting jobs, experiences of interviews and their future plans. On the demand side, information has been gathered from 45 private enterprises from various industry groups to understand the nature and forms of employment on offer by employers, their job signalling, matching and hiring methods, hiring preferences, strategies of promot-ing social diversity in their recruitments, employees' turnover/attrition, and wages and challenges they face in hiring and retaining of workers.

For understanding the role of labour market intermediaries in formal sector urban labour market, the study has collected data from 50 select labour market intermediary firms such as private placement agencies and educational institutions placement cells. Thus, the author uses a unique approach to address the issues of informational asymmetries, equity, access and discrimination in the urban labour markets with an exclusive focus on formal private sector in India.

The book comes up with several interesting findings. It finds job search a widespread activity which is not limited to the unemployed persons in the labour market. A majority of those working in different occupations also search jobs with substantive differences in job search intensity across gender, social group and location. Most of them are people in their 30s and 40s who are searching other jobs due to a variety of reasons, the predominant being the quest for higher income, career progression and workplace environment. The study underlines the crucial role of information and its access to both job seekers and employers in determining access to quality jobs from the perspective of job seekers, and a productive and competent human resource from the perspective of employers.

The most insightful finding of the study is that despite significant IT-enabled changes in methods of job search and hiring over the years along with a weakening public employment services system, particularly after the mid-1980s, social network contacts continue to be the prime source of job information and job access for the vast majority of job seekers. This implies that the emergence of new institutions in labour market has not undermined the significance of social networks for seeking jobs, which are iniquitous by their very nature. Social networks continue to remain the dominant channel in getting access to low-end entry-level jobs in the urban labour market. At the same time, employee referrals are gradually becoming an important source of job information and entry in enterprises. Due to weak referrals, particularly in the case of SC/ST job seekers, they are generally crowded in low-paying occupations and also face a situation of high unemployment. Such dependence on social networks is relatively low for unemployed graduates, an overwhelming majority of whom uses print and electronic media such as free electronic portals (Naukri.com, DevNet), social sites (LinkedIn and Facebook) and services of relatives and friends more frequently for their job search.

Amid the larger dependence on informal social networks in urban labour market, the study finds significant changes in recruitment processes and hiring methods in private sector enterprises in urban labour market as employers apply various methods of job posting information and hiring in order to tap the best human resource at most competitive cost, ensuring their efficiency, quality and profits as well. Surprisingly, in this entire process of recruitment by employers, the access to information to job seekers has become rather limited, particularly at lower-level jobs, thereby reducing the likelihood of giving employment opportunity to those persons or group of persons who do not have such sources of information. The increasing use of employee referrals by employers in recruitment benefits only the members of specific social networks, thus denying opportunities by barring access or excluding those who are not part of such networks.

Yet another important observation of the study is a rapid increase in labour flexibility wherein employers are able to hire and fire human resources depending on their requirements. The high turnover of workers due to high attrition rates and resultant new recruitments is a common phenomenon in modern enterprises. At the same time, finding competent human resources has emerged a big challenge for many enterprises even amid significant improvements in the educational level of Indian population and information technology (IT)-enabled flow of information on employment opportunities as well as job applicants. Employers are struggling in a situation where talent oversupply and low employability are leading to underemployment on the one hand and to a supply deficit for the industry on the other.

The criticism of the private sector for its inability to promote social diversity in workplaces is also underlined in the book, which shows how employers are obsessed with the concerns of merit and profitability; and factors such as caste, region, gender and class are irrelevant for them. But the merit argument ignores the social and economic factors that produce 'meritorious' candidates in the first place, especially the continuing monopoly of a small proportion of socially and economically privileged groups over the best educational institutions and a large majority of others including marginalised groups being deprived of such advantage. This has obvious implications for the efficacy of current education and skill development system.

The study also cites some chilling experiences of discrimination by job seekers in the form of job information, job interviews, job mobility, harassment at workplace and salary offers by employers in the urban labour market. Uncomfortable questions about caste, religion and beliefs are asked many times to ascertain the social identity of a job seeker, which are used as screening processes indirectly by employers indicating the subtle forms of discrimination cloaked under the garb of merit.

The findings of the study have important policy implications for reducing informational asymmetries in the labour market along with promoting decent employment and educational development opportunities from the perspective of equality and non-discriminatory accessibility to such opportunities. I am convinced that the book will immensely help policymakers to develop a regulatory framework so that all social groups receive equal access to job information and non-discriminatory access to job opportunities. I congratulate Professor Rajendra P. Mamgain for undertaking extensive research on such an important issue and sharing the findings in the form of the book for the benefit of a larger audience. His study provides a lead for further research on emerging new institutions in the labour market in India.

—Sukhadeo Thorat
Professor Emeritus, Jawaharlal Nehru University
Former Chairman, University Grants Commission and
Indian Council of Social Science Research

Preface

During the last six and a half decades of development planning, India has achieved remarkable progress on several fronts, ranging from ending food starvation to acquiring scientific and technological capabilities. However, the country's experience of creating decent employment and income opportunities has been less than desirable despite achieving high economic growth since the 1990s. Rising unemployment among the youth with higher levels of education has become a matter of concern for both policymakers and job hunters alike. It is now a hot topic of raging policy debates. Regular salaried jobs ensuring stability and security are shrinking alarmingly as decent employment has become a painful casualty of liberalisation. In 2011–2012, regular salaried jobs were limited to only 18.4 per cent of the Indian workforce. If the recent trends in the growth of employment opportunities are any indicator, the situation should not have changed significantly in the favour of creating decent employment ensuring tenurial and social security to the country's workforce.

Although there has been a reasonably high growth in regular employment opportunities in recent years, particularly in the private sector, the benefits of such job opportunities have not been equally distributed among various regions and social groups. An overwhelming 80 per cent of the regular salaried jobs in the private sector are located in urban areas. Nearly 63 per cent of the regular salaried jobs in urban private enterprises are provided by those employing more than 20 workers. Further, the social composition of regular employees in big private enterprises (employing more than 20 workers) is highly biased in the favour of 'Other' castes comprising mainly of upper castes in the caste hierarchy. More importantly, a significant increase (over 10% per annum) in regular employment opportunities for SC/ST graduates and also for OBCs has been witnessed in these enterprises in urban areas during the period 2005–2010, as compared to Others (7% per annum). This is definitely a positive feature of our growth story. However, this high growth in employment has not been sufficient enough to improve the share of the marginalised groups in private sector employment in proportion to their share in population. Also, the quality of regular salaried employment is a matter of concern as over half of such employment opportunities are created in informal enterprises which are bereft of any social security benefits. SCs and OBCs are proportionately more in such jobs. A rather worrisome feature has been the increasing informalisation of regular employment opportunities in private as well as public sectors in recent years, indicating the deteriorating quality of regular employment opportunities. The access to regular employment fulfilling the broad conditions of decent jobs is proportionately far less for SCs, Muslims and OBCs, particularly in the private sector. What makes the situation more precarious is the evolution of job search from an entry-seeking activity in the job market to a career-progression endeavour. Thus, we now not only have unemployed people searching for jobs but also a majority of those employed actively looking for better jobs.

The answers for better understanding such unequal access to employment opportunities to various socio-religious groups, particularly in the private sector, could be contextualised in a broad framework of demand and supply in labour market under which job search and hiring methods play a critical role in shaping the labour market outcomes. Little is known about the job search methods and processes of hiring by employers, particularly in the formal sector in the urban labour market from the perspective of marginalised groups who still face various forms of discrimination in their socio-economic development process and access to quality employment opportunities. This book attempts to bridge this gap in the available literature on the urban labour market in India by undertaking a holistic approach of understanding the functioning of job search and hiring practices in the labour markets in four Indian cities, namely Delhi, Lucknow, Pune and Coimbatore, with a focus on marginalised groups. It is based on an intensive research of about 3,000 urban households, 45 enterprises and 50 labour market intermediary firms such as private placement agencies and educational institutions placement cells.

The book comes up with several interesting findings pertaining to access to job opportunities, job search methods, and the intensity of job search, job mobility, wage inequality, hiring practices and discrimination in the urban labour market in India. It finds job search as a widespread activity which is not limited to the unemployed persons only in the labour market. A majority of those working in different occupations also search jobs with substantive differences in intensity across gender, social group and location. Most of them are in their 30s and 40s looking for other jobs due to variety of reasons. The predominant ones are the quest for higher income, career progression and workplace environment. The study underlines the crucial role of information and its access to both job seekers and employers in determining access to quality jobs from the perspective of job seekers and a productive and competent human resource from the perspective of employers. It is observed that despite significant changes in methods of job search over the years, along with a weakening system of public employment services, particularly after the mid-1980s, social network contacts still remain the major source of job information and job access to about 64 per cent job seekers. The access to jobs and earnings are significantly influenced by the nature of such contacts. The author's analysis of job search method used by employed persons for their current job reveals a comparatively higher dependence on social networks such as friends among SCs and OBCs as compared to other social groups (OCs—upper castes). This is in contrast to the earlier studies which showed how due to weak social networks, SC job seekers in urban labour market suffered with higher unemployment incidence. However, social networks are crucial in getting access to low-end entry-level jobs for a majority of workers in the urban labour market. There has been an ever-increasing use of IT in both job signalling and hiring in the recent years, thereby reducing information asymmetries in the labour market to a certain extent. At the same time, employee referrals are gradually becoming an important source of job information and entry into the corporate sector. Due to weak referrals, particularly in the case of SC/ST job seekers, they get crowded in low-paying occupations. In the case of unemployed persons, an overwhelming majority depends on print and electronic media, including free job portals such as Naukri.com and DevNet, social sites such as LinkedIn and Facebook, and services of relatives and friends more frequently for their job search. Employee referrals and college campus placement cells are also important modes of job search for them.

From the perspective of job seekers from the marginalised social groups, they face major constraints related to lack of job information, lack of desired education and skill training, poor communication skills and weak self-confidence that are in demand in the labour market. Other constraints include lack of quality social networks, employee referrals, and poor family and social background in getting access to jobs in the urban labour market.

The recent years have also witnessed a rapid increase in labour flexibility wherein employers are able to hire and fire human resources depending on their requirements. The high turnover of workers due to high attrition rates and resultant new recruitments is common in modern enterprises. At the same time, finding competent human resources has emerged as a formidable challenge in spite of significant improvements in the educational level of Indian population and IT-enabled information flow about employment opportunities as well as job applicants. Employers find themselves struggling with a situation where talent oversupply and low employability are leading to underemployment on the one hand and supply deficit for the industry on the other. The book reports significant changes in the recruitment processes and hiring methods of private sector enterprises in the urban labour market as employers adopt various means of posting job information and hiring in order to get the best human resource at most competitive costs while ensuring their efficiency, quality and profits as well. As a result, recruitment practices by employers have undergone a sea change which differ in various economic sectors/sub-sectors and geographical/administrative regions. Information asymmetries in the labour market are being eased with the emergence of commercial jobs boards (such as Naukri.com, DevNet and Monster) for posting job advertisements. Technology-supported social networks such as Facebook, LinkedIn and WhatsApp also have emerged as important sources of job information. Employers are increasingly depending on private human resources (HR) companies who provide them with workers but are not on their payrolls (third-party workers). Campus recruitments and job fairs are other channels of recruitment. Apart from these methods, social networks and employee referrals are very common sources of job information and recruitment. Surprisingly, in this entire process of recruitment by employers, information access to job seekers has become rather limited, particularly at lower-level jobs, thereby reducing the likelihood of employment opportunity to those persons or group of persons who do not have such sources of information.

The private sector has also been criticised for its inability to promote social diversity at workplaces. The representation of SCs/STs and Muslims in private sector employment is proportionately much low as observed in some recent studies. Similar is the case with women. Arguments for such lower representation of these marginalised groups are varied. Employers commonly argue that they practise highly competitive recruitment processes wherein they hire employees only on the basis of merit, and that factors such as caste, region, gender and class are irrelevant. The merit argument, however, ignores the social and economic factors that produce 'meritorious' candidates in the first place, given the continuing monopoly of a small proportion of socially and economically privileged groups over the best educational institutions to the disadvantage of the vast majority of the marginalised groups. The author exposes how private sector employers' obsession for workers with better education and knowledge along with soft skills such as communication, language proficiency, self-esteem, team spirit, etc., which have little relevance to performance in many cases, works in the favour of candidates with better social and economic endowments (e.g., fluency with spoken English), basically the upper caste.

The study also presents experiences of discrimination suffered by job seekers while accessing job information during job interviews, harassment at workplace and differential salary offers in the urban labour market. Uncomfortable questions about caste, religion and beliefs are often asked to ascertain the social belonging of a job seeker, which are used for screening out traditionally ostracised candidates indirectly by employers. The increasing use of employee referrals by employers in recruitment only benefits the members of network, thus excluding those lacking presence in such networks from coveted employment opportunities, especially in the IT sector. The affirmative action policy aimed at promoting employment of SCs/STs could hardly make any impact towards improving the employment opportunities for SCs/STs due to its own limits.

The book is based on a larger research study with generous financial support from the Indian Council of Social Science Research (ICSSR), New Delhi, under its sponsored research programme. I would like to thank ICCSR for its valuable support. I am immensely indebted to Professor Sukhadeo Thorat, former chairperson of ICSSR and Professor Emeritus, Centre for the Study of Regional Development, Jawaharlal Nehru University, New Delhi, for encouraging me to undertake the study on this complex theme. I have immensely benefitted from his valuable guidance and encouragement.

There are many intellectuals and institutions who provided me their valuable support during different stages of the study. My deep sense of gratitude goes to late Professor T. S. Papola for his vital mentoring during the early stages of the present study. I have immensely gained from the invaluable guidance of the members of Advisory Committee comprising Professors K. P. Kannan, Arup Mitra, Binoo Paul, Amaresh Dubey, G. Raveendran and Rajesh Chauhan. The comments by Professors K. P. Kannan, Amitabh Kundu, Arup Mitra, S. Madheswaran, A. K. Singh and Bhim Reddy were very useful in revising the study. I put on record my sincere thanks to all of them for their priceless time and crucial guidance. The herculean task of data collection in urban areas from diverse situations was possible due to eight teams of dedicated research assistants under the supervision of senior researchers in the four sample cities. I am thankful to their painstaking efforts and valuable support in the timely collection of data. My sincere thanks and appreciation are due to Dr K. K. Singh, Dr R. Nagarajan, Dr Parmeshwaran Jadav and Dr Shivakar Tiwari for coordinating the data collection work in Delhi NCR, Coimbatore, Pune and Lucknow, respectively. I would like to thank various industry organisations and the HR heads of private enterprises for extending their critical cooperation in providing information for the study. In particular, I would like to thank Mr B. P. Pant of the Federation of Indian Chambers of Commerce and Industry (FICCI); Mr D. S. Rawat, Secretary-General, Associated Chambers of Commerce and Industry (ASSOCHAM); Mr Sameer Gupta, Chairman-Uttar Pradesh, State Council, Confederation of Indian Industry (CII); Mr S. C. Bahuguna, Director, Indian Society of Training and Development, New Delhi; Mr V. Thirugnanam, Honorary Secretary, the Coimbatore District Small Industries Association (CODISSIA), Coimbatore; and Mr Milind Kamble, Founder Chairperson, Dalit Indian Chambers of Commerce and Industry (DICCI), Pune, for sharing valuable information and providing useful support to reach the HR heads of various companies.

The Giri Institute of Development Studies (GIDS) provided excellent support in the smooth conduct of the study. The research assistance by Dr Shivakar Tiwari, Mitali Gupta, Pragya Sharma and Sanjaya Malik at various stages of the study has been very critical. For this, I thank all of them. Last but not least, I am grateful to all respondents of the study as without their active support this work would not have been possible.

CHAPTER 1

Introduction
Labour Market

The Context

The question of employment has always been at the centre stage of the development discourse across the globe due to its multiplier impact on the well-being of humankind. It is argued that structural rigidities and imperfections in an economy tend to slow down the process of its structural transformation and growth in employment. Towards addressing such structural rigidities and accelerating the growth process, the neoliberal policies propagated free market economies. However, the neoliberal policies and programmes aimed at achieving high economic growth by removing distractions in factor markets are increasingly coming under fire across the world for their inability to remove structural imbalances and create ever-growing inequalities in factor incomes (Atkinson, 2015; Ostry, Loungani, & Furceri, 2016; Piketty, 2014). Albeit such policies helped bring about significant structural changes in the favour of the service sector, they resulted in disproportionate increase in the share of capital as compared to labour as a factor of production. Moreover, the gains in labour earnings are mostly shared by those at the top 1 percentile, thereby creating sizeable income inequalities in recent years. The increased policy support for the private sector at the cost of the public sector under the neoliberal policy regime could hardly create employment opportunities to clear the backlog of unemployment at the desired pace.

In India, while the neoliberal policies resulted in higher economic growth and significant changes in the economic structure since the early 1990s, they have been rather slow in creating employment opportunities. Over half of the Indian workforce is still dependent on the self-employed form of employment, mostly as own account workers (who do not employ any hired worker on wage payment basis) contributing about 14 per cent to the gross domestic product (GDP) of the country (IHD & ISLE, 2014, p. 26). The decline in the proportion of such occupations has rather been slow. Wage paid employment, constituting about 48 per cent of the total employment, is largely in the form of casual wage work. Regular employment, characterised as steady and secure, paying well, meeting labour standards and offering social protection (Fields, 2011), contributes just about 18 per cent of the total employment in the country. The share of regular wage employment in India is much lower as compared to many other countries such as China, Malaysia, South Africa and Brazil (ILO, 2014) due to predominance of informal activities. The demand for regular employment in the public sector and reservation therein is huge, invoking agitations as seen recently by the Patel community in Gujarat, the Marathas in Maharashtra and the Jat community in Haryana. Most of the growth in employment opportunities is led by casual and contractual jobs without any social security, in both public and private enterprises. Thus, the informal mode of employment, with low earnings and limited or no social protection, still accounts for about 84 per cent of the total employment in India (IHD & ISLE, 2014; Srivastava & Naik, 2017). In brief, the fastest economic growth witnessed during the late 1990s till 2013–2014 could hardly ameliorate the persistent deficit of quality employment, thus perpetuating the problems of underemployment and educated unemployment in India.

The Indian labour market is also characterised by unequal access to employment opportunities to women and those belonging to the socially marginalised groups such as scheduled castes (SCs), scheduled tribes (STs) and Muslims. Apart from the low participation in the labour force, most of the women are engaged in elementary occupations. Similarly, despite their higher labour force participation rates, historically disadvantaged groups such as SCs and STs are proportionately over-represented in casual wage works. Although their share in the public sector employment has improved due to affirmative policies, they remain under-represented in the private organised sector employment despite the improvement in their education and training (Mamgain & Tiwari, 2017). These population groups face discrimination in their human capital formation and later on in the labour market as well (Thorat & Newman, 2010).

Unemployment is a major policy challenge. It is more severe among the youth, particularly who are better educated and are mainly looking for regular salaried employment. A high one-fifth of the youth labour force with graduate-level education is unemployed, thus posing a serious challenge for creating productive jobs in the Indian economy (Mamgain & Tiwari, 2016).

These broad features of employment and unemployment at the national level are also true for urban areas where about 31 per cent of the country's population resides. However, a few distinct features of the urban labour market are worth highlighting. Urban India has lower share of economically active population (labour force) than rural India mainly due to the very low labour force participation of women therein. Over two-thirds of the regular employment opportunities are located in urban areas. Among the urban workforce during the year 2011–2012, the share of regular workers was highest (43%), closely followed by self-employed (42%), while the lowest was that of the casual wage labour (15%).

Regular employment, however, suffers from informality and lack of social security as nearly half of such employment is generated in private informal enterprises. A large proportion of regular employment that was created between 2004–2005 and 2011–2012 in public and private organised sectors was devoid of tenurial and social security benefits. Moreover, access to regular salaried jobs in the private organised sector yet remains very low for SCs and STs as compared to other social groups (OCs; Mamgain & Tiwari, 2017). Such informality in employment has increased over the years, particularly after the economic reforms of the early 1990s, thereby worsening the conditions of employment in the labour market.

Yet another important challenge in the urban labour market is high unemployment rates among both young men and women. There were 3.94 million unemployed persons in urban areas, constituting 43.1 per cent of the total unemployed in India in 2011–2012. The unemployment rate in urban areas is almost double for men and triple among women as compared to rural areas. Many unemployed youth migrate to urban areas in search of employment due to lack of job opportunities in rural areas. Such rising stock of unemployed persons is well recognised in the neoclassical economic theory, and has serious economic, social and political consequences if it remains unaddressed for a long time (Cramer, 2010).

Unlike in the past, job search is becoming a widespread activity which is not limited to the unemployed persons only in the labour market. A fairly high majority of working population in their 30s and 40s are on the lookout for a new job with substantive differences in their job search intensity across gender, social group and city of location. They search other jobs due to a variety of reasons, the predominant being the quest for higher income, career progression and workplace environment.

The rapid penetration of information technology (IT) is reshaping the landscape of labour markets. E-job portals, private placement agencies, recruitment process outsourcing (RPOs), social network platforms (such as LinkedIn, WhatsApp and Facebook), online platform-based labour market for service delivery (Ola, Uber, e-retailing, repair and maintenance works) and college campus placement cells have become new mediums of job information in the labour market. Traditional labour market intermediaries like the National Employment Service in its earlier form have lost their relevance. Keeping pace with the changing times, the National Employment Service was redesigned into National Career Service (NCS) in 2015. The NCS portal facilitates the registration of job seekers, employers, skill providers and career counsellors, and thus is distinct from other private sector job portals in that it provides job-matching services to job seekers as well as employers. These developments have definitely improved the access of job information to both employers and job seekers. However, information asymmetries in labour market still remain a major concern in segmented labour markets, which were likely to disappear with the rapid penetration of IT in recent years. A fairly high proportion of job seekers still depend on its social networks for job information, thereby dwarfing the potential of IT in the labour market. Employee referrals are gradually becoming an important source of job information and entry in enterprises. The use of social networks is comparatively more important for those searching contractual/casual jobs in the middle- and low-end occupational hierarchies in both formal and informal sector enterprises. However, such networks are exclusionary by their very nature, resulting in inefficiency in resource use (Kannappan, 1977; Papola, 1981).

On the demand side, employers tend to economise their costs by reducing costs of their human resources including recruitment costs towards improving their competitiveness. They are demanding flexibility in hiring and firing of workforce. Although such flexibility has become one of the indicators of 'ease of doing business,' it is being criticised for its insensitivity towards labour as a distinct factor of production. Employers are able to hire and fire human resources depending on their requirements. At the same time, finding competent human resources by the enterprises has emerged as a big challenge in spite of the significant improvements in the educational level of Indian population and IT-enabled flow of information on employment opportunities as well as job applicants. Employers are struggling with a situation where talent oversupply and low employability are leading to underemployment on the one hand and a supply deficit for the industry on the other (World Bank, 2011). Employers apply various methods of job posting information and hiring in order to get the best human resources at competitive cost, ensuring their efficiency, quality and profits as well. As a result, recruitment practices by employers have undergone a sea change which differ in various economic sectors/sub-sectors and geographical/administrative regions.

Along with information asymmetries, the prevalence of discrimi-nation in recruitment processes based on caste, ethnicity and religion creates inefficient outcomes in the labour market. Many a time, such imperfect information creates segmentations and duality in labour markets and becomes a source of discrimination. Studies show how discriminatory practices used by employers in the screening and selec-tion processes are adversely affecting the chances of employment and wage earnings of the discriminated groups such as SCs in the labour market (Thorat & Newman, 2010). Job seekers belonging to the mar-ginalised groups, poorer sections as also migrants from rural areas often experience discrimination on the basis of their medium of education, as most of them do not have proficiency in English language and com-munication skills—considered important in the era of globalisation.

The Indian education system has perpetuated the duality in edu-cational outcomes and accordingly affected the employability of job seekers. In such a dual educational system, particularly at school level, access to quality education is extremely poor for most of the poor and disadvantaged sections of the society (SC/ST and Muslim popula-tion, and those from the rural background). Moreover, discriminatory practices in many such institutions make learning uninteresting and painful. In such situations, their transition to the labour market is again painful and generally puts them in low-paying jobs (Banerjee, Bertrand, Datta, & Mullianathan, 2009; Thorat & Newman, 2010).

These developments in the urban labour market need to be under-stood critically in the context of available theoretical frameworks and empirical evidences, particularly relating to changes in job search and hiring practices from the perspective of social and gender inclusion.

While rich empirical work is unfolding the understanding of functioning of labour markets in India, most studies are centred around understanding the dualism and segmentation associated with gender, caste, industry, location and region, their consequences and policy implications for better planning. This is briefly explained in the next section.

Labour Market: Theoretical Insights and Empirical Evidences

The neoclassical economic theory treats labour (measured as work done by an individual) as one of the factors of production, the price of which is determined by its demand and supply in the market. This simple characterisation of the labour market in a demand and supply framework has been criticised as labour being distinct from other factors of production (like the markets for goods or the financial market) in several ways. In particular, unlike other markets, the labour market may act as a non-clearing market at an equilibrium price. The persistent level of unemployment is a testimony of this fact (Campbell & Ahmad, 2012). Contrasting the labour market to other markets also reveals persistent compensating wage differentials among similar workers, that is, the additional amount of income that a given worker must be offered in order to motivate them to accept a given undesirable job, relative to other jobs that a worker could perform. Employment and wage earnings are important outcomes of labour market, which also influence the economic and social well-being of individuals. Sociologists attach dignity as an important constituent of employment.

In the context of the urban labour market in lower-middle income countries like India, this would help us in developing our own framework of analysis related to job search and hiring practices in the urban labour market from the perspective of social and gender inclusiveness. It is also well known that apart from economic factors, non-economic factors play a critical role in determining the labour supply in labour market, thereby creating rigidities and inequalities. In developing countries like India, labour markets are not fully developed as a large number of activities, in fact, remain outside of a 'market' altogether. Examples of some such activities are subsistence farming and petty self-employment activities like street vending, which can be understood as an 'employment-led', survivalist strategy, rather than a 'growth-led' demand for labour (Campbell and Ahmed, 2012). Labour markets are also segmented on the lines of formal and informal sectors, rural and urban areas, gender, and social belonging of labour force. A typical example is that of caste-based occupations such as priest, cobbler and washerman, where occupational choices are determined by birth or caste and not by other attributes of a person. The simple dualistic model of labour market is thus inadequate to explain the interplay of such features in the labour market. The Indian labour market is characterised by the persistence of informality in urban areas, the continuing share of workers in subsistence agriculture, low pay and poor working conditions, along with the disparities faced by the women, youth and socially marginalised sections of the society (Campbell and Ahmed, 2012; NCEUS, 2007). Such informality in the labour market has grown with the increasing informalisation of formal employment opportunities, thereby resulting in vulnerability and insecurity of employment (NCEUS, 2007).

Theoretical Insights

The economic literature is replete with a variety of models explaining labour markets and related employment, unemployment, job search situations and hiring practices in an economy. These models can be grouped into two subgroups: those that treat unemployment as a generalised phenomenon for the economy and those that are sector-specific. The first group can be divided into three subgroups based on the different views of what causes labour market imbalance: aggregate demand deficiency models, technical lack of substitution models and models that rely directly on the fixity/stickiness of real wages to explain unemployment. Similarly, the sector-specific models can be divided into two categories: those that see the wedge driven between earning and the marginal product of labour within a sector as the root of the problem and those that view the difference between sectors in earnings for economically homogeneous labour as the root of the problem (for details, see Harris & Sabot, 1982).

However, these five categories of models, except that of the labour market segmentation models, do not address the dynamics of urban unemployment in developing countries like India. The Lewis model (1954) and subsequently Harris and Todaro model of segmentation (1971) do explain to some extent the transfer of workers from traditional agrarian economy to modern sectors in urban areas. They argue that high and institutionally determined urban wages make migration attractive even in the presence of urban unemployment. While the wage gap continues to explain rural–urban migration in developing countries (Lucas, 2015), Harris and Todaro model does not explain why people belonging to various social groups such as SCs in India could not migrate freely with the wage-associated signals (Harris, Kannan, & Rodgers, 1990; Mamgain, 2004). The neoclassical theory hardly provides adequate explanations for the existence of several labour market rigidities, especially multiple levels of segmentation and discrimination in hiring and wage inequality (Ruwanpura, 2005; Taubman & Wachter, 1986).

Many economists reject a predominantly competitive analysis and emphasise, instead, a fragmented nature of labour markets and the importance of institutional and social influences upon hiring of workers and wage rate. Accordingly, a wide range of theoretical perspectives have emerged with varying viewpoints around the neoclassical, institutionalist, Marxist and feminist streams of economic theories (Arrow, 1972; Becker, 1957; Darity, 1975; Doeringer & Piore, 1971;, Stiglitz, 1973; Taubman & Wachter, 1986).

The dual labour market and labour market segmentation schools of thought (Doeringer & Piore, 1971; Reich, Gordon, & Edwards, 1973) developed by political economists showed how market imperfections are institutionalised, resulting in inequality in employment and wage outcomes. They argue how labour market is segmented in a variety of ways, for example, formal–informal, rural–urban, men–women and modern–traditional. The underlying theme of these approaches views labour market as a collection of parts or segments, for example, well-paid, male, higher caste workers, and another of low-paid, female, lower caste workers, region, occupation, etc. Analyses differ in the outcomes of interest (access to jobs, pay, employment stability or mobility, social security, rights and dignity), in the delineation of segments (by job, industry, gender, caste, race or age) and in the methodology of investigation, whether qualitative or econometric (McNabb & Ryan, 1990).

Becker's theory (1957) of 'taste of employers' and Arrow's model (1972) of 'statistical discrimination' are two important works in neoclassical economics which theorise discrimination in the labour markets. Becker (1957, pp. 15–17) argues that 'employers taste for discrimination, including prejudice, ignorance and nepotism, leads to a misallocation of resources and is economically inefficient'. Arrow (1972) argues that employers have 'preconceived notion' about productivity of a group of workers rather than 'actual information' on their productivity, thus denying them work. He argues that only the absence of such misperceptions supported by complete information symmetries will eliminate discrimination in the labour market in the long run. These neoclassical perspectives argue how labour mobility and occupational flexibility increase by eliminating discrimination, which also leads to reduction in the shortages of particular types of labour (Bergmann, 1971, p. 308). Most of these pioneering studies show how discrimination results in wage inequality (Becker, 1957) and occupational segregation (Arrow, 1972; Bergmann, 1971). Such segregation often results in oversupply of labour in certain occupations, leading to situations of reduced marginal productivity and decrease in wage earnings (Bergmann, 1971, p. 310).

With the persistence of segmentation and discrimination in labour markets, new explanations around the human capital theory emerged from the neoclassical economists. They explained that education and skill attainments (human capital) of people served as major drivers for their participation in the labour market, marginal productivity and wage earnings. The wage differentials are seen as differences in the human capital levels of workers. The human capital theory is criticised for its limitations in not being able to explain the wage gaps between two groups of workers from different race/caste/ethnicity even after controlling other variables (Darrity, 1975; Madheswaran & Attewell, 2007).

The Marxist and institutional models also do not pay enough attention to the social, political and historical factors that may equally deserve consideration (Ruwanpura, 2005). The early theoretical insights about caste acting as one of the important institutions in the allocation and use of labour is traced in Dr B. R. Ambedkar's writings on the economic situation of Dalits (SCs) in India (Ambedkar, 1936). He showed how caste as an important social institution puts barriers in economic and social mobility of persons and results in inefficiency in resource allocations, thereby reducing the productivity. The roles of social relations and networks along with technology are found to be important in determining labour productivity and wage earnings (Mason, 1999, p. 281; Williams, 1987, p. 9). Interaction of institutional factors could lead to multi-discrimination in the labour market (Ruwanpura, 2005, p. 14). More recently, the seminal identity model by Akerlof and Kranton (2010) postulates how individuals mostly follow prescriptions associated with their identities because it is a way of maintaining concepts of the self, though there may also be positive externalities and pay-off by following identity-related actions. However, the model fails to explain the overlapping identities and intersectionality. In such situations, it is difficult to analyse whether a person faced discrimination on one pretext or other, because these differing pretexts intersect and interact with each other and are specific (Ruwanpura, 2005, p. 14). The experience of Dalit women in India being discriminated on the basis of intersection of gender and caste is a case in point. For these reasons, deciphering the connections among diverse social positions, features and relations is not easy, and the literature is scarce on the topic (Ruwanpura, 2005, p. 11). Hence, the alternative framework for explanations of multi-discrimination in the labour market, as advocated in recent years, is largely based on the approach of feminist economists.

The feminist economists approach acknowledges the interlinked nature of social identities in the contexts of market and non-market relationships, which requires analysing the relationship between social and political-economic structures (Brewer, Conard, & King, 2002). This allows the interplay between agency and social structures, where the analysis of social construction of identities is noted as specific to time, place and historical location. Related to this approach, a recent approach in the framework of social exclusion and discrimination is gaining ground in the analysis of inequality in the labour market.

Theoretical Insights into Social Exclusion and Caste Discrimination

For explaining multiple discrimination-induced inequalities in the labour market, the social exclusion framework has emerged as an important stream in recent decades. It recognises (a) the multiple aspects of discrimination and the societal processes in historical contexts and (b) various forms of social, political, economic, cultural and religious institutions that create and perpetuate exclusion and discrimination. Sen (2000) conceptualises social exclusion in the framework of capability deprivation and poverty, wherein he categorises various forms of exclusions and inclusions. He draws a distinction between the situations in which some people are kept out (or at least left out) and wherein some people are being included (may be even being forced to be included) in deeply unfavourable terms. He describes the former as 'unfavourable exclusion' and the latter as 'unfavourable inclusion'. The latter with unequal treatment may carry the same adverse effects as the former. Such exclusion/inclusion can be practised at different levels, such as for individuals, group of individuals, gender, caste, ethnicity, religion and spatial. The notion of unfavourable inclusion appears to be quite close to the concept of 'market discrimination' developed in the mainstream economic literature related to race and gender (Becker, 1957). Discrimination, thus, manifests as a situation, which involves exclusion or outright restriction on various market entries and/or selective inclusion with unequal and unfavourable treatment in various market transactions (Sen, 2000).

Theoretical attempts to unfold the economic logic of caste as an institution and related inclusion/exclusion are not many. There are at least three readily identifiable approaches, which try to understand the governing economic rules or principles of the caste system. These include (a) neoclassical, (b) Marxian and (c) Ambedkar's approach to the institution of the caste system. Detailed reviews of economic theory and its insights into caste discrimination are given in Thorat (2007) and Thorat and Newman (2010).

The insights of mainstream economic theory of caste-based exclusion and discrimination, though limited in numbers, indicate how individuals from the lower castes in the caste hierarchy are unable to interact freely and productively with others, inhibiting their full participation in the economic, social and political life of the community (Bhalla & Lapeyere, 1997). Akerlof's formal model (1976) of caste equilibrium was the first among the few attempts to apply the neoclassical economic theory to the institution of caste system. The later writers (Lal, 1984; Scoville, 1991) made some improvement in Akerlof's theoretical formulations. In the caste economy conceived by Akerlof, occupations are supposed to be hereditary, compulsory and endogenous. These typical features of the caste system bring about immobility of labour across (caste) occupations and segmentation in the labour market, the consequence of which is the lack of free and fair competition. The model also yields discriminatory outcomes. In Akerlof's view, the caste system imposed penalties on workers, employers and customers for violating caste employment rules resulting in workers being segregated into their caste-specific occupations or jobs. In equilibrium, no employer has an incentive to hire an outside caste worker.

Scoville (1991) modified Akerlof's model, particularly with respect to the cause for the survival of the caste system. He identified the factors which created barriers in the free effective participation in labour market. Scoville argued that the caste system (through the system of penalties) created enormous and virtually insurmountable transition costs to break the restrictions on labour or occupational mobility. Thus, the major difference between Akerlof and Scoville is that while the former argues that caste-based labour segmentation is maintained through the system of penalties, the latter goes beyond the penalties and locates the reasons into enormous insurmountable transaction and enforcement costs to break the caste-based occupation or employment structure (Madheswaran, 2017).

Based on Akerlof's model (1976, 1980), Deepak Lal (1984) developed an economic model of the caste system. He observed,

> The caste system has been both unique, and one of the most enduring . . . its direct effect is on the labour in terms of occupational segregations and imperfectly (though not completely) immobile endogenous groups. The division of labour by caste and its enforcement by local ostracism were central to the scheme.

> The social ostracism involved in breaking the caste code, either as consumers or producers (at each level of caste hierarchy) would entail higher cost than any gains from performing any profitable arbitrage in the labour market that the caste induced-segmentation of labour might entail.

In the Marxian approach towards institutions, the economic structure of society is considered to be the foundation of all institutions—legal, social, religious and political. And although the focus is on the dialectical relationship between the changes in the forces of production (means of production and technology) and the relation of production (institutions), it is the former (with the consideration of surplus appropriation by the dominant class) which is supposed to provide more potent and dynamic source of institutional change. Recognition of the forces of production under the Marxist framework as critical driving force behind institutions such as caste and religion has shifted the attention from efficiency aspects of institutions to the distribution aspects, and also the considerations of surplus appropriation and explorative character of the caste system (Ruwanpura, 2005).

However, in the Marxian analysis, there is a tendency to avoid microeconomic analyses of the formation of these institutions in the first place, and to explain the changing nature, adoption and survival of the caste like relations (Bardhan, 1989). The lack of microeconomic analysis has limited our capacity to understand the dynamics of institutions like caste under the mode other than feudal, like capitalistic and even the state sector. How the social and religious ideologies through reverse interaction influence the economic structure and, at the same time, preponderate in determining their form has not been explored and understood properly. These are, in fact, the gaps or issues on which Ambedkar's conceptualisation of caste system provides useful insights.

Ambedkar (1987a) provides a powerful explanation of caste as an economic system in his writings. He argues that the primary unit of the Hindu society is not an individual but caste; hence, the rights and privileges (or the lack of them) of an individual are on the account of the latter's membership of a particular caste (Ambedkar, 1987b). The caste system forms the basis of entitlements to civil, economic and educational rights of various groups or castes. Such entitlements become narrower or even completely denied to certain caste groups as one moves down in the caste hierarchy. For example, Shudras and Ati Shudras or 'untouchables' (now called SCs or Dalits) were denied the right to acquire education. Similarly, assigning occupations on caste lines by the virtue of birth and not on the basis of education and skills rendered inter-caste occupational mobility rather impossible. The system also provides for a community-based regulatory mechanism to enforce the system through the instrument of social ostracism as well as social and economic penalties, and is further reinforced with justification from some philosophical elements in the Hindu religion (Ambedkar, 1987b). Those forced into occupations considered as 'polluting' or 'impure' based on their caste group and, therefore, socially degrading do not derive job satisfaction and indeed constantly provoke them to aversion, ill will and the desire to evade. The caste system also puts a low value on 'physical' work, as compared to 'mental' work, as a result of which the dignity of physical labour is nearly absent in the work ethics of the caste system. Consequently, the lack of dignity of labour adversely affects the incentive to work. Thus, caste exists as a system of endogenous groups that are interlinked with each other in an unequal measure of rights and relations in all walks of life.

Ambedkar argues that such unequal distribution of rights in a caste system creates distortions in the allocation of resources, resulting in factor immobility and segmentation in various kinds of markets by not permitting factors of production to participate equally. This causes gross inefficiency in resource allocation and economic outcomes (Ambedkar, 1936, 1987b). Thus, in caste-based segmented markets, economic efficiency is generally lower than in a situation of perfectly competitive market economy (Birdsall & Sabot, 1991). Restrictions on factor mobility may create a situation of higher unemployment among those who are restricted to participate freely in the market economy (Thorat & Newman, 2010). Thus, in view of the standard mainstream theories of discrimination, and also in view of Ambedkar (1936), judged by the standard criterion of economic efficiency, the caste system as an economic organisation lacks all those elements or assumptions which are required to fulfil the conditions for optimum economic outcome in neoclassical economic theories (Thorat & Newman, 2010).

Empirical Evidence in the Indian Context

Few path-breaking studies that have emerged during the 1970s and 1990s in India analyse the relationship between labour market segregation, hiring of labour and the wage differential in the Indian context (e.g., Deshpande, 1979; Harris, Kannan, & Rodgers, 1990; Kannappan, 1977; Mazumdar, 1983; Papola & Rodgers, 1992; Rodgers, 1993). It is argued in these studies that labour markets are segmented not only on the sectoral (traditional rural and modern urban) paradigm but also across industry, occupation, gender and social/ethnic groups. All these studies point out that the labour market

structure is partly embedded in the overall pattern of social organisation which determines, along with the dominant labour institutions,
the nature of access to the labour market and the distribution of benefits from the economic development. A simple dualistic conception
of labour markets such as formal–informal and organised–unorganised
sectors in the neoclassical and Marxian theoretical frameworks is criticised for being too simplistic, as they ignore the complex social realities
of urban production systems and labour processes in the multi-layered
segmented urban labour markets (Harris, Kannan, & Rodgers, 1990).
The emphasis, therefore, has been on a thorough understanding of the
labour market (beyond the prevalent dualistic conceptions), not only
for analytical purposes but also for effective labour market interven-
tions and policies. It was also shown how segmented labour markets
acted as a hindrance in the free flow of labour across various sectors
and industries, thereby creating inefficiency in the allocation of labour,
resulting in low employment, low productivity, low-income earnings
and increasing income inequality (IHD& ISLE, 2014; Papola &
Rodgers, 1992).

Regarding employment opportunities, the Lewisian perception of
an ever-expanding demand for labour in the urban industrial sector
seems to be rudely shattered by empirical realities in the Indian context
as well (Bhardwaj, 1994; Randhawa, 1989). The 'institutionalist' characterisation of the industrial sector as 'competitive' and of agriculture
as the 'pre-capitalist' reservoir of surplus labour not only oversimpli-
fies the existing scenario but also leads to analytically misleading
conclusions (Bhardwaj, 1994). For example, agrarian studies in India
have amply demonstrated that the peasantry cannot be treated as a
homogenous mass of producers, either as a passive reservoir of surplus
labour or as independent producers facing competitive markets.[1] On
the other hand, the industrial growth-led development strategy could
not generate enough employment opportunities and there persisted
the backlog of unemployment and underemployment. The evidence

---

[1] For a critique of such exercises, see Rudra (1967); Bhardwaj (1974); Rao
(1992); Dasgupta and Laishley (1975); Reddy (2002).

of increasing poverty and income inequalities triggered the critical view of the industry-led growth philosophy. The persistence of a large share of informal sector and informal employment belies the arguments by advocates of liberal policies about a gradual decline in informality with a corresponding rise in formal jobs (Agarwala, 2013; Breman, 2010, 2013; NCEUS, 2007). The regime of high economic growth after the economic reforms of the early 1990s and thereafter could hardly generate enough jobs in the formal sector, thus resulting in the concentration of additional labour force in the informal sector at the low level of productivity and earnings (OECD, 2007). Thus, the informal sector has proved to be the overwhelming and enduring reality of the Indian urban economy (Breman, 1996).

There are a few studies which explore the processes of caste- and religion-based segmentation and associated exclusion, and discrimination in employment, reasons thereof and consequences on income and social status of workers (Banerjee & Knight, 1985; Madheswaran & Attewell, 2010; Siddique, 2008; Thorat & Newman, 2010; Upadhya, 2007). These studies show significant influence of the social background of labour force in determining their access to job opportunities in the urban labour market. In an audit study, Thorat and Newman (2010) show how SC and Muslim applicants, who are equally or better qualified than higher caste applicants, are less likely to pass through the hiring screen among employers in the modern formal sector in India. Such caste and religious prejudices among employers seriously hamper the employment opportunities for SCs and Muslims. The managers in the private organised sector bring to the hiring process a set of stereotypes that makes it difficult for very low-caste applicants to succeed in the competition for position (Jodhka & Newman, 2010; Woodard & Saini, 2006). Mamgain (2017) shows how the probability of SCs entering into emerging occupations (those growing at over 3.5% annually and fetching more than national mean income) is significantly lower than 'higher' castes after controlling for endowment factors such as education and experience, and location factors such as rural–urban residence and regions. Based on the National Sample Survey Organisation (NSSO) data on employment and unemployment, he shows how the education level of graduate and above increases the chance of 'Other' (high) caste Hindus of getting into emerging occupations by around 36 per cent as against 27 per cent for SCs in comparison to the reference category (ST illiterates).

While segmented labour markets generally result in income inequalities, a substantive part of such inequalities arises due to social discrimination in both job access and wage determination. Recently, Singhari and Madheswaran (2016) measured about 36 per cent of the difference in the occupational and wage inequalities due to the discrimination of SCs in finding access to private sector jobs in the urban labour market in India. Banerjee and Knight (1985), in their study in Delhi, explain the wage and earning differentials between SCs and others partly due to discrimination. They show how an additional year of urban experience of non-SC (NSC) migrants increases their earnings 6.6 times over SC migrants. They also show that most SCs in private enterprises are employed in low-rung jobs, which is most likely due to the discrimination in the allocation of workers to jobs. However, the wage differentials between SCs and NSCs are largely due to differences in endowment (education, age, experience, location, etc.) and partly due to job discrimination (differential access to certain occupations; Singhari & Madheswaran, 2016).

Access to urban jobs is not as automatic even in informal jobs as postulated by earlier works on informal economy (Hart, 1973). In fact, access to urban jobs has been restricted due to lack of social networks (Lucas, 2015; Papola & Subamanian, 1975; Upadhya, 2007). Social networks are found to be important in migration decisions to cities (Banerjee & Knight, 1985; Mitra, 2006). However, it does not strictly function on caste-class lines but on location-specific co-villagers. In contrast, Holström (1984), Panini (1996) and others suggest that employment in many Indian industries has been monopolised by members of certain castes, thereby restricting the entry of other groups such as SCs/STs. Munshi and Rosenzweig (2006) find sub-caste or *jati* as the powerful boundary for labour market networks, which help them to garner proportionately larger representation in employment in various industries.

The under-representation of marginalised groups in private corporate sector jobs (Mamgain & Tiwari, 2016; Sharma, 2008) is a testimony of biases in the hiring of workers belonging to these groups by employers even in the formal labour market. The reasons for such low social diversity in private sector jobs are yet to be studied intensively. The limited evidence shows how the private sector holds merit-based selection as the prime criterion in hiring workers and blames the current dual education system for causing unequal outcomes and low representation of SCs/STs. It is particularly so in growing industries such as IT and information technology-enabled services (ITeS), wherein certain social and cultural attributes are thought to be necessary (Jodhka & Newman, 2010; Upadhya, 2007). However, such arguments by the industry are misplaced, as a sizeable proportion of job hiring in the industry is made through employee referrals (Ramesh, 2004) and the marginalised groups are highly disadvantaged in such networks.

Some scholars argue that the new liberal policies have made a significant change in the organisation of work processes led by technological changes and have provided more employment opportunities to marginalised groups like SCs (Kapur, Prasad, Pritchett, & Babu, 2010). As a result, there has been convergence among SCs/STs and Others in their occupational distribution, relative wages, educational attainments and faster intergenerational mobility in both education and work (Hnatkovska, Lahiri, & Paul, 2012). Some studies argue that in the modern technology-savvy sectors such as software and business process outsourcing (BPO) or call centres, no such discrimination exists as is observed in Delhi's labour market (Banerjee, Bertrand, Datta, & Mullianathan, 2009). However, evidence also suggests that SCs/STs have suffered most during the period of economic liberalisation, as they lost more secure and decent employment in public enterprises and also faced discrimination in getting private corporate sector jobs. In fact, they have become more vulnerable to employment and income fluctuations (Kannan, 2012; Mamgain & Tiwari, 2017).

The rising inequality in urban as well as rural areas has added to their woes and adversely affected the overall human development levels of the country (Suryanarayan & Agrawal, 2013). The boom in IT industry employment has been largely realised by the urban middle class, as they possess better education, knowledge of written and spoken soft skills like English, and some degree of Westernised social orientation (Upadhya, 2007, p. 41).

Affirmative measures have, no doubt, improved the access of SCs and STs to jobs over the past 60 years, particularly in the public sector employment and educational development (Borooah, Sadana, & Naik, 2013). The 'patronage effect' based on caste is also significant in securing public sector jobs at lower positions, thereby underscoring the importance of social networks (Gille, 2013). However, social exclusion and discrimination in labour markets against these groups still continue to be widespread and to a significant extent partly due to poor effectiveness of the existing measures and partly because of the absence of any affirmative action (AA) in the private sector where most of the Indian workers are employed (Papola, 2012).

Part of the exclusion in the labour market takes place because of the dissemination of information on jobs, which is often exclusionary: Information becomes available only to those who have someone 'inside'; and the 'insiders' mostly happen to be from among those socially and economically better placed. In the process, equality of opportunity is denied. Also, discriminatory processes can extend beyond the access to information and to processes of selection in which attributes which have little relevance regarding job performance but tend to favour candidates with better social and economic endowment (e.g., facility with spoken English) are emphasised. Another necessary condition to reduce exclusion and discrimination, therefore, is to ensure equality of opportunity in access to information and use of non-discriminatory methods and criteria in selection (Papola, 2005).

The brief overview of the literature on the labour market in India is to show that most of the studies have focused on supply side dynamics, whereas demand side perspectives remain rather sketchy. There is hardly any recent study that exclusively analyses the issues covered in this book on both the demand and supply side dynamics of urban labour market in the formal sector in India with an exclusive focus on the access and inclusivity issues. As stated earlier, urban labour markets have undergone a tremendous change during the recent period and thus have become more complex to understand. New forms of work organisations and related employment such as third-party manpower services and IT-enabled platform works are emerging, resulting in a faster growth in the contractualisation and casualisation of labour. Keeping this in view, it would be interesting to critically understand the job search and hiring of workers in urban labour markets from the perspective of marginalised groups such as SCs, STs and Muslims in a comparative manner with other better-off socio-religious groups with an objective to contribute to the available literature on labour market and provide policy prescriptions for promoting faster growth in quality employment opportunities with more inclusiveness. Towards this objective, we have undertaken a holistic analysis of urban labour market from the perspective of access and inclusion in the demand and supply of labour force. We have also done a critical analysis of job search strategies of employed as well as unemployed persons in the framework of information asymmetries in the labour market. We argue that segmentation in urban labour market continues to persist on the lines of gender, caste, ethnicity, location and occupations. We show how social networks and employee referrals are critical in job search and job mobility, thereby undermining the chances of those equally or more competent for the job in the labour market. We provide an in-depth analysis of job postings and hiring practices by employers and their impact on participation as well as employment of marginalised social groups. We make a critical analysis of the argument of 'meritocracy' by the private sector and weak social diversity of workplaces in the private sector, which are then juxtaposed to explain discriminatory practices by employers in the private sector. Income inequalities are explained in terms of employment inequality and wage inequality. We argue that marginalised groups continue to remain mostly in low-end-low-paying jobs in urban areas, which is mainly due to their disadvantage in human capital endowment as compared to other social groups along with weak institutional support and unequal access to job market information. Finally, we offer useful suggestions to improve the quality of employment and its access to socially marginalised groups and ensure redistributive justice through affirmative measures. This book is largely based on a large primary sample survey of job seekers, final-year students of graduate programmes, employers and labour market intermediaries in four cities of Delhi National Capital Territory (NCT), Pune, Lucknow and Coimbatore. It also uses the NSSO unit-level data on employment and unemployment for under-standing the broad features and structural changes in employment in urban India. The details about the methodology and sample selection are presented in Annexure 1A. It merits mention here that the results of the study do not take into consideration the issue of selection bias. Hence, they are applicable not to the average of different social groups in the sample cities but only to those survey respondents. Nonetheless, this technical limitation does not dilute the broad policy conclusions emerging from the study.

Chapter Plan

The book spans eight chapters. After briefly presenting the broad features of employment, the current chapter provides theoretical developments and empirical evidences in the context of urban labour market in India. It argues that there are very few studies which have analysed the job search and hiring practices in urban India, particularly when both job seekers and employers are equipped with IT. Even in such a changing milieu, there remain information asymmetries, and caste dynamics still play an important role in determining the outcomes in the urban labour market in the country. Chapter 2 delineates the trends and patterns in employment in India with a focus on urban areas. Based on the NSSO data on employment and unemployment, it examines in detail the access of quality employment to labour force belonging to various social groups. It also analyses the determinants of access to such quality employment opportunities. Based on the sample survey data, we have analysed the city-level features of employment and unemployment across four sample cities in Chapter 3. This chapter thereafter sets stage for understanding the job search methods and access to jobs among the sample labour force in Chapter 4. Based on the framework outlined in Chapter 1, it further elaborates the discussion around information asymmetries and discrimination. Chapter 4 studies the characteristics of job seekers, their job search strategies and access to jobs in the urban labour market. It also attempts to understand the role of networks and labour market intermediary institutions in job search and access to quality jobs. Chapter 5 attempts to examine job mobility in the urban labour market. It covers various forms of job mobility, the role of social networks in job mobility, determinants of job mobility and the impact of job mobility on the earnings of workers with a special focus on marginalised groups. The issue of wage earnings and inequality are analysed in Chapter 6. The chapter also decomposes wage inequality into job inequality and wage inequality in a framework of discrimination in urban labour market. It argues that while job inequality is the major contributor to wage inequality, the prevalence of discrimination in access to various occupations also contributes significantly to wage inequality in the Indian urban labour market. Recruitment or demand for workers is an important aspect of the functioning of the labour market. The changes in recruitment processes and their implications for hiring are critically analysed in Chapter 7. The chapter attempts to understand the role of labour market intermediaries such as job portals, social networks, private placement agencies and staffing companies in the recruitment strategies by employers. It argues that switching to new forms of recruitment practices by employers is largely to save their time and monetary costs while at the same time securing access to a relatively larger pool of suitable applicants for different kinds of jobs. The growing use of employee referrals and social networks in hiring decisions and underlying rationales are also discussed in Chapter 7. We attempt to understand the dynamics of discrimination in urban labour market based on the information collected from sample job seekers and employers in Chapter 8. The chapter delineates the nature and forms of discrimination faced by job seekers. It also juxtaposes such discrimination revealed by job seekers with the responses from employers and argues that with several hidden forms of job signalling, screening, selection criteria and pay offers by the employers, job seekers from poor social backgrounds and marginalised communities generally get excluded in such recruitment practices. It also outlines select policy imperatives for the creation of quality employment opportunities, improving employability and promoting social diversity in private industry through well-defined affirmative programmes.

Annexure 1A. Research Methodology

The study is largely based on primary data. It also uses unit record-level secondary data from various NSSO rounds on employment and unemployment to understand the broad trends in employment/unemployment, its characteristics, structure and participation of marginal groups therein. Intersectionality between gender and social groups constitutes cross-cutting comparatives to understand the gender and caste dynamics in urban labour markets. However, as mentioned earlier, a large part of the study is based on primary survey data to answer several questions mentioned in the preceding sections. Given the wide yet complex set of research questions, the information has been collected from both demand and supply side actors. This is thus a unique approach to address the underlying questions pertaining to urban labour markets.

On supply side, information is collected on labour supply side characteristics of urban households. This includes participation in labour market, job search strategies, household members' experiences of participation in hiring by employers, job mobility, nature and quality of employment, and income along with their various socio-economic characteristics. We have also collected information from the final-year graduates/postgraduates from select higher educational institutions (new entrants to labour market) to know about their job search methods, including their experiences of participation in campus placement drives, success rate of hitting job, experiences of interviews and their future plans along with socio-economic details of their parents.

On demand side, the information is gathered to understand the nature and forms of employment on offer by employers, their job-matching and hiring methods, hiring preferences, strategies of promoting social diversity in their recruitments, employees' turnover/ attrition, wages and challenges they face in the hiring of workers. Equally important would be to study the functioning and efficacy of campus placement cells of educational institutions to know the strategies and criteria for campus placements, the challenges which they face and the selection rate. Firms are increasingly adopting RPOs and a number of RPO firms have emerged in urban labour markets. These also include the placement agencies and private employment agencies directly recruiting and supplying labour to firms. It will be interesting to understand and analyse their role, processes of recruitment, criterion for placement, counselling/guidance to job seekers and social protection to labour from the perspective of marginalised groups. Job portals such as Naukri.com and Babajob and social networking portals such as Facebook and LinkedIn have emerged recently as major actors in the labour market for job signalling and job matching. We could not collect the information from such portals due to no sharing of data policy of these portals. However, we draw our analysis from related studies and also from the information collected from select human resource (HR) managers/firms.

Sample Selection

Selection of City

Our strategy has been to draw the sample from among the three megacities and other cities with million-plus population. From among the three megacities (or now being called the global cities) of Delhi, Greater Mumbai and Kolkata, we selected Delhi NCT for our study. In 2011, there were 53 million-plus cities/urban agglomerations. The selection of the city from this list was made purposively. Three million-plus cities, namely Lucknow in Uttar Pradesh, Coimbatore in Tamil Nadu and Pune in Maharashtra, were selected purposively for the study. The reasons for this purposive selection are as follows: The population growth in Delhi has considerably decelerated (26.7%) between 2001 and 2011 as compared to the earlier decade (52.7%). It is an important centre of both public and private sector enterprises having second highest per capita income in the country. It has seen a highest inflow of in-migrants from its adjoining states. The city has also witnessed a very high growth of population as urban agglomeration in its National Capital Region (NCR) consisting of Gurgaon, Faridabad, Noida and Ghaziabad cities. Lucknow urban agglomeration has witnessed a rapid increase in its population and expansion of economic activities in recent years. This city is also the capital of the most populous state of India. Similarly, Coimbatore and Pune are important hubs of manufacturing and services industries, including education. Pune witnessed an impressive growth in employment opportunities in both manufacturing and services sectors such as IT and education. Coimbatore has also been an important hub for export-oriented firms which also witnessed fluctuations in its industrial activities due to global recession. More so, labour markets of all the sample cities of Delhi, Lucknow, Pune and Coimbatore have been studied in the past focusing on processes of migration, segmentation, informality, recruitment practices and earnings (for Delhi, see Banerjee, 1984; Banerjee & Knight, 1985; Desi, 1998; for Coimbatore, see Harris, Kannan, & Rodgers, 1990; for Lucknow, see Papola, 1982; for Pune, see Lambert, 1963).

Selection of Wards

Using the 2011 Census list of wards, all wards in each city were arranged according to the percentage of SC population therein. A sample of 20 wards for Delhi and 10 wards each for Lucknow, Coimbatore and Pune was selected purposively, keeping in view the concentration of SC/ST population. From each sample wards, 3 census enumeration blocks (CEB) consisting of 150–200 house-holds were selected using the probability proportional to size (PPS) method.

Selection of Job Seekers in Urban Households

The next step consisted of the selection of job seekers in urban households as sample units. All the households located within the boundaries of the sample CEB were listed and certain auxiliary information was collected during the listing to form second-stage strata (SSS). While forming SSS, SC/ST and other households were grouped under separate SSS (four in number) in the following manner:

Household Type	SSS Number
SC/ST/Muslim Households:	
• Households with at least one unemployed person in the age group 15–35 years and actively searching job	1
• Households with at least one employed person in the age group 15–45 years and actively searching job	2
Other Households:	
• Households with at least one unemployed person in the age group 15–35 years and actively searching job	3
• Households with at least one employed person in the age group 15–45 years and actively searching job	4

A sample size of 20 households in a sample CEB was allocated over the respective SSS in proportion to the total number of listed households in the respective SSS with a minimum allocation of 2 households for each SSS, subject to the availability of the required number of households in the respective frame. In other words, if H_i be the number of listed households in the ith SSS ($i=1, 2, \dots, 4$), the number of households to be selected from the ith SSS is given by $20 \times (H_i/H)$, rounded off to the nearest integer with a minimum of 2, where H denotes the total number of households listed in the CEB, that is, the selected block or sub-block, as the case may be. The required number of sample households from any SSS was selected by systematic random sampling without replacement (SRSWOR).

Selection of Educational Institutions and Final-Year Students

Students passing out from various categories of educational institutions and searching for job formed another segment on the supply side information. The sample of students consists of those belonging to technical, management, professional and general education streams (in degree and diploma/certificate-level institutions) who are in their final year of degree programme and are planning to join the labour market for their job search. Public as well as private educational institutions were selected purposively for the interview of final-year degree/diploma students.

We have also collected information from the placement cells of the sample educational institutions on placement services, placements of students during last year, nature of employment on offer through placement services, industry of employment and selection criteria. The purpose of the information is to illustrate the role of placement cells not only being intermediary labour market institutions but also helping in brand building for the educational institutions themselves so as to create more demand for their education. This is more so in the case of private educational institutions. Most of the private institutions were reluctant to share the detailed data about the placement of their students by their gender, social groups and industry of employment. We have to satisfy ourselves with the limited information through personal discussions with the placement officers. This information is used to triangulate the information collected from the final-year students from these institutions. In all, our sample included 25 placement cells of sample educational institutions.

Sample Selection for Demand Side Variables

Selection of Private Firms

For understanding the demand side dynamics of the recruitment of persons in urban labour market, we have collected information randomly from the HR managers of major employing private sector firms in each city. For the selection of enterprises, a list of companies from Fundoodata.com was used. This data provided vital information about companies, including their sub-entities covering manufacturing as well as services sector, total turnover, size of employment and contact address. Based on the list of companies obtained from Fundoodata.com for each sample city and discussions with the city-level industry associations, we categorised firms into three categories based on the size of employment, that is, big, medium and small separately for manufacturing and services industries. We selected 15 enterprises from each sample city randomly. In all, we could succeed in collecting detailed information from 45 private sector firms. Both quantitative and qualitative information was collected on various methods of hiring and retainment of employees along with their plans to promote social and ethnic diversity in their enterprises.

Selection of Private Placement Agencies/Recruitment Firms

As mentioned earlier, private placement agencies are increasingly playing an important role in the labour market in helping job seekers in their job search, job matching and recruitment for public as well as private sector firms, mostly for lower- and middle-level jobs. Other intermediaries in the labour market that are emerging fast are staffing companies and recruitment firms. We attempted to collect information from placement agencies and staffing companies for understanding their role in the labour market from the perspective of social inclusion. It has been difficult to get the data for private placement agencies and staffing companies for drawing a sample for the study. In the case of private placement agencies and staffing companies, we used the limited information available from the internet for sample selection in each city. In all, 20 private placement agencies, staffing companies and recruitment firms were selected for an in-depth study. The information provided by the placement agencies and staffing companies, particularly about the job seekers, placements and wages offered, was quite broad, giving little scope for detailed analysis.

City-wise details about sample size are as follows:

S. No.	Sample Unit	Delhi	Lucknow	Coimbatore	Pune	Total
1	Job-seeking households	1,150	760	492	806	3,208
2	Private firms	15	10	10	10	45
3	Private placement agencies/recruitment firms/staffing companies	10	5	5	5	25
4	Educational institutions and their placement cells	10	5	5	5	25
5	Final-year students and pass-outs of sample educational institutions	600	350	350	350	1,650

Source: Author.

CHAPTER 2

Employment and Unemployment Situation in Urban India

(with Special Focus on Regular Salaried Employment)

Introduction

The question of employment has always remained centre stage in the development policy debate across the globe. In India, it has featured as an element of development policy since the beginning of Five-Year Plans, albeit with varying degree of emphasis. Improving the quality of employment in terms of reasonable and rising level of income, and a minimum measure of social security against the common risks of work and life, was, however, considered an important concern of the state policy. Despite such concerns, the progress on the front of employment generation has been a mixed one. The experience of a consistently high rate of economic growth of over 6 per cent in India since the 1980s, and its accelerated pace after the economic reforms of the 1990s, has had limited impact on creating employment oppor-tunities for its growing labour force outside the farm sector (Papola &

Sahu, 2012). In fact, the pace of employment creation was quite dismal during the 1990s, which was termed as a period of 'jobless growth'. The situation worsened further after the advent of the economic crisis in 2007–2008, causing a faster deceleration in the employment growth. There is a growing deficit of decent employment, which is regarded as instrumental in achieving the economic and social development across the globe (ILO, 2014; World Bank, 2011, p. 2).

Unlike many developed as well as developing countries, the incidence of open unemployment is proportionately less in India. The real issue instead is the nature and quality of employment available to the labour force, owing to which the biggest challenge is that of the high incidence of underemployment and the accrual of very low earnings from the available employment opportunities for a large section of Indian workers. About half of the Indian workforce is engaged in occupations related to agriculture and allied activities at abysmally low levels of income, contributing a mere 14 per cent of the GDP of the country (IHD & ISLE, 2014, p. 26). Further, the decline in the proportion of such occupations in total employment has been rather slow.

The opportunities for regular salaried employment are also extremely limited as over half of the Indian workforce is engaged as self-employed workers, while another one-third works as casual wage labourers. Moreover, the new wage employment opportunities that have emerged in recent years have largely been casual in nature without any social security (Mamgain & Tiwari, 2017). Thus, the informal mode of employment, with low earnings and limited or no social protection, still accounts for about 86 per cent of the total employment in India (IHD & ISLE, 2014; ILO, 2015). More so, employment generation is significantly being influenced by the technological revolution in recent decades that has been reshaping the methods of production, distribution and services, and the resultant skill landscape of organisations (Aedo, Hentschel, Luque, & Moreno, 2013). In brief, the rapid economic growth witnessed during the period from the late 1990s till 2012 hardly succeeded in bringing about any significant structural changes in employment.

Based on the National Sample Survey data on Employment–Unemployment Surveys (EUS), this chapter attempts to analyse the nature, form and growth of employment in urban India since 1983 with a focus on social groups (such as STs, SCs, Muslims and Others including Other Backward Classes [OBCs]) and regular salaried employment. It also critically examines the magnitude and challenges of unemployment in urban India. As is well known, over 30 per cent of the Indian population now resides in urban areas. The growth in urbanisation has accelerated in the last decade, 2001–2011, and is expected to increase to 40 per cent by 2030, thereby adding 250 million people—many migrants from rural areas—in the urban population (McKinsey Global Institute, 2010). The present form of urbanisation is supported by the rapid increase in services and the deindustrialisation of cities with factories being moved to the urban periphery or the agricultural hinterland. These trends have important implications for employment and earning situation in the urban areas.

Trends in Labour Force and Employment in Urban India

Labour Force

Labour force constitutes economically active population including the working population and those searching employment. Over 36.6 per cent of the urban population constitutes labour force. The corresponding figure for rural areas is much higher. Gender-wise, over 56 per cent of the male and 15.5 per cent of the female population constitute labour force in urban India. The long-term trend in labour force participation rates (LFPRs) for males in urban areas has been increasing, whereas it was declining for females, particularly during the post-reform period (Table 2.1). The decline in female LFPRs has been more pronounced in rural areas, more so in the 15–29 years age group. The reasons for such withdrawal of females in rural areas are well documented in the recent literature. These largely include increasing participation in education and withdrawal from low-income

Table 2.1 Gender-Wise Trends in LFPRs in Urban and Rural India (%)

Year	Rural			Urban		
	Male	Female	Person	Male	Female	Person
1983	55.49	34.19	45.04	53.93	15.88	35.86
1993–1994	55.95	32.73	44.70	54.28	16.37	36.38
2004–2005	55.33	33.04	44.48	57.03	17.88	38.39
2011–2012	55.17	25.06	40.48	56.29	15.48	36.64

Source: Calculated from NSSO unit-level data on employment and unemployment for different rounds. Employment/unemployment figures are based on the NSSO's usual status (UPS; principal status including subsidiary status) approach.

activities (see Gang, Sen, & Yun, 2012; Rangarajan, Iyer, & Kaul, 2011; Verick & Chaudhary, 2017).

There have been considerable variations in the LFPRs across the social groups, the highest being for STs, closely followed by SCs, Muslims and lowest among Others including OBCs. A similar pattern has been observed for both urban and rural areas (Table 2.2). While LFPRs are generally higher in rural areas than in urban areas, the difference is substantively higher for STs, SCs and Muslims, whereas such difference is not revealing for Others. This suggests the relatively weak economic situation of former three groups, forcing them to opt for work than leisure or educational development. Such differences also emerge due to the relatively very low LFPRs of women, particularly among Others as compared to the remaining groups, both in urban and rural areas.

The LFPRs tended to decline in both urban and rural areas among population from different social and religious groups but more rapidly in rural areas in the recent period 2004–2005/2011–2012. In urban areas, while LFPRs of STs and SCs have declined by around 2 percentage points, it almost remained unchanged for Others. In fact, as

Table 2.2 *Trends in LFPRs of Different Social Groups in Urban and Rural India (%)*

Year	ST	SC	Others	Muslim	Total
			Rural		
1983	53.59	47.24	36.33	44.25	45.00
1993–1994	53.60	46.06	33.83	44.48	44.70
2004–2005	51.79	44.71	34.72	45.06	44.49
2011–2012	46.72	40.98	33.58	40.54	40.48
			Urban		
1983	42.04	37.24	32.23	36.16	35.86
1993–1994	39.56	37.78	33.32	36.65	36.38
2004–2005	39.66	39.96	34.68	38.88	38.39
2011–2012	37.79	37.68	34.11	37.02	36.64

Source: Calculated from NSSO unit-level data on employment and unemployment for different rounds.

Notes: Others include OBCs and other socio-religious groups such as Hindus, Christians, Jains, Buddhists and Sikhs, except Muslims. STs, SCs and Muslims are generally considered as marginal groups in terms of their numbers in population of the country and stand at the bottom in various socio-economic indicators of development.

compared to 1983, it has been higher by around 2 percentage points for Others in urban areas.

Growth in Employment

After arguing that India has comparatively low LFPRs as compared to developed countries, largely due to the low yet declining female participation in labour market, let us first briefly look into broad patterns in the growth in employment in India since 1983. The long-term growth in employment over the period of nearly three decades has been around 2 per cent (slightly lower than the growth in labour force). It tended to decelerate in recent years—from 2.02 per cent per annum during 1983–1993/1994 to 1.84 per cent during 1993–1994 to 2004–2005, but at a sharp pace between 2004–2005 and 2011–2012 (0.45%). The deceleration in the growth in employment has been accompanied by an acceleration in the economic growth, clearly suggesting the decline in the employment component of growth (IHD & ISLE, 2014). This has been true for workers belonging to various social groups.

This period of high growth has also been accompanied by a period of rapid structural transformation in employment, probably at a rate not witnessed during any past period since Independence. For the first time in India's history, the absolute number of workers in agriculture declined by 32.3 million between 2004–2005 and 2011–2012. As compared to an overall low employment growth rate of only 0.5 per cent, the non-agricultural workforce grew by 3.1 per cent annually over this period. Moreover, the number of regularly employed wage/salaried workforce grew by a highest 3.2 per cent per year, as compared to an annual decline of 0.7 per cent in the self-employed workforce, and a modest increase of 1.1 per cent per year in the casually employed workforce. Although these changes appear partially magnified due to the hump in the year 2004–2005 in both the agricultural workforce and the numbers of self-employed, nevertheless they represent real and significant changes in the structure of employment (Srivastava & Naik, 2017).

Let us look into the trends in the growth in employment in urban areas. There were 111.30 million workers in urban areas accounting for 26.5 per cent of the total workforce in India during the year 2011–2012. Nearly one-fifth of the women workers in the country were located in urban areas. Similarly, a highest 36 per cent of the Muslim workforce and one-fifth of the SC workforce lived in urban areas (Figure 2.1).

Among the total workforce in urban areas, an overwhelming majority were men (80%) in 2011–2012. Nearly 15 per cent were SCs and another 16 per cent Muslims (Figure 2.2). The share of women in urban workforce declined by nearly 2 percentage points between 2004–2005 and 2011–2012. There had been no substantive change in

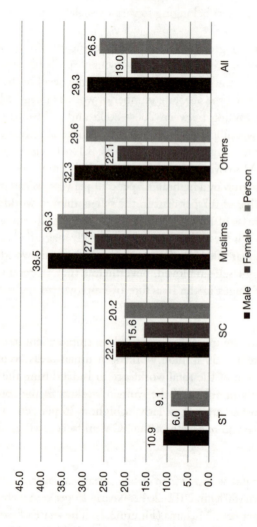

Figure 2.1 *Percentage Share of Workers in Urban Areas in All-India Workforce, 2011–2012*

Source: Calculated from NSSO unit level data on employment and unemployment, 68th Round, 2011–12.

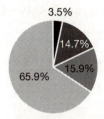

■ST ■SC ▨Muslims ▨Others

Figure 2.2 Distribution of Urban Workforce by Their Social Group, 2011–2012

Source: Based on NSSO unit level data on employment and unemployment, 68th Round, 2011–12.

the relative share of different social groups in urban workforce except for a marginal increase in the share of Muslims during the period 2004–2005 and 2011–2012.

The long-term growth in employment opportunities in urban areas had been almost growing at double the rate than in rural areas during 1983/2011–2012. Urban areas fared relatively better in creating employment opportunities during the post-reform period by recording an annual growth of over 3 per cent as compared to around 1 per cent in rural areas. However, the growth in employment decelerated during the post-reform period, in both urban and rural areas, more so during 2004–2005/2011–2012. The major impact has been noticed in rural areas where the annual growth of employment dipped steeply from about 1.6 per cent during 1993–1994/2004–2005 to 0.11 per cent during the subsequent period 2004–2005/2011–2012 (Table 2.3). This had largely been due to the sharp decline in female participation in the labour market in rural areas.

Gender-wise, the growth in female employment decelerated sharply in urban areas as well. This has been quite contrary to the pattern observed in the case of their counterparts residing in rural areas, where they witnessed an absolute decline in employment during the period 2004–2005/2011–12 (Table 2.3).

Table 2.3 *Gender-Wise Growth of Workers (CAGR)*

Period	Rural			Urban		
	Male	Female	Person	Male	Female	Person
1983/1993–1994	2.93	2.23	2.67	4.04	4.02	4.03
1993–1994/2004–2005	1.49	1.78	1.59	3.23	3.72	3.33
2004–2005/2011–2012	1.36	–2.39	0.11	2.82	1.54	2.56
1993–1994/2011–2012	1.44	0.14	1.01	3.07	2.86	3.03
1983/2011–2012	1.97	0.88	1.60	3.41	3.28	3.39

Source: Calculated from NSSO unit-level data on employment and unemployment for different rounds.
Note: CAGR: Compound annual growth rate.

How did the growth in employment opportunities vary for the population across various social and religious groups in urban India? While SCs experienced a fairly high growth of over 4 per cent in their employment in urban India as compared to other castes till 2004–2005, it decelerated the most in the later period 2004–2005/2011–2012 to nearly 2 per cent. Contrary to this trend, the growth of employment of Others picked up during the post-reform period, more so during 2004–2005/2011–2012. In the case of STs, the annual growth rate in employment tended to improve during the post-reform period. In the case of Muslims, the growth in employment decelerated in the post-reform period but not as sharply as observed in the case of SCs (Table 2.4). In brief, employment opportunities for SCs tended to worsen in the recent period in urban areas. The possible causes for such decline in employment opportunities, particularly for SCs despite their almost stable LFPRs between 1993–1994 and 2011–2012, may be largely associated with the sharp decline in manual job opportunities in urban areas coupled with their higher participation in education in the 15–29 years age group.

Table 2.4 *Growth of Workers by Their Social Groups in Urban India (CAGR)*

Period	STs	SCs	Others	Muslims	Total
1983/1993–1994	2.59	4.27	3.78	4.21	4.10
1993–1994/2004–2005	3.42	4.76	3.65	2.96	3.33
2004–2005/2011–2012	3.56	1.98	4.06	2.31	2.56
1993–1994/2011–2012	3.47	3.67	3.80	2.71	3.03
1983/2011–2012	3.16	3.89	3.80	3.24	3.41

Source: Calculated from NSSO unit-level data on employment and unemployment for different rounds.

Growth of Employment across Major Economic Activities

The tertiary sector dominates employment opportunities (58.7%) in urban areas, followed by the secondary sector that absorbs about one-third of the workforce in urban India (Table 2.5). The manufacturing sector employed nearly one-fourth of the urban workforce. Another 9.4 per cent of the urban employment is provided by the construction sector. Within the tertiary sector, trade, hotel and the restaurant sector accounted for nearly one-fourth of the urban employment. Another 16 per cent of the urban employment was contributed by the financial services sector in 2011–2012. Gender-wise, the structure of urban employment varies significantly for men and women. While more women than men are employed in manufacturing, financial services and community services, men are predominantly employed in trade and transport, although manufacturing and financial services are also popular among them. The share of women in trade, transport and construction is significantly lower than males (Table 2.5). Also, over one-tenth of the women were employed in agriculture and allied activities in urban areas during 2011–2012.

Table 2.5 Sector-Wise Composition of Employment in Urban Areas between 2004–2005 and 2011–2012 (%)

National Industrial Classification (NIC) One Digit/Year	2004–2005			2011–2012		
	Male	Female	Person	Male	Female	Person
Agriculture and Allied	6.2	18.1	8.7	5.7	10.9	6.7
Mining and quarrying	1.0	0.2	0.8	0.9	0.3	0.8
Manufacturing	23.3	27.4	24.2	21.9	28.2	23.1
Utilities	0.8	0.2	0.7	1.3	1.0	1.3
Construction	9.3	3.8	8.1	10.8	4.0	9.4
Secondary Sector	33.4	31.4	33.0	34.0	33.2	33.9
Trade, hotel and restaurant	27.9	12.5	24.6	26.1	12.9	23.5
Transport storage and communication, etc.	10.7	1.4	8.7	11.8	2.8	10.0
Financing, insurance, real estate and business services, etc.	16.8	22.1	17.9	15.2	20.9	16.3
Community, social and other services	4.1	14.4	6.3	6.3	19.0	8.8
Tertiary Sector	59.5	50.3	57.5	59.4	55.7	58.7
Total	100.0	100.0	100.0	100.0	100.0	100.0

Source: Calculated from NSSO unit-level data on employment and unemployment for different rounds.

How did employment opportunities grow across various economic sectors in urban areas, particularly during the recent period 2004–2005/2011–2012? While the urban employment registered a CAGR of around 2.56 per cent during 2004–2005/2011–2012, it considerably varied across different economic sectors (Table 2.6). The highest growth of over 12 per cent was witnessed in utilities. However, the share of utilities in total employment was very low at 1.3 per cent, thereby not affecting the overall growth rate in urban employment. The other sectors registering a sizeable employment growth in urban areas included community and social services, construction and transport. The boom in construction industry during the post-reform

Table 2.6 *Sector-Wise Growth of Urban Employment between 2004–2005 and 2011–2012 (CAGR %)*

Sector	Male	Female	Person
Agriculture	1.63	−5.58	−1.18
Mining and quarrying	1.45	6.73	1.79
Manufacturing	1.88	1.96	1.90
Utilities	10.63	28.33	12.35
Construction	5.10	2.03	4.81
Secondary	*3.05*	*2.37*	*2.91*
Trade, hotel and restaurant	1.89	2.02	1.90
Transport storage and communication	4.19	12.17	4.53
Financing, insurance, real estate and business services	1.40	0.77	1.24
Community, social and other services	9.30	5.70	7.64
Services	*2.81*	*3.01*	*2.85*
Total	2.82	1.54	2.56

Source: Calculated from NSSO unit-level data on employment and unemployment for different rounds.

period in urban areas has, in fact, created multiplier effect on community and transport services growth, resulting in higher growths in employment therein.

Gender-wise, the growth in employment of women in urban India has been nearly half than that for men. However, their number in utilities, transport storage and communication, and community services significantly increased during the period 2004–2005/2011–2012. For men, apart from these three sectors, their employment in construction increased by over 5 per cent per annum. The number of women employed in agriculture and allied activities declined at an annual rate of 5.6 per cent during the period (Table 2.6). The decreasing importance of agriculture in women employment is an appreciable development given the low productivity in this sector. However, it is intriguing that women participation in urban labour market is abysmally low and that too tended to decline over the years. A growing number of women in urban areas are neither in employment nor in education and training (NEET). The deceleration in women's participation in urban labour market is mainly associated with the lack of employment opportunities for them outside agriculture both in rural and urban areas (Chatterjee, Murgai, & Martin, 2015).

While making gender-wise analysis of employment, it needs to be kept in mind that the participation of women in labour market is inadequately covered by the population Census and NSSO's EUS. Unpaid activities such as 'attended domestic duties' (code 92) and 'attended domestic duties', and 'also engaged in the free collection goods,' largely undertaken by women are categorised as domestic work and not as 'economic activity' in EUS by NSSO. By including these activities, the LFPR of women turns out to be higher than men both in urban and rural areas, and there is no significant decline in women LFPRs. Such a pattern is explained as a shift for women, across both rural and urban locations, from remunerated and/or recognised work to unpaid and largely unrecognised domestic duties in recent periods (Ghosh, 2017). This situation occurs when the opportunities for stable employment with reasonable income grow less than the desired rate, thereby compelling women to shift to unpaid and largely unrecognised domestic duties.

The sector-wise composition of urban employment varies significantly across different social groups. A highest one-third of the Muslim workers are working in the manufacturing sector, whereas nearly 30 per cent of the SC/ST workers are working in community and other services (including financial and business services) in 2011–2012 (Table 2.7). The construction sector employs about 16 per cent of the total SC/ST workforce in urban areas, which is more than double than the corresponding share of workers from OCs (higher caste). Opposite is the scenario in the trade and hotel sector which employs much less percentage of ST/SC workforce as compared to Others

Table 2.7 *Industry-Wise Distribution of Employment in Urban India for Each Social Group, 2011–2012*

Industry	ST	SC	Muslims	Others	Total
Agriculture	12.2	7.1	3.9	7.0	6.7
Mining and quarrying	1.7	1.1	0.3	0.7	0.7
Manufacturing	14.6	19.0	33.6	22.7	23.6
Electricity, water, etc.	1.1	1.7	1.1	1.3	1.3
Construction	15.5	16.1	10.1	7.3	9.3
Trade, hotel and restaurant	13.4	15.9	27.0	24.7	23.4
Transport storage and communication	10.2	9.8	11.1	9.7	9.9
Other services	31.2	29.2	12.9	26.6	25.0
Total	100.0	100.0	100.0	100.0	100.0

Source: Calculated from NSSO unit-level data on employment and unemployment for different rounds.

and Muslims. As stated earlier, there are evidences of discrimination against SCs in employment in the trade and hotel sector.

In brief, urban areas witnessed a moderately high growth in employment, mainly for men. Unlike rural areas, the participation of women in urban areas although remained low yet it did not decline as significantly as in rural areas between 2004–2005 and 2011–2012. Construction, utilities and the service sector such as transport and community, social and other services have been the major drivers of employment growth in urban areas during the period. The growth of employment for population groups such as SCs and Muslims had been significantly lower than Others and STs, indicating the challenges of access to employment opportunities faced by these marginalised groups in the urban labour market. This is mainly due to the lower education and skill levels of labour force belonging to SCs and Muslims, and also partly due to the discrimination in the labour market (Madheswaran, 2017).

Nature of Available Employment

The nature and form of employment significantly varies between urban and rural areas. While, self-employment predominates in the rural areas, wage employment is the major form of employment in the urban areas employing about 59 per cent of the workers therein. About 42 per cent of the workers in urban areas were engaged as self-employed workers in 2011–2012. Another 43 per cent of the workers were working in regular salaried jobs in urban areas (Table 2.8). The corresponding figure for rural areas was far less at 8.8 per cent. In other words, over 64 per cent of the regular salaried jobs were located in urban areas, whereas nearly 87 per cent of the casual labourers and 78.7 per cent of the self-employed workers were based in rural areas (Figure 2.3). This shows the disproportionately higher dependence on casual wage and self-employment in rural areas as compared to urban areas.

Table 2.8 *Gender-Wise Nature of Employment in Urban India*

Nature of Employment	1983	1993–1994	2004–2005	2011–2012
		Male		
Self-employed	40.66	41.52	44.71	41.90
Regular salaried	44.18	42.56	40.74	43.06
Casual labour	15.16	15.92	14.57	15.04
		Female		
Self-employed	45.56	44.56	46.75	42.67
Regular/Salaried	26.21	29.71	36.27	43.04
Casual labour	28.23	25.73	16.98	14.29
		Person		
Self-employed	41.66	42.15	45.14	42.05
Regular/Salaried	40.53	39.93	39.78	43.05
Casual labour	17.84	17.93	15.08	14.89

Source: Calculated from NSSO unit-level data on employment and unemployment for different rounds.

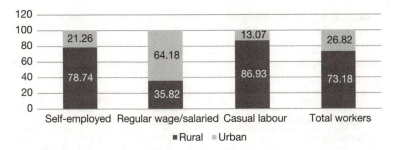

Figure 2.3 *Rural–Urban Distribution of Workers by Their Type of Employment, 2011–2012*

Source: Based on NSSO unit level data on employment and unemployment, 68th Round, 2011–12.

How the nature of employment changed in urban areas over the period is illustrated in Table 2.8. The share of self-employed persons among total workers in urban areas hovered around 42 per cent, except for a rise of around 3 per cent in 2004–2005. Similar has been the trend in other forms of employment, except for a substantive rise in the share of regular employment by 2011–2012 (around 3%) with a corresponding decline in the share of self-employed. Across genders, while the nature of male employment did not change much, there has been a steady rise in the share of females in regular salaried jobs with a corresponding decline in their share in casual wage labour in urban areas. In other words, despite the overall lower participation of women in urban labour market, their access to regular salaried jobs improved significantly, particularly during the post-reform period. A part of this rise in their share in regular salaried jobs is explained by a rapid growth in domestic paid work, which is largely menial and low paid. Similar pattern of rise in the share of regular salaried workers and a corresponding decline in the share of self-employment is also observed in the composition of employment across each social group of workers between 2004–2005 and 2011–2012. Such trend has been more pronounced in the case of ST workers as most of their women work as domestic helps on a monthly salary basis.

Social group-wise, Muslims are largely engaged in self-employment activities as compared to SCs, STs and Others. Most Muslim workers

Table 2.9 *Social Group-Wise Nature of Employment in Urban Areas (%)*

Nature of Employment	ST	SC	Muslims	Others
2004–2005				
Self-employed	35.1	32.4	57.6	45.9
Regular/Salaried	38.5	40.6	26.7	42.2
Casual labour	26.3	26.9	15.7	11.8
2011–2012				
Self-employed	26.4	30.1	54.3	42.4
Regular/Salaried	47.7	45.3	27.9	46.3
Casual labour	25.9	24.6	17.8	11.3

Source: Calculated from NSSO unit-level data on employment and unemployment for different rounds.

in urban areas are engaged in informal manufacturing and petty business. Nearly 45 per cent of the workers other than Muslims are in regular salaried employment. Such share is lowest for Muslims. Almost one-fourth of the SCs/STs are working as casual wage labourers in urban areas in 2011–2012 (Table 2.9).

Unemployment in Urban India

There were 3.94 million unemployed persons in urban areas, constituting 43.1 per cent of the total unemployed in India in 2011–2012. Unemployment is prevalent predominantly among youth as over 85 per cent of them were in the 15–29 years age group in urban areas, and about 88.6 per cent youth in rural areas in 2011–2012. Table 2.10 presents the incidence of unemployment among youth across their gender and educational attainments. Overall, the incidence of unemployment is almost double among urban youth as compared to their rural counterparts. Gender-wise, the rate of unemployment is highest among females in urban areas.

Table 2.10 Unemployment Rate among Youth (15–29 Years) by Their Educational Level, 2011–2012

Education Level	Rural			Urban			Total		
	Male	Female	Person	Male	Female	Person	Male	Female	Person
Illiterate	2.29	0.81	1.61	2.60	1.50	2.27	2.35	0.89	1.72
Primary	3.21	0.52	2.43	5.02	4.74	4.97	3.69	1.19	3.03
Middle	4.17	4.12	4.16	5.06	6.72	5.31	4.43	4.65	4.47
High school and higher secondary	5.28	10.12	6.27	8.42	16.30	9.72	6.34	11.86	7.40
Diploma and certificate	15.82	27.70	17.92	12.58	18.92	14.03	14.25	22.77	15.98
Graduate and above	18.91	29.18	21.45	16.46	24.47	19.01	17.37	25.86	19.86
Technical degree	29.72	71.51	40.35	16.09	21.24	17.90	18.07	26.08	20.79
Diploma not equivalent to degree	17.50	35.36	20.77	13.46	24.17	16.15	15.33	28.28	18.20
Diploma equivalent to degree	22.46	47.16	29.81	15.18	12.13	14.20	16.54	18.08	17.03
Total	4.94	4.45	4.80	8.25	14.05	9.49	6.01	6.83	6.23

Source: Calculated from NSSO unit-level data on employment and unemployment for different rounds.

Mismatch between Education and Employability

Youths having graduate degree including technical and professional educational attainments suffer with the highest incidence of unemployment both in rural and urban areas. The next highest incidence of unemployment is among those having diploma-level professional and technical education (Table 2.10). Young females with higher level of education face higher incidence of unemployment compared to their male counterparts, more so in rural areas. For example, about 24.5 per cent females with graduate and above education were unemployed in urban areas as compared to 16.5 per cent of their male counterparts in 2011–2012. Due to the lack of employment opportunities in rural areas, the incidence of unemployment is substantially higher among those with higher levels of education. It is more so for young women. Reasons for such high incidence of unemployment among young women include responsibilities of home care economy, limited mobility due to various socio-economic constraints and gender discrimination in recruitment and wages (IHD & ISLE 2014).

Overall, the employability of youth has declined over the years, which is largely due to the rising incidence of unemployment among those with education levels up to or below middle school. The reduction in unemployment rates among those with educational levels up to secondary school and higher except graduates with technical degrees, largely confirms that an improvement in the education levels of youth has led to a concomitant improvement in their employability since the early 1990s. However, the prevalence of a high rate of unemployment among graduates and technical degree/diploma-holders is still a matter of concern. This also justifies the concerns of employers regarding the poor education and skill levels of youngsters passing out of higher and technical educational institutions (FICCI, 2010; NASSCOM, 2014). It is also reflective of a huge disconnect between theoretical learning and practical knowledge being imparted in the educational institutions. Moreover, the mushrooming of technical education institutions during the last two decades has grossly undermined the quality of vocational and technical education in the country. As a result, the demand for degree-level technical education offered by private institutions has significantly come down as evidenced in a sizeable number of seats remaining vacant therein in recent years. Many private institutions offering degree-level technical education are now also offering diploma-level education. The demand for such diploma-level courses is increasing as the industry is getting technically qualified undergraduates at comparatively low salaries. The emphasis of Prime Minister, Narendra Modi, on imparting skills to Indian youth to help them improve their employment prospects, coupled with the ongoing initiatives under the National Skill Development Mission, could ensure that the gap between the current education levels and industry needs is bridged by ensuring both the quality, and the relevance of technical education in the country.

After examining the characteristics and broad trends in employment in urban areas, the following section examines the nature and access of regular salaried employment both in rural and urban areas. This has been examined in detail, as one of the objectives of the present study is to assess the nature and access of such employment to job seekers belonging to various socio-religious groups.

Nature and Access of Regular Salaried Employment

This section is based on the unit record data of large sample round of NSSO on Employment–Unemployment Survey (EUS) for the years 1983, 1993–1994, 1999–2000, 2004–2005 and 2011–2012. NSSO provides information on the type of enterprises where workers are employed. For understanding the nature and patterns in regular employment across the types of enterprises, we have categorised the employers of such regular workers into three categories, that is, (a) public sector enterprises consisting of all kinds of government departments, autonomous/sub-ordinate organisations supported by government finances, etc. (b) private sector enterprises consisting of public and private limited companies/organisations, voluntary and other firms/organisations (broadly matching the features of the private organised sector) and (c) informal sector enterprises including proprietary/partnership firms and individual employer households employing domestic helps, security guards, etc. The data thus grouped for the years 2004–2005 and 2011–2012 are comparable across these categories, whereas the same is not strictly comparable for earlier period 1999–2000. Given this limitation, we shall confine our in-depth analysis for the period 2004–2005 to 2011–2012 only. Various social and religious groups considered here include SCs, STs, OBCs excluding Muslim OBCs, Others excluding Muslims (OCs) and Muslims (including both OBCs and general categories). Minority religious groups such as Christians, Sikhs, Jains and Buddhists excluding those reporting as STs and SCs among them are included in OCs. STs, SCs and OBCs are generally categorised as vulnerable groups who have been given reservation in the public sector employment through government's affirmative policies.

About 87 million of workers in India were working in regular salaried jobs, constituting over 18.4 per cent of the total workforce during 2011–2012. This share tended to improve over the years but more rapidly in recent period of high economic growth. For the first time in India's history, the absolute number of workers in the agriculture sector declined by 32.3 million between 2004–2005 and 2011–2012. As compared to an overall low employment growth rate of only 0.5 per cent, the non-agricultural workforce grew by 3.1 per cent annually during this period. Moreover, the number of regular wage/salaried workforce grew by 3.2 per cent per year, as compared to an annual decline of 0.7 per cent in the self-employed workforce, and a more modest increase of 1.1 per cent per year in the casually employed workforce (Srivastava & Naik, 2017).

Such growth in regular employment opportunities was experienced by workers belonging to various social groups, thereby improving their shares in regular employment. However, other social groups lagged behind OCs in their shares in regular employment (Table 2.11). Thus, the dependence on casual wage labour is highest among SCs

Table 2.11 *Share of Regular Employment in Total Employment in India (%)*

Employment Type / Socio- Religious Group	1983	1993–1994	1999–2000	2004–2005	2011–2012
STs	7.9	6.3	7.0	7.4	9.0
SCs	11.3	9.6	10.9	13.2	15.8
Muslims	13.2	12.7	13.8	13.5	16.6
OBCs	–	–	11.8	13.0	16.2
OCs	15.3	16.4	24.7	25.2	30.0
All	13.6	13.7	14.6	15.3	18.4

Source: Calculated from NSSO unit-level data on employment and unemployment for different rounds.

workers, followed by STs. Among OBC and Muslims workers, the proportion of casual workers was about 28 per cent each, and lowest at 13 per cent among OCs.

How are regular employees distributed across various types of employers? Based on the categorisation of employers as mentioned previously, around 30 per cent of the regular salaried workers were employed in the public sector, another 22.6 per cent in the private sector and the remaining 47.5 per cent in the informal sector, including about 1.4 per cent with employer households in 2011–2012 (Table 2.12). There are significant differences in the opportunities of regular salaried employment across the social groups.

For STs, the public sector emerges as a major source of their regular employment opportunities. For Muslims, a lowest 16.7 per cent of their regular salaried workers get jobs in the public sector. Nearly 12 per cent of the regular employment among STs and around 16 per cent that of SCs and Muslims is provided by the private sector. Thus, regular employment opportunities for two-thirds of Muslim workers and for over half of the SC and OBC workers are created

Table 2.12 Distribution of Regular Salaried Employment by the Type of Enterprises

Socio-religious Group	Public Enterprises	Private Enterprises	Informal Enterprises[a]	Total
		1999–2000		
STs	51.21	11.70	37.09	100
SCs	41.42	13.37	45.20	100
Muslims	22.22	12.23	65.56	100
OBCs	31.31	15.33	53.36	100
OCs	37.51	19.95	42.54	100
Total	35.62	16.69	47.69	100
		2004–2005		
STs	52.63	9.42	37.95	100
SCs	35.96	12.33	51.71	100
Muslims	23.53	9.73	66.74	100
OBCs	29.56	16.27	54.17	100
OCs	36.16	22.13	41.71	100
Total	33.54	16.93	49.54	100
		2011–2012		
STs	53.17	11.96	34.87	100
SCs	32.59	16.69	50.72	100
Muslims	16.72	16.03	67.25	100
OBCs	27.79	21.30	50.91	100
OCs	31.65	29.86	38.49	100
Total	29.98	22.56	47.46	100

Source: Calculated from NSSO unit-level data on employment and unemployment for different rounds.

Note: [a] Includes employer's households accounting for a negligible share in total regular employment. This note also applies to the rest of the tables wherever applicable.

outside the public and the private sector, that is, the informal sector, which are mostly menial in nature. The situation of OCs is much better than SCs, OBCs and Muslims as the former's share is much higher in the public and the private sector regular employment (Table 2.12).

How did the opportunities of regular salaried employment grow over the years for different social groups? Let us first look into the trends in the growth of regular employment opportunities in the public sector. Regular employment in the public sector increased by about 2 per cent annually during the period 2004–2005/2011–2012. The growth in the public sector employment has been significantly higher in the earlier period, 1999–2000/2004–2005. However, the growth in the number of regular workers in the public sector belonging to various social groups varied significantly over the years. In the recent period, 2004–2005/2011–2012, it has been the lowest for OCs and Muslims (about 0.7%), followed by SCs (1.7%), but highest for OBCs (6.6%) and STs (6.1%). There has been a fast deceleration in the growth rates of regular employment in the public sector for SCs and Muslims between two periods, that is, 1999–2000 and 2004–2005, and 2004–2005 and 2011–2012, whereas the trend was opposite for STs (Table 2.13). The growth of employment opportunities for OBCs in the public sector, however, decelerated marginally. Such vast differences in the growth in regular employment in the public sector could be due to the better reinforcement of OBC and ST quota in government jobs in recent years.

The private sector consistently performed better than the public sector and the informal sector in creating regular employment opportunities since 1999–2000. This could be due to the neoliberal policies promoting the increasing role of the private sector since the early 1990s. The private sector alone contributed a highest 61.6 per cent to additional regular employment (totalling 11.07 million persons) opportunities generated during the period. This acceleration in the growth in employment has also been observed by recent studies on the organised manufacturing sector after an almost jobless growth

Table 2.13 *Trends in Annual Growth Rates in Regular Salaried Employment for SCs and Others*

Socio-religious Group	Public Enterprises	Private Enterprises	Informal Enterprises	Total
		1999–2005		
STs	1.29	−1.50	0.48	0.70
SCs	5.61	7.78	10.69	8.35
Muslim	5.36	−0.33	3.60	3.56
OBCs	7.06	10.67	8.46	8.37
OCs	−0.11	4.59	0.33	1.02
All	3.09	6.12	4.91	4.47
		2005–2012		
STs	6.17	9.70	4.74	6.01
SCs	1.69	7.68	2.85	3.13
Muslim	0.72	13.57	5.87	5.75
OBCs	6.66	22.07	11.12	11.55
OCs	0.74	7.17	1.50	2.68
All	2.07	8.05	3.08	3.71
		1999–2012		
STs	4.11	4.88	2.94	3.77
SCs	3.31	7.72	6.05	5.27
Muslims	2.63	7.56	4.92	4.84
OBCs	4.87	9.31	5.44	5.95
OCs	0.39	6.09	1.01	1.98
All	2.49	7.24	3.84	4.03

Source: Calculated from NSSO unit-level data on employment and unemployment for different rounds.

during the 1990s (Goldar & Suresh, 2017). Interestingly, all social groups benefitted with this high growth but OBCs benefitted the most. Growth in their numbers in private sector jobs almost doubled from 10.7 per cent per annum during 1999–2000/2004–2005 to over 22 per cent during the later period, 2004–2005/2011–2012

(Table 2.13). Next to OBCs, Muslims experienced a phenomenal growth of about 14 per cent in their employment in the private sector during 2004–2005/2011–2012. This also suggests an inclusive growth in the private sector employment but at the cost of decent work which ensures tenurial as well as social security.

In the informal sector, the growth in regular employment opportunities was comparatively high as compared to the public sector, and OBCs and Muslims experienced faster growth in employment therein since 1999–2000. For SCs, the growth in regular employment opportunities in the informal sector was highest at about 11 per cent during 1999–2000 to 2004–2005, which decelerated steeply to 2.8 per cent during the later period, 2004–2005/2011–2012. For Muslims and OBCs, growth in such employment accelerated (Table 2.13). The reasons for such varying growth in regular employment opportunities among SCs in the informal sector could be linked to their corresponding higher growth in casual wage employment during 2004–2005/2011–2012, thereby implying a very thin difference in switching between regular jobs in the informal sector and casual wage labour. Many a time, casual wage employment fetches higher wages for such workers in comparison to those in so-called regular jobs in the informal sector. In such situations, workers withdraw themselves from the informal sector regular jobs and work as casual labour. A case in point is the recent boom in construction industry, which offered casual wage for a long duration at relatively higher wages than those prevailing in the informal sector activities.

Representation of Various Groups in Regular Salaried Jobs

How are SCs/STs and Muslims represented in regular employment as compared to OBCs and OCs in the public and the private sector? The representation of SCs/STs in the public sector regular employment has been fairly proportionate to their respective shares in all-India population. This has largely been possible due to the reservation of employment for these two groups in the public sector employment. It has fairly improved since the 1990s after the active involvement of judiciary in the implementation of reservation in the public sector. However, Muslims are grossly under-represented in the public sector employment and their relative share in such jobs has not improved much over the years. The reasons for their under-representation in the public sector jobs and the need for affirmative measures to promote their share have been well outlined in the reports of both the Sachar Committee (GoI-Cabinet Secretariat, 2006) and, recently, the Kundu Committee (GoI-Ministry of Minority Affairs, 2014).

In private sector regular employment, the share of SCs, STs and Muslims is still low in proportion to their share in population, but more so in the case of STs and Muslims. OBCs also remain under-represented in private sector jobs but their representation tended to improve due to the faster growth in their employment during recent years. In the informal sector regular wage employment, SCs and Muslims are fairly represented (Table 2.14).

The case of OBCs is worth mentioning here in the context of their representation in regular employment in the country. Although they experienced a rapid improvement in their share in regular wage employment in the public as well as the private sectors, they remain under-represented in proportion to their share in the total population. The rise in the share of OBCs in the public sector could be directly due to reservation (Table 2.14). But it is also worthwhile to mention the rise in their share in the private and informal sectors as it is associated with the significant improvement in their education levels in recent years and faster withdrawals from farm-related jobs. In brief, although OCs represent a proportionately larger share in regular employment in the public as well as the private sectors, the higher growth in employment for SCs, STs and OBCs is gradually bridging the gap in their relative share in such employment (Table 2.14). This is definitely a positive trend which can be associated with the higher economic growth that created regular employment opportunities in the private as well

Table 2.14 Representation of SCs/STs in Regular Salaried Employment by the Type of Enterprise (%)

Socio-religious Group	Public Enterprises	Private Enterprises	Informal Enterprises	Total	As % of Total Workers in India
1999–2000					
STs	7.06	3.33	3.92	4.95	11.1
SCs	16.15	11.46	13.56	14.16	20.3
Muslims	5.82	7.27	13.26	9.66	9.9
OBCs	23.26	24.83	29.5	26.53	33.1
OCs	47.71	53.12	39.77	44.7	25.8
All	100	100	100	100	100
2004–2005					
STs	6.47	2.29	3.16	4.12	9.8
SCs	18.22	12.38	17.73	16.99	19.9
Muslims	6.48	5.31	12.45	9.24	10.3
OBCs	28.08	30.62	34.84	31.86	37.5
OCs	40.75	49.4	31.82	37.79	22.5
All	100	100	100	100	100
2011–2012					
STs	8.52	2.55	3.53	4.8	10.2
SCs	17.75	12.08	17.45	16.33	19.1
Muslims	5.91	7.53	15.01	10.59	11.7
OBCs	30.63	31.2	35.44	33.04	37.6
OCs	37.19	46.64	28.56	35.23	21.4
All	100	100	100	100	100

Source: Calculated from NSSO unit-level data on employment and unemployment for different rounds.

as informal sectors particularly after 1999–2000, benefitting the marginalised groups.

Regular Salaried Employees across the Industry of Employment

Which are the major industries in terms of providing regular employment opportunities to workers belonging to various social groups? As shown in Table 2.15, over three-fourths of the public sector jobs are concentrated in other services including public administration, whereas nearly half of the regular jobs in the private sector are available in manufacturing industries. Another one-fourth of the regular jobs in the private sector are contributed by other services, mainly consisting of education, health and other basic services. The structure of regular employment is significantly diversified in informal enterprises, which employed almost half of the regular salaried workers in 2011–2012. The industry sectors such as trade and transport have a sizeable share in employment apart from manufacturing and other services in informal enterprises. This pattern of distribution of regular workers across industry groups is almost similar for SC and OC groups (Table 2.15). A notable difference, however, exists among SC and OC regular workers with respect to their relative shares in trade, hotel and other services in the informal sector. The share of SCs in hotel and restaurant jobs is proportionately very low as compared to OCs. Their share is comparatively much higher in transport-related jobs and other services. Such smaller share of SCs in hotel industry-related jobs could partly be associated with the discrimination which SCs generally face in accessing jobs in eateries and hotel industry (Iversen & Raghavendra, 2006). The reverse is the case of other services where SCs are employed in cleaning and other menial jobs as workers from OCs are generally not willing to take up such tasks considered as 'polluting' ones.

Quality of Regular Employment

As mentioned previously, we have categorised regular salaried employment as the most desirable form which provides fixed tenurial written

Table 2.15 Percentage Distribution of Regular Salaried Employees across Industry of Employment and the Type of Enterprise, 2011–2012

Industry	SCs				OCs			
	Pub.	Pvt	Inf.	Total	Pub.	Pvt	Inf.	Total
Agriculture	0.32	0.29	0.29	0.3	0.71	0.27	1.21	0.80
Mining and quarrying	2.31	1.67	0.46	1.27	2.14	1.14	0.32	1.10
Manufacturing	2.6	48.69	26.51	22.4	3.31	44.04	29.52	25.73
Electricity, water, etc.	5.61	1.72	1.34	2.8	5.52	1.07	0.49	2.16
Construction	1.16	3.06	4.75	3.3	1.20	3.39	3.56	2.80
Trade, hotel and restaurants	0.91	6.98	17.14	10.14	1.23	7.60	23.65	12.40
Transport, storage and communication	10.19	12.00	16.83	13.85	8.98	15.01	12.63	12.20
Other services	76.9	25.59	32.68	45.94	76.92	27.47	28.63	42.81
Total	100	100	100	100	100	100	100	100

Source: Calculated from NSSO unit-level data on employment and unemployment for different rounds.
Notes: Pub.: public enterprises; Pvt: private enterprises; Inf.: informal enterprises.

job contract along with social security benefits such as paid leaves, medical benefits, insurance, gratuity and provident fund to wage/salaried workers. Such categorisation also meets two important conditions of 'decent work'. The NSSO data allow us to work out such workers for two periods, that is, 2004–2005 and 2011–2012.

Given the relatively higher increase in private sector jobs, it is warranted to know the quality of regular employment generated in the private sector. It is expected that all employees working in the public as well as private organised sectors should have at least written job contracts. Surprisingly, a significant share of regular workers working in the public sector does not have any written job contract. The proportion of such workers has increased in the public sector from about 23 per cent in

Table 2.16 *Percentage Share of Regular Workers without Any Written Job Contract*

Type of Enterprise	2004–2005	2011–2012
Public	22.98	28.06
Private	50.06	60.08
Informal	88.56	89.85
Total	60.01	64.62

Source: NSSO EUS.

2004–2005 to over 28 per cent in 2011–2012. This is perhaps due to the fact that these workers are purely ad hoc with no fixed period of appointment. Furthermore, in the private sector, over 60 per cent of the regular workers do not have any written job contract, and this proportion has substantially increased between the period 2004–2005 and 2011–2012. Surprisingly, a whopping three-fourths of the additional regular employment opportunities generated in the private sector and 61 per cent of that in the public sector during the period 2004–2005/2011–2012 did not provide any written job contracts to workers (Table 2.16). The variations have been clearly spread across social groups as well.

The proportion of workers without any written job contract in the private sector is comparatively higher among STs (68%) and SCs (64%), followed by OBCs (62%) and lowest among OCs (57%). The Annual Survey of Industries (ASI) data also clearly show a steep rise in the proportion of contractual workers in private sector enterprises (from 14% in 1995 to 34% in 2010; Goldar & Suresh, 2017). These workers often do not have a written job contract and social security coverage, and their working conditions are poor. Neither the contractor nor the principal employer takes the responsibility of workers' welfare (NCEUS, 2009).

Written Job Contracts with Social Security

All regular employees in the public sector do not enjoy both tenurial security and social security benefits. Only about 62 per cent of the regular employees working in the public sector have some kind of written job contract along with social security benefits. Thus, a substantial percentage (about 38%) of the public sector regular employees have precarious nature of job without any social security, and which can be terminated at any time without any notice. This has been true for all regular employees belonging to various social groups but more so for Muslims, SCs and STs.

In the case of the private sector, the proportion of regular workers having some form of job contract along with social security is expectedly very less as compared to the public sector, thereby indicating the vulnerability of almost 70 per cent of the regular employees in the private sector in the hands of their employers. Similar to the public sector, the extent of such vulnerability is more so in the case of Muslim, ST and SC regular workers as compared to OBCs and OCs in the private sector. As obvious, almost all regular workers in the informal sector are most vulnerable from the perspective of their job contract and social security (Table 2.16). In brief, an overwhelming majority of regular salaried employees in India did not have any form of written job contract and social security, implying the magnitude of precariousness of such employment opportunities. Muslim and SC regular workers suffer maximum with such vulnerability.

Has such vulnerability of workers reduced over the years? No, in fact, it has significantly increased during 2004–2005/2011–2012, as the proportion of workers without job contract and social security increased by almost 10 percentage points in both public and private sectors. This general deterioration in the quality of regular employment has been witnessed by workers across all social groups but more so among Muslims (Table 2.17).

Regional Disparities in Quality of Regular Employment

It would be equally interesting to analyse the regional disparities in the access to regular employment opportunities and their quality in India. For this, we have analysed the data pertaining to the year 2011–2012

Table 2.17 *Percentage of Regular Employees Having Written Job Contract and Social Security*

Socio-religious Group	Public Enterprises	Private Enterprises	Informal Enterprises	Total
		2004–2005		
STs	64.66	24.49	4.50	38.05
SCs	66.27	29.42	2.94	28.98
Muslims	63.95	30.81	3.61	20.45
OBC	68.61	37.52	5.74	29.49
OCs	72.50	48.88	8.88	40.73
Total	69.21	41.47	5.94	33.17
		2011–2012		
STs	59.98	20.25	5.71	36.30
SCs	58.63	24.04	3.20	24.74
Muslims	52.55	17.91	1.57	12.71
OBC	57.19	30.44	4.34	24.59
OCs	68.81	34.85	7.83	35.20
Total	61.73	30.52	4.77	27.66

Source: Calculated from NSSO unit-level data on employment and unemployment for different rounds.

only. The share of regular workers in total workers varies from a highest 28 per cent in Punjab to a lowest 6 per cent in Bihar. Industrially advanced states such as Punjab, Tamil Nadu, Maharashtra, Gujarat, Haryana and Karnataka have proportionately high share of workers in regular employment as compared to relatively less developed states such as Bihar, Chhattisgarh, Uttar Pradesh, Jharkhand, Rajasthan, Orissa, Madhya Pradesh and Assam (Table 2A.1). In most of such less developed states, the public sector stands a major source of regular employment. Understandably, these states have comparatively very low share of the private sector in regular jobs, ranging from 6 per cent in Bihar to 18 per cent in Madhya Pradesh. In relatively developed states such as Karnataka, Haryana, Tamil Nadu, Maharashtra and

Gujarat, the private sector contributes about 25–38 per cent of the regular employment therein.

Over half of the regular employment in Punjab, Tamil Nadu, Andhra Pradesh, West Bengal, Gujarat, Uttar Pradesh, Kerala and Rajasthan is contributed by informal enterprises. There is a significant positive correlation between the shares of private and informal enterprises in regular employment (0.49) among states, indicating strong linkages between the two sectors in generating regular employment opportunities.

How do regular employment opportunities conform to the select features of decent work, that is, security of job tenure and social security benefits of over 80 per cent of the regular workers are covered by tenurial security and social security in public sector enterprises as well as in most Northeastern states, Jammu & Kashmir, Bihar, Rajasthan, Himachal Pradesh and Uttarakhand. The proportion of such regular workers is far less (50–65%) in relatively developed states such as Tamil Nadu, Haryana, Punjab, Maharashtra, Gujarat and Karnataka, thereby showing an unsecured regular employment in the public sector for a sizeable number of regular workers. In other words, privatisation has pushed the public sector to switch to unsecured jobs mostly in the industrially developed states. The situation of quality employment in the private sector is grave and widespread across India as the proportion of regular workers enjoying both tenurial security and social security therein do not exceed 30 per cent in most states (Table 2A.2). Understandably, the informal sector lacks such quality jobs across all the states.

Determinants of Access to Decent Regular Employment

As mentioned earlier, the quality of regular employment is assessed in terms of regular jobs providing tenurial security along with some social security. The likelihood of access to such 'quality regular employment' is analysed through personal and household characteristics of an individual measured through the educational levels of workforce, social belonging, gender, place of residence and enterprise type. The dependent variable quality regular employment (Q_{re}) is a binary variable with the value 1 if a particular regular worker has defined the characteristics and 0 otherwise. Symbolically, it can be written as

$$Q_{re} = \begin{cases} Q_{re} = 1 & \text{if WC} > 1 \quad \text{SS} < 8 \\ Q_{re} = 0 & \text{if WC} = 1 \,\&\, \text{SS} > 7 \end{cases}$$

$$P_i = P\{Q_{re} = 1 | X_i\}$$

$$\ln\left(\frac{P_i}{1 - P_i}\right) = \Lambda(X'\beta)$$

where $\Lambda(\cdot)$ is a logistic distribution, X is $(K \times 1)$ the vector of explanatory variables discussed previously. It is to be mentioned that the model is estimated with the state fixed effect. β is the vector of unknown parameters which has been estimated through the maximum likelihood method from the NSSO unit record data of EUS for the years 2011–2012. At the all-India level, there were around 40,197 persons in the individual sample of regular workers. Among them, a total of 39,565 persons provided information about the type of enterprise where they were working in.

The maximum likelihood estimate results of the Logit model discussed previously have been given in Table 2.18. All estimated coefficients are significant at the 1 per cent level, and the robust standard error has been reported along with the confidence interval. In getting decent regular employment, education emerges as a crucial factor after controlling for other variables. As expected and as per the human capital argument, in reference to the not literate individual, the likelihood of getting quality regular job increases with the education level as all the coefficients are positive and increase with the level of education. Predicted probabilities of getting such job with the educational achievements are shown in Figure 2.4 to substantiate the argument. The negative sign of the coefficient for females shows the prevalence of gender bias in quality regular jobs with reference to their male

Table 2.18 Estimation Results of Logit Model

Dependent Variable Education Level	Coefficient	Std Error	P > z	Confidence Interval Lower	Upper
Literate (Primary)	0.225	0.002	0.000	0.2214	0.2282
Middle	0.382	0.002	0.000	0.3785	0.3851
Secondary	0.894	0.002	0.000	0.8910	0.8970
High secondary	1.395	0.002	0.000	1.3910	1.3985
Diploma and certificate	1.492	0.002	0.000	1.4887	1.4949
Graduate and above	1.800	0.002	0.000	1.7964	1.8031
Gender					
Female	−0.393	0.001	0.000	−0.3942	−0.3909
Social Status					
STs	0.118	0.002	0.000	0.1150	0.1210
Muslims	−0.501	0.001	0.000	−0.5030	−0.4980
OBCs	0.020	0.001	0.000	0.0190	0.0220
OCs	0.072	0.001	0.000	0.0700	0.0740
Enterprise					
Private	−1.422	0.001	0.000	−1.4234	−1.4205
Others	−3.242	0.001	0.000	−3.2438	−3.2402
Sector					
Urban	0.276	0.001	0.000	0.2751	0.2778
State Fixed Effect	Yes				
Constant	−0.992	0.003	0.000	−0.9986	−0.9859

Source: Mamgain and Tiwari (2017).

Notes: Reference groups in education level, gender, social status, enterprise type and sector are not literate, male, public enterprises and rural area, respectively. All the coefficients are significant at the 1 per cent level of significance.

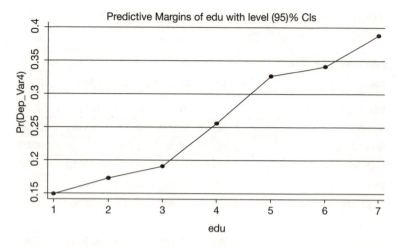

Figure 2.4 *Average Predicted Probabilities of Getting Quality Employment and Education*

Source: Based on NSSO unit level data on employment and unemployment, 68th Round, 2011–12.

counterparts. Also, most of the quality regular jobs are concentrated in urban areas as compared to rural areas. This improves the chances of workers in urban areas getting decent jobs.

Despite declining the share of employment in the public sector, this sector remains the best source of quality jobs. The likelihood of getting decent jobs in the private sector as compared to the public sector is 14 times less ($P > -1.42$ for private enterprises and $P > -3.24$ for informal enterprises). Thus, the likelihood of getting a decent employment is higher for a better-educated male individual residing in an urban area and employment in the public sector (Figure 2.5).

In order to see the level of education effect on decent regular jobs between different social groups and gender, the mean predicted probability has been estimated in Table 2.19. The aggregate predicted probability shows that the chance of getting quality regular employment has been around 0.35. However, as the coefficient (Maximum Likelihood estimate) above shows, the probability is the lowest for the not literate and highest for the individuals with the education level of graduates and above. Among different social groups in regular

Table 2.19 *Predicted Probabilities of Estimated Logit Model for Different Social Groups by the Level of Education*

Education Level/Social Group	SCs	STs	Muslims	OBC	OCs	Total
Illiterate	0.123	0.144	0.041	0.081	0.112	0.097
Primary	0.158	0.235	0.061	0.115	0.151	0.137
Middle	0.194	0.305	0.107	0.150	0.184	0.183
Secondary	0.343	0.457	0.233	0.297	0.345	0.337
High Secondary	0.471	0.581	0.321	0.381	0.483	0.443
Diploma	0.523	0.591	0.415	0.468	0.520	0.509
Graduate and above	0.589	0.649	0.494	0.523	0.595	0.572
Total	0.300	0.456	0.213	0.302	0.397	0.344

Source: Mamgain and Tiwari (2017).

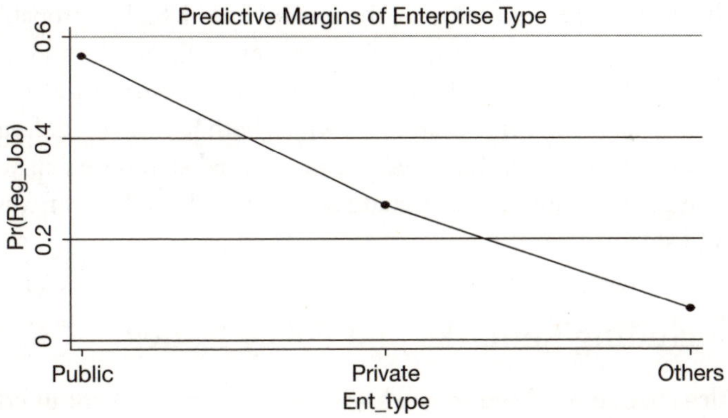

Figure 2.5 *Average Predicted Probabilities of Getting Quality Employment and Enterprise Type*

Source: Based on NSSO unit level data on employment and unemployment, 68th Round, 2011–12.

employment, the probability of getting quality jobs has been the highest for the STs, followed by Others, OBCs and lowest for SCs. However, the intergroup probability estimate shows that there has been considerable variation at the 'level of education'. For example, the likelihood of ST graduates getting decent jobs is higher than graduates belonging to OBCs, SCs and OCs.

Table 2.20 *Predicted Probabilities of Estimated Logit Model for Male and Female by the Level of Education*

Educational Level/Gender	Male	Female	Total
Illiterate	0.107	0.079	0.096
Primary	0.140	0.116	0.135
Middle	0.182	0.181	0.182
Secondary	0.339	0.332	0.338
High secondary	0.454	0.407	0.443
Diploma	0.535	0.417	0.511
Graduate and above	0.605	0.490	0.574
Total	0.354	0.305	0.345

Source: Mamgain and Tiwari (2017).

Between males and females, the former have a higher probability of being in quality regular jobs. At different levels of education, the probability for females has been lower than males except for the middle and secondary levels of education for which both have an equal level of probability. However, the difference in the predicted probability has been higher for diploma and graduate and the above level of education (Table 2.20).

Concluding Remarks and Policy Issues

In this chapter, we have shown how growth in employment in urban as well as rural areas has been much less than the desired pace to clear the backlog of unemployment and absorb the new additions to the labour force. The higher rate of economic growth since the post-reform period of the early 1990s has been characterised with the deceleration in employment growth, more so in rural areas. Wage employment constitutes about 59 per cent including 43 per cent regular employment in urban areas. Such composition of employment in urban areas has not changed substantially over the last three decades except in the recent period. Though the growth of regular employment accelerated in urban areas between 2004–2005 and 2011–2012 as compared to other forms of employment such as casual wage labour and self-employment, it suffered in terms of quality pertaining to its regularity and social security, and also equal access to various socio-religious groups. Majority of such regular employment opportunities suffer from informality, characterised by the precarious nature of jobs with no tenurial security, poor working conditions, extremely low levels of earnings and negligible social security during the phase of the neoliberal policies. Even in the private organised sector, which registered the highest growth in regular employment opportunities in recent years, a large majority of regular workers are bereft of tenurial and social security benefits, and the proportion of such workers is increasing over the years. Although the private sector has emerged as an important source of regular employment for all including SCs since the decline in the public sector employment, it has yet to improve the representation of SCs, STs and Muslims in their workforce proportionate to their population. Access to regular jobs is further constrained by the educational and social background of individuals, and the prevailing discrimination in labour market. There are strong evidences of discrimination of SCs in job offers and wages in the private sector, necessitating the private sector to act on a priority basis to desist from such practices in the garb of meritocracy.

Average wage earnings of regular workers vary hugely across the public, private and informal sectors, and also among social groups. A large number of regular employment on offer falls short of quality, characterised as poor working conditions, low earnings and lack of social security, thereby making them vulnerable to income fluctuations and exploitation by the employers.

The prevalence of low quality of employment, particularly among the SCs, STs and Muslims, has created a vicious circle of low-productivity occupations, poor remunerations, and the limited ability of the family to invest in education and healthcare, which dampens the overall prospects for both development and growth. A positive feature in recent years, however, has been the phenomenon of an increasing proportion of SC youths studying in the educational institutions. However, this transition in favour of education has also widened the gap among SCs/STs and Others in their participation in both work and education.

The challenge, therefore, is to create remunerative employment opportunities at a faster pace, particularly for youths who are increasingly becoming impatient with the inability of the political systems to generate employment opportunities for them. With the faster rise in urban population, mainly associated with migration from rural areas, urban India stands to face the challenge of employment generation at a much higher pace in next two decades. Therefore, employment generation should be made central to the development strategy, as it is an important pillar for achieving inclusive development. This calls for the measures to increase investment in the labour-intensive sectors, especially in the industrially backward and remote areas, which include the measures for the ease to do business, infrastructure development, safety, good governance, and sound corporate social responsibilities and ethical practices on the part of industry.

The major challenge is to formalise the huge informal sector by scaling up its technology, production, productivity and employment. The big industry can play a role of facilitator to transform the microunits into small, medium and large in a steady fashion, thereby creating a proactive path of industrial development in the country. The growing profit margins of big industries enabled by capital-intensive production processes, intensive marketing but disproportionate rewards to labour may not lead to a healthy relationship between capital and labour for a long time. The strategy should be to redistribute the benefits of growth by the industry by creating more jobs with social security to workers. This will accelerate the effective demand for the goods and services, and create a virtuous cycle.

It is thus imperative to intensify policy initiatives to promote enterprise development, particularly among SCs/STs/Muslims in a big way under the current 'Make in India' programme. This would require more intensive implementation of the 'mentorship programmes for SC/ST entrepreneurs' as promised under the affirmative action policy (AAP) by the private sector in 2006. The Public Procurement Policy of 2012 needs to be operationalised in a big way by effectively allocating and using the funds under Scheduled Caste Sub-Plan (SCSP) and Tribal Sub-Plan (TSP) along with the access to general funds. So far the experience of effective allocation of resources under SCSP and TSP is far less than satisfactory; and there are evidences how these funds have been diverted to other uses, not benefitting the SCs/STs (NCDHR, 2016).

Public policy should aim at extending the credit points similar to carbon points to the private sector for improving the diversity of their workforce by employing persons from SCs/STs communities, particularly at the supervisory and managerial level regular positions. These credits can be used for tax and other kinds of exemptions by the government. However, this would require the monitoring of workforce which the private sector may like to avoid.

Another major challenge is to improve the educational development of youths. An alarming aspect is the increasing deficit of quality education and skill training. The deterioration in the quality of public educational institutions at primary, secondary and higher educational levels have most adversely affected the SCs/STs who are most dependent on these institutions. The major challenge is to improve the access to quality education to all and to SCs/STs in particular. Thus, public educational institutions at both the school and higher levels need to be strengthened and made accountable for their quality and relevance. Private educational and training institutions also need to be monitored closely for the quality of teaching they offer and their fee structures. The current measures of skill development under the National Skill Development Mission need to be scaled up in a big way in order to address the skill shortages being faced by the Indian industry. More so, there is hardly any comprehensive study and concurrent evaluation to understand the impact of skill development programmes in employment and employability of youth in India.

We must not forget that unlike the past, today's youth including SCs are more informed and keen to be a part of the IT revolution. They are justifiably asserting their concerns for a decent and dignified life. Politicians and policy-makers must, therefore, come forward in a big way to facilitate their overall development and ensure decent employment opportunities for them.

Finally, employment expansion should be undertaken under the 'decent work' framework, ensuring fair and equal opportunities to everyone, increased productivity of workers, better working conditions, fair wages, skill development and social security. It also calls for building a morally sound responsible environment along with the usual business environment by employers as well as workers to leap into the next stage of inclusive development. Equally important would be to strengthen the database at the disaggregated level for group-specific planning, monitoring and quality control.

Annexure 2A

Table 2A.1 *Regional Trends in the Composition of Regular Employment, 2011–2012*

State	% Share of Regular Employment in Total Employment in the State	Distribution of Regular Employment by the Type of Enterprise (%)		
		Public	Private	Informal
Andhra Pradesh	18.24	28.52	16.08	55.40
Arunachal Pradesh	19.80	80.79	4.71	14.50
Assam	15.09	52.00	17.14	30.87
Bihar	6.02	51.20	6.20	42.60
Chhattisgarh	10.16	47.61	13.87	38.51
Delhi	62.02	26.22	21.03	52.75
Gujarat	25.70	19.03	27.84	53.13

State	% Share of Regular Employment in Total Employment in the State	Distribution of Regular Employment by the Type of Enterprise (%)		
		Public	Private	Informal
Haryana	25.57	29.80	36.27	33.92
Himachal Pradesh	18.00	53.95	17.95	28.11
Jammu & Kashmir	21.62	56.79	8.04	35.17
Jharkhand	10.83	49.42	15.78	34.80
Karnataka	23.29	23.49	37.58	38.93
Kerala	26.34	30.57	19.68	49.75
Madhya Pradesh	11.96	44.85	18.77	36.39
Maharashtra	26.47	22.75	32.20	45.05
Manipur	14.83	80.02	4.22	15.76
Meghalaya	16.75	66.52	11.34	22.15
Mizoram	23.08	85.93	2.31	11.76
Nagaland	22.26	89.51	1.29	9.20
Orissa	10.94	45.26	17.14	37.61
Punjab	27.88	24.61	18.29	57.10
Rajasthan	13.31	34.74	16.09	49.17
Tamil Nadu	26.77	19.65	24.93	55.42
Tripura	16.40	61.60	7.01	31.39
Uttar Pradesh	10.82	31.53	15.81	52.66
Uttarakhand	18.69	44.30	16.36	39.34
West Bengal	18.22	31.94	14.41	53.65
Total	**18.41**	**29.98**	**22.56**	**47.46**

Source: Calculated from unit record data of NSSO's 68th round on employment and unemployment.

Table 2A.2 Regional Trends in the Quality of Regular Employment, 2011–2012

State	% of Regular Workers Having Written Job Contract and Social Security by the Type of Enterprise		
	Public	Private	Informal
Andhra Pradesh	69.5	15.98	14.52
Arunachal Pradesh	89.23	1.28	9.49
Assam	75.33	20.79	3.89
Bihar	92.49	3.78	3.73
Chhattisgarh	83.57	8.46	7.97
Delhi	53.73	26.26	20.01
Goa	41.29	50.79	7.93
Gujarat	65.02	26.86	8.12
Haryana	63.99	29.69	6.33
Himachal Pradesh	87.17	8.14	4.69
Jammu & Kashmir	94.85	0.83	4.32
Jharkhand	78.33	16.62	5.04
Karnataka	51.26	38.04	10.69
Kerala	72.46	18.56	8.99
Madhya Pradesh	76.69	17.19	6.12
Maharashtra	50.74	39.71	9.54
Manipur	95.67	1.68	2.65
Meghalaya	89.29	4.66	6.04
Mizoram	98.58	0.33	1.1
Nagaland	98.67	1.15	0.18
Orissa	79.16	16.37	4.47
Punjab	65.00	28.15	6.85
Rajasthan	89.94	6.33	3.73
Tamil Nadu	60.91	29.86	9.23
Tripura	94.96	3.31	1.74

State	% of Regular Workers Having Written Job Contract and Social Security by the Type of Enterprise		
	Public	Private	Informal
Uttar Pradesh	77.75	16.81	5.44
Uttarakhand	82.44	13.37	4.2
West Bengal	70.25	23.33	6.42
Total	**66.92**	**24.89**	**8.19**

Source: Calculated from the unit record data of NSSO's 68th round on employment and unemployment.

CHAPTER 3

City-Level Features of Employment and Unemployment

Development Pattern in Sample Cities—A Brief Overview

Having examined the broad features of urban employment in Chapter 2, let us now analyse the features of employment and unemployment in our four sample cities, that is, Delhi, Lucknow, Pune and Coimbatore. These cities are distinct in their broad characteristics and hence have become relevant for a comparative analysis. A brief development pattern of these cities is discussed in this section from the perspective of labour market. This section also provides select demographic features of the sample cities based on the population Census 2011 data. In the next section (Select Demographic Features of Sample Cities), the demographic characteristics of sample households including migration are discussed. In Section 'Broad Features of Sample Households', broad features of employment and unemployment are analysed for the sample population. It needs to be clarified here that the broad employment pattern observed among the sample households may not necessarily represent the employment pattern in the sample cities due to our purposive sampling of households where any member in a household was actively searching a job.

Delhi National Capital Territory

Delhi's demographic and economic evolutions have highly been influenced by its glorious past, especially during the 20th century when it became the capital of British India and later of Independent India since 1947. Today's Delhi is characterised as a global city with its unique blend of the ancient and modern. Post Independence, modern growth and development efforts in general, and those that took place at the dawn of the new millennium in particular, have contributed towards making Delhi a global capital city state. As a result, Delhi is endowed with state-of-the-art infrastructure facilities, enabling it to serve as the seat of the government at both the Union and state levels. However, Delhi is also inhabited by a large number of poor slum-dwellers, street children, homeless and differently abled people. The city attracted a large number of migrants till the 1990s. Almost two-thirds of the population living in Delhi is from the neighbouring states of Uttar Pradesh, Haryana, Punjab and Rajasthan (Dupont, 2000).

Delhi, akin to other Indian megacities such as Mumbai and Kolkata, has recorded a significant decline in the population growth rate during the period 2001–2011. This has largely been linked to the faster growth of satellite townships in NCR such as Gurgaon, Noida, Faridabad, Ghaziabad, Sonipat and Meerut. The Census data show that during the decade 2001–2011, the population growth rates in the urban areas of the constituent regions of NCR other than Delhi, such as Haryana (61%), Uttar Pradesh (52.3%) and Rajasthan (50.5%), were very high (IHD, 2013).

Economic growth and the accompanying livelihood and educational opportunities in Delhi have attracted people from all over the country. Migrants not only from neighbouring states but also from distant states such as Bihar, West Bengal, Madhya Pradesh and several other states made Delhi their home with dreams of building a better future. Although they form the backbone of Delhi's economy in many ways by providing invaluable labour and services, they also exert pressure on the civic services and other urban infrastructure that is already strained (IHD, 2013). Like the population growth decline in Delhi, the migrant population growth in the city has also declined. The reasons for such decline may be many, including the emergence of economic opportunities in NCR area and the high cost of living in Delhi.

The major sources of employment in Delhi are three sectors: trade, other services (including financial, business services, public administration, education and health care) and manufacturing. Manufacturing is an important sector of employment in Delhi, but its importance over the years has gradually declined with the shifting of such activities in NCR townships. Like other states in India, employment opportunities in the organised sector in Delhi have declined over the years, as most of the employment is generated in the unorganised sector. The poor, who end up getting jobs in the unorganised sector, often find themselves vulnerable due to the lack of both job and social security, often working in conditions detrimental to their health. They largely end up earning their livelihood from sectors such as construction, retail trade, transport and solid waste management (IHD, 2013).

The rapid growth in satellite towns in Delhi NCR was contributed by the fast growth in manufacturing, construction and services such as education, health, banking, hotels, transport, communication and IT services, leading to a significant rise in the per capita income since the late 1990s. Gurgaon, Greater Noida and Manesar represent new centres for global automotive manufacturing, finance and call centres (Barnes, 2014). Gurgaon and Faridabad are the bases of many domestic and foreign companies, and half of the income tax collected in Haryana comes from these two urban regions (Debroy & Bhandari, 2009). The Haryana and Uttar Pradesh state governments played a major role in the development of Gurgaon, Noida and Greater Noida to attract the industrial development therein.

Along with industrialisation, there was an expansion of the large-scale industrial production and mushroom growth of small, micro and medium ancillary industries in NCR area. This led to the demand of huge informal labour and continuous decline in the wage labour in the organised sector (Barnes, 2014). In NCR's auto assembly and components plants, there was continuous replacement of formal workers with informal workers. Most of the workers were appointed through the networks of labour contractors. The reason being that there was a huge supply of workers from the rural areas who were unable to earn their livelihood from agriculture. They started migrating to the urban regions in NCR in search of livelihood and earned their living as daily wage labourers. The improvement in transport network further enabled large magnitude of daily commuting within the NCR region including Delhi.

The nature and form of work have also changed with such development in recent years in Delhi NCR, with increasing informalisation of work including home-based work with low incomes bereft of any social security. This has aggravated the vulnerability of workers to various types of shocks such as slipping into poverty, poor health and poor human capital formation.

Lucknow

Lucknow is the capital of Uttar Pradesh, India's most populous state. It is the second most populated city in the state after Kanpur. Lucknow Urban Agglomeration (LUA) became a million-plus city in 1981. The population of LUA increased nearly threefold from 1.06 million in 1981 to 3.04 million in 2011. According to one estimate, migration added 36 per cent of the population to the city between 1991 and 2001. The prominent economic reasons for migration were employment, business and education.

Lucknow has always been known as a multicultural city, and it flourished as the cultural and art capital of North India during the

18th and 19th centuries. It was well known as a centre of production and trade from the early years of the 17th century in Oudh region. It also remained a main centre of manufacturing and trade during the British Raj. The city is famous for its chikankari and zardozi—two forms of embroidery, which flourished during the Mughal period but tended to decline over the years.

In post-Independent India, Lucknow is a state capital. Construction, trade and service sectors emerged as major sources of employment to the city's population. The industrial landscape of the city and its periphery is dominated by the micro and small enterprises—mostly informal enterprises consisting of readymade garments and embroidery, handicrafts, repairing, engineering works and agro-based units. The big industries are Hindustan Aeronautics Ltd and Tata Motors. During 2012–2013, there were 556 factories (registered under the Factories Act, 1948) and 1,925 small enterprises, together employing 32,186 people in urban areas of Lucknow (Lucknow Statistical Diary, 2015). However, of the 603 total registered factories in Lucknow district in 2012–2013, only 179 were working indicating high sickness level in the factories (GoUP-DES, 2016). In other words, employment opportunities in the industrial sector are dwindling in the city. Of late, Lucknow is also witnessing growth as another hub of IT/ITeS. IT and ITeS companies currently operating in Lucknow include Tata Consultancy Services (TCS), HCL Technologies and local open source technology companies.

There has been a significant growth in the construction and real estate businesses in the city during the last two decades or so. There are many new projects such as the Lucknow–Agra Expressway, Lucknow–Azamgarh–Ballia Expressway (now known as Purvanchal Expressway) and the metro rail which seek to add world-class infrastructure to the old city. For agricultural produce logistics, Lucknow is a *mandi* (wholesale market) for mangoes, melons and food grains that are grown in the surrounding areas.

The city is also home to major research and development (R&D) centres such as the Central Drug Research Institute (CDRI), the

National Dairy Development Board (NDDB), Industrial Toxicology Research Centre (ITRC), National Handloom Development Corporation (NHDC) Ltd, Central Institute of Medicinal and Aromatic Plants (CIMAP), National Botanical Research Institute (NBRI), Research Design and Standards Organisation (RDSO), Pradeshik Cooperative Dairy Federation Ltd (PCDF) and the UP Export Corporation. The city also witnessed a rapid growth in the number of educational institutions and health facilities since the 1990s.

According to 2011 population census, the major sectors of employment in Lucknow included manufacturing (16.1%), menial services including domestic help (16%), trade (14.2%), public administration (14.2%) and construction (7.1%), together employing more than two-thirds of the city's workforce (i.e., main workers). In brief, although Lucknow city has expanded in terms of its population, employment opportunities in the city remain limited.

Pune

Located in Maharashtra on the leeward side of the Sahyadri mountains (Western Ghats), Pune is one of the leading Indian cities in terms of industrialisation and urbanisation. Pune was a small village for centuries. Urbanisation in Pune started in the era of Peshwas during the late 17th and the early 18th centuries. Pune was the de facto capital of Peshwas for the short duration (Diddee & Gupta, 2003, quoted in Carsten et al., 2017). This was the first phase of urbanisation. The second phase of urbanisation began with the defeat of Peshwas in the early 1800s by the Britishers, who developed a military base in Pune (Carsten et al., 2017). The history of industry began in Pune with the establishment of an ammunition factory in 1869. Subsequently, the Deccan Paper Mill came up in 1885, followed by a copper and brassware factory in 1888 and a textile mill in 1893 (Benninger, 1998).

The third phase of urbanisation in Pune started in the 1960s when industries started shifting from Bombay in a big way after a legislation prohibiting the establishment of new industries in Mumbai

(Carsten et al., 2017). Since 1960, with the promotive policy environment of the government, the city witnessed a rapid increase in its industrial growth. Later on, Pune became the site of bicycle manufacturing and food processing (Sinha, 1972). This resulted in the subsequent growth of industries, and related housing and other services all over the city (Dandekar & Sawant, 1998). With the growth of the twin city of Pimpri-Chinchwad near Pune, and growth in IT and education services sector, the city witnessed a significant increase in the migrant population (Diddee & Gupta, 2017, cited in Carsten et al., 2017). At present, it is an auto industries' hub. It has more than 3,200 industrial units which are in production. The major industries are Bajaj, Tata Motors, Dgp Hinoday, Philips India Limited, etc. The Maharashtra Industrial Development Corporation (MIDC) has also played an important role in facilitating the develop-ment of small and medium enterprises (SMEs). These SMEs supply auto products and other engineering goods and services to the major industries in Pune.

Pune became a million-plus city in 1971 with a population of 1.14 million people. The 1991 Census report quoted Pune as the fastest growing city in India and the eighth largest city in the country. By 2011, the population of Pune (urban agglomeration) increased to 5.06 million people, almost three times over 1981. A sizeable growth in population is contributed by migration, induced by industrialisation and the demand for labour.

Pune has emerged as a major hub for IT and ITeS services. It has rambling software parks, which are mushrooming all over the city. The industrial growth in Pune has provided employment opportunities to skilled, semi-skilled and unskilled labour force. It has also created a multiplier effect on the consumer goods industries, housing, education, health, financial and transport services. As a result, it has also merged a major education hub since mid-1980s. Such development has also attracted a large migrant population pouring into the city in search of better opportunities.

According to Population Census of 2011, Pune's employment landscape is dominated by the manufacturing sector, contributing one-fourth of city's employment (main workers) in 2011. The other important sector of employment includes public administration (13.6%), trade (12.3%) and construction (11.0%). Education and health sector also provided employment to nearly 7 per cent of the city's workforce.

Coimbatore

Called the textile capital of south India, Coimbatore is a major city in Tamil Nadu located at the banks of Noyyal River. It became a million-plus city in 1991. The population of Coimbatore increased by 2.3 times from 0.92 million to 2.14 million between 1981 and 2011. It is one of the most industrialised cities and was once popular as the 'Manchester of South India'. This city also has a rich history of its development which started initially during the British Empire in the 19th century. In the year 1865, Coimbatore became the capital of the newly formed Coimbatore district and acquired its municipal status in 1866. Industrialisation began in the Coimbatore district in the year 1888. This city also experienced a textile boom in the period 1920–1930. Coimbatore witnessed a rapid industrialisation after Independence, with major industries such as textiles and allied industries, and units manufacturing motor pumps used for the irrigation of cotton farming (Census of India-District Census Handbook, Coimbatore, 2011). Coimbatore is also called the 'pump city of India', meeting the demand of nearly 40 per cent of the India's motor and pump industry.

Other major industries in and around Coimbatore include cement, rubber, transport equipment, jewellery, foundry engineering, auto parts and a variety of engineering industries. Service industries include ITeS, BPOs, health care and trade. The city is the second largest software producer in Tamil Nadu, next only to Chennai. Two industrial estates, one at Peelamedu and the other at Kurichi, are the hubs for the majority of these industries. The other major industrial areas are located at Singanallur and Uppilipalayam. Such large industrial development of Coimbatore is a part of the Coimbatore–Tirupur–Erode Industrial corridor. Other growing businesses include software services, entertainment services, e-commerce, etc. The industrial landscape of Coimbatore is dominated by SMEs. Coimbatore has more than 55,000 small-, medium- and large-scale industries, according to the Indian Chamber of Commerce and Industry (ICCI), Coimbatore. The district of Coimbatore is well known for its entrepreneurial activities, with strong farm–non-farm linkages of development.

The city has also emerged as a major technical education centre catering to HR needs of industries. Coimbatore has a number of trade associations which facilitate the investment in Coimbatore. These include Coimbatore District Small Industries Association (CODISSIA), Coimbatore Industrial Infrastructure Association (COINDIA) and ICCI. The South India Textile Research Association (SITRA) has a chain of laboratories providing services and research facilities in textile industries.

Such an industrially developed city generates huge demand for a variety of skilled and unskilled job opportunities in both organised and unorganised sectors. As a result, Coimbatore attracted a large number of migrant workers not only from surrounding districts but also from far-flung states such as Bihar and Assam. Harris, Kannan and Rodgers (1990) observed that the labour market in Coimbatore city is highly segmented not only on the lines of traditional versus modern but also across the types of industries, occupations, gender and social/ethnic groups. They found caste and social networks playing a major role in access to labour market information, job mobility and hiring decisions by employers.

Manufacturing thus is a major sector of employment, employing about 28 per cent of the city's workforce in 2011. The other major sectors of employment include trade (14%), construction (10.4%) and other services including domestic employers. In other words, over 61 per cent of the workers in Coimbatore were working in these four industry groups in 2011.

Select Demographic Features of Sample Cities

All sample cities are million-plus cities with Delhi (NCT-urban) being the largest one. The average household size is lowest in Coimbatore and highest in Lucknow (5.2 persons). With a sex ratio of 997 women per 1,000 men, Coimbatore is characterised as a city with reasonably favourable gender balance as compared to other sample cities. Delhi has the lowest sex ratio (868).

With regard to the socio-religious composition of the population, the share of SC/ST population ranges between a highest 16.7 per cent in Delhi and 10.3 per cent in Coimbatore (Table 3.1). Over 80 per cent of the population is Hindu in all the sample cities except Lucknow where over 26 per cent of the population is Muslim. Around 8–9 per cent of the population in cities such as Pune and Coimbatore belong to other religious minorities. In brief, Pune and Coimbatore are relatively more diversified cities in terms of the socio-religious composition of population therein.

The literacy levels of population also vary across the sample cities with Coimbatore having the highest literacy rates among their male and female populations. Lucknow remains at the bottom on this count. The gender difference in literacy is highest (about 9 percentage points) in Delhi reflecting the general regional character of low female literacy in the northern regions of the country.

Apart from the general literacy rate, the educational levels of population are important, which help them in improving their employability and earnings (Mathur & Mamgain, 2004) more so, after secondary level, when various streams open out for specialisation at higher education level. Viewed from this perspective, we have clubbed the percentage share of population with secondary and above level education (generally referred as educated persons) for each gender. The information is given in Figure 3.1a.

Nearly 57–60 per cent of the population in the 15–59 years age group in sample cities is educated; the share being comparatively

Table 3.1 *Select Demographic Features of Sample Cities, 2011*

Variable	Delhi (NCT-Urban)	Lucknow (M Corp.)	Coimbatore (M Corp.)	Pune[a]	Total
Total Population (Million)	16.37	2.82	1.05	5.00	25.24
Average household size (No.)	4.90	5.20	3.70	4.20	4.70
Sex ratio	868	928	997	904	887
Socio-Religious Composition (in %)					
SC/ST	16.68	10.98	10.34	15.78	15.60
Hindu	81.40	71.70	83.30	81.10	80.20
Muslims	13.00	26.40	8.60	9.60	13.50
Others	5.60	1.90	8.10	9.30	6.30
Literacy Rate (in %)					
Person	76.00	73.90	82.40	79.30	76.70
Male	80.10	77.00	85.10	81.80	80.30
Female	71.30	70.60	79.80	76.50	72.60
% Working Persons in Total Population (Main Plus Marginal Workers)					
Person	33.34	33.52	40.46	38.81	34.70
Male	53.08	51.68	60.99	56.47	53.90
Female	10.60	13.95	19.87	19.28	13.10
% Working Persons in Total Population (Main Workers)					
Person	31.70	26.85	38.26	36.33	32.30
Male	50.90	43.52	58.79	53.64	50.90
Female	9.59	8.90	17.68	17.18	11.40
High School and above Education (15–59 yrs; in %)					
Person	55.91	57.18	55.90	59.84	56.90
Male	59.46	59.77	58.38	63.82	60.30
Female	51.77	54.40	53.42	55.40	53.00

Source: Population Census, 2011-Primary Census Abstract and C8 Series Tables.

Note: [a] Includes Pune and Pimpri-Chinchwad Municipal Corporation.

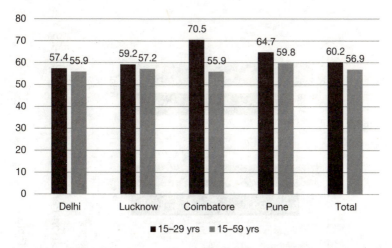

Figure 3.1a *City-Wise Share of Educated (Secondary and above Education) Persons among Youth (15–29 Years) and Adult Population (15–59 Years), 2011 (%)*

Source: Population Census 2011-Primary Census Abstract and C8 Series Tables.

higher in Pune city—also known as one of the education hubs of the country. The youth have comparatively higher educational levels in all the sample cities. The highest among sample cities—70 per cent—of the youth in Coimbatore is educated. Delhi lags behind in the educational attainments of youth. Surprisingly, the proportion of graduates is the highest at 27.5 per cent in Lucknow and the least in Coimbatore. This is despite the fact of the low literacy rates in Lucknow as compared to other sample cities. It also indicates that due to the lack of employment opportunities in Lucknow as compared to other three cities as reflected in the lowest work participation rates (WPRs), a larger proportion of population in Lucknow continue to improve their educational levels. It is true for both men and women (Figures 3.1a and 3.1b).

Gender-wise data on education brings out an interesting pattern. The proportion of education among men in the 15–59 years age group

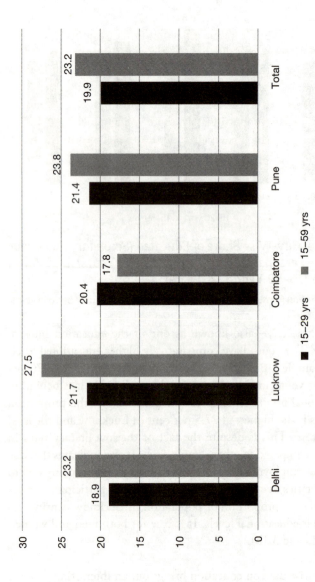

Figure 3.1b City-Wise Share of Graduate and above Education Persons among Youth (15–29 Years) and Adult Population (15–59 Years), 2011 (%)

Source: Population Census 2011-Primary Census Abstract and C8 Series Tables.

is definitely higher than women, but the gender differences are comparatively on a larger side in Delhi and Pune. Such gender differences are not substantive among those with the graduate level of education (Table 3.2). The gender gap in the educational attainments among educated youth is less revealing. However, such gender gap is more in the case of those with graduate and above education—the proportion of graduate and above among young females is much higher than their male counterparts in all the cities. In brief, with the improvement in access to education, proportionately, more young females are seeking higher education, which is an all-India feature as well in the recent years.

Table 3.2 City-Wise Share of Educated and Graduates among Youth and Adult Population by Their Gender, 2011 (%)

City	Male		Female	
	High School and Above	Graduate and Above	High School and Above	Graduate and Above
Youth (15–29 yrs)				
Delhi	57.37	17.79	57.42	20.20
Lucknow	57.90	19.78	60.61	23.87
Coimbatore	69.48	19.42	71.38	21.29
Pune	65.61	20.31	63.60	22.62
Total	60.06	18.66	60.33	21.23
Adult Population (15–59 yrs)				
Delhi	59.46	23.50	51.77	22.78
Lucknow	59.77	28.30	54.40	26.68
Coimbatore	58.38	18.28	53.42	17.41
Pune	63.82	24.21	55.40	23.32
Total	60.31	23.68	53.00	22.77

Source: Population Census 2011-Primary Census Abstract and C8 Series Tables.

Participation in Work

The population Census defines work as any gainful economic activity undertaken by a person during the year. Based on the duration of engagement in economic activity, a worker is further classified as main (working for more than 180 days in a year) and marginal workers (less than 180 days). According to the 2011 population Census, there were 8.75 million workers (main plus marginal) in our sample cities, constituting about 34.7 per cent of the total population therein. City-wise, the highest 40.4 per cent of the population in Coimbatore forms its workforce. On the other extremes, in Delhi and Lucknow nearly one-third of the population are workers. The proportion of workers among women is sizeably low in India and more so in urban areas. It ranges between nearly 20 per cent in Coimbatore and 10.6 per cent in Delhi. Both Delhi and Lucknow have lower participation rate of women in work than the other two sample cities. The reasons for such lower participation of women in the labour market, particularly in the urban areas, are generally traced to the lack of employment opportunities, overburdened with homecare work, restriction on mobility, and safety at work and public places (Rustagi, 2017; Verick & Choudhury, 2017). More so, the present definition of work in Population Census and NSSO are inadequate to capture women's work due to their preoccupation with the economic activity (Ghosh, 2017; Hirway, 2014).

Unlike rural areas, the proportion of marginal workers is comparatively low in urban areas. This is due to the availability of work in urban areas for a relatively longer duration. However, this may be not true for all the cities. For example, the proportion of marginal workers is highest in Lucknow constituting over 7 per cent of the city's population. This share is much low in other cities (Table 3.1).

The economy of any region can be deduced broadly from the distribution of workers employed in different economic activities therein. Since urban areas are characterised predominantly with the non-agriculture economic activities, such activities vary in their importance significantly across different cities. In Delhi NCT, trade, public administrative services and manufacturing are the three major economic activities, employing nearly 58.5 per cent of the workforce in 2011. The other important sectors are education, health, construction and other services like domestic help. Pune and Coimbatore are manufacturing hubs; alone employing over one-fourth of the workforce therein. Construction and trade are other major sectors in these two cities, employing another one-fourth of the workforce. Public administrative services are also important employing between 14 and 19 per cent of the workforce in all cities except Lucknow.

Lucknow is comparatively a different city in terms of the structure of economic activities. Though a highest number (about 39%) of its workforce is working in three sectors, namely public administration, education and health, and other services, a sizeable number are also engaged in trade (Table 3.3). The information and communication sector employs about a highest 5 per cent of the workforce in Pune, and about 3 per cent that in Delhi NCT and Coimbatore. In brief, the economic structure in Pune and Coimbatore is dominated by the manufacturing, construction and trade activities, whereas that in Delhi NCR is dominated by the trade, public administrative services and manufacturing activities. Lucknow is a mixed case of the spread of economic activities across various sectors.

Occupation-Wise Distribution of Workers

Occupational pattern of workers (other than cultivators and agriculture labour) varies substantively across sample cities. Top three occupational divisions in the occupational hierarchy employ nearly 30 per cent of the workforce in Pune, followed by Delhi NCT (24.9%), Coimbatore (22.5%) and least (20.6%) in Lucknow (Table 3.4a). Service and sales occupations are equally important in Delhi NCT and Lucknow, employing 18–20 per cent of the workforce. Craft and related occupations are important in Coimbatore employing a highest one-fifth of its workforce. Surprisingly, a highest 27.5 per cent of the workforce in Lucknow is working in miscellaneous occupations which are not classified in the standard occupational classification framework.

Table 3.3 *Distribution of Main Workers in Select Urban Areas by Their Industry of Employment, 2011 (%)*

Industry	Delhi	Lucknow	Pune	Coimbatore
Agriculture, forestry and fishing	1.03	5.05	2.20	11.01
Mining and quarrying	0.01	0.05	0.11	0.13
Manufacturing	17.79	16.13	25.18	27.85
Electricity, gas, steam, air conditioning and water supply, sewerage, waste management, etc.	1.39	1.55	0.39	0.53
Construction	6.53	7.34	11.00	10.44
Wholesale and retail trade (repair of motor vehicles and motor cycles)	21.88	15.29	12.29	14.10
Transportation and storage	7.72	6.53	7.10	5.75
Accommodation and food service activities	1.92	1.50	2.25	2.11
Information and communication	2.46	2.06	4.99	3.00
Financial and insurance activities, real estate activities, professional, scientific and technical activities	4.92	5.69	4.22	3.64
Administrative and support service activities, and public administration and defence, compulsory social security	18.83	14.20	13.62	6.40
Education, health and social work activities	7.20	8.61	6.87	6.15
Arts, entertainment and recreation, other service activities, activities of household as employers, activities of extra territorial organisations and bodies.	8.33	16.00	9.78	8.89
Total	100	100	100	100

Source: Population Census (2011; B-series Tables).

Notes: The data pertains to the urban areas of Delhi NCT, Lucknow, Pune and Coimbatore districts. The urban areas of Lucknow, Pune and Coimbatore districts are broadly assumed as a proxy of the sample city, as the city-wise data on industrial and occupational distribution of workers is not available in the Population Census.

Table 3.4a Occupation-Wise Distribution of Main Workers Other than Cultivators and Agriculture Labour in Select Urban Areas, 2011 (%)

Occupation	Delhi	Lucknow	Pune	Coimbatore
Legislators, senior officials and managers	7.94	5.58	10.40	7.50
Professionals	7.16	8.25	11.12	7.70
Technicians and associate professionals	9.76	6.80	7.78	7.28
Clerks	4.05	4.36	7.32	4.73
Service and sales workers	19.85	17.68	10.38	12.94
Skilled agriculture and fishery works	0.47	1.13	0.47	1.01
Craft and related works	14.02	14.25	12.58	21.04
Plant and machine operators and assemblers	9.50	4.49	10.58	11.55
Elementary occupations	16.08	10.00	20.18	18.74
Workers not classified by occupations	11.15	27.45	9.19	7.52
Total	100.00	100.00	100.00	100.00

Source: Population Census (2011; B-series Tables).

This also means that such workers are working in multiple occupations to support their livelihoods. Generally, income earnings from such occupations are very low.

Although, proportionately, women are much less in workforce as compared to men, they are largely employed in top-end occupations in Delhi, Pune and, to some extent, Lucknow. For example, in Delhi NCR, more than 41 per cent women are employed in the top three occupations, namely senior officials and managers, professionals and technicians. In Coimbatore, the proportion of men and women in these top-end occupations is almost similar, that is, one-fourth of their respective workforce. The cities of Delhi NCR and Pune have attracted migrant women workers to work in their IT and other service-related industries in the recent years. The proportion of women in sales and service occupations, craft, and machine operator-related occupations is comparatively much less than men in all the four cities. The lesser number of women in these occupations is partly due to the difficulty in their mobility needed to work in jobs such as sales and service-related occupations, and partly due to social taboo and related bias to work as machine operators. This pattern has been observed across all the four sample cities referred here (Table 3.4b). Women are proportionately more in elementary occupations such as domestic help and labourers. In brief, women are concentrated in top-end and bottom-end occupations with under-representation in mid-level occupations. The highest 45.4 per cent women workers in Lucknow are engaged in elementary occupations and also in unclassified occupations. This is closely followed by Coimbatore and Pune employing about 39 per cent of their women workers therein, and Delhi NCR (33%), respectively. Similar pattern of proportionately higher share of women in top and bottom-end occupational groups can be seen in Table 3.4c. This occupational pattern also indicates inequality in earnings for both genders but more so in the case of women as compared to men (Papola & Kannan, 2017).

Broad Features of Sample Households

The broad features of the sample households are presented in Table 3.5. The sex ratio broadly follows the pattern across the cities as observed in Table 3.1. Over 60 per cent of the population belonged to the 18–45 years age group—the focus age group of the present study. Since our focus population group is SC and ST, a substantive proportion of the sample population constituted SCs and STs. In Coimbatore, the proportion of OSG was very small (5.1%), thus both SCs/STs and OBCs constituted about 95 per cent of the sample population therein (Table 3.5). As regards the religious background of the sample population, a large majority comprised Hindus. Due care is also given for the representation of Muslims in our sample. About 12 per cent of the sample population was Muslim.

Table 3.4b Gender-Wise Occupational Distribution of Main Workers Other than Cultivators and Agriculture Labour in Select Urban Areas, 2011 (%)

Occupation	Delhi		Lucknow		Pune		Coimbatore	
	Male	Female	Male	Female	Male	Female	Male	Female
Legislators, senior officials and managers	8.01	7.47	5.98	3.42	11.61	6.13	8.84	3.44
Professionals	6.18	13.12	7.70	11.25	10.29	14.06	7.11	9.50
Technicians and associate professionals	7.99	20.65	5.32	14.78	6.20	13.36	6.08	10.89
Clerks	3.62	6.70	4.35	4.39	6.72	9.43	3.95	7.05
Service and sales workers	21.25	11.32	18.62	12.64	10.73	9.16	13.98	9.82
Skilled agriculture and fishery works	0.52	0.18	1.24	0.56	0.49	0.42	1.05	0.89
Craft and related works	15.43	5.42	15.67	6.61	14.48	5.86	22.94	15.32
Plant and machine operators, and assemblers	10.68	2.27	5.15	0.95	12.81	2.72	13.88	4.53
Elementary occupations	15.61	18.95	10.34	8.17	18.83	24.94	16.52	25.42
Workers not classified by occupations	10.70	13.91	25.64	37.23	7.85	13.93	5.65	13.15
Total	100	100	100	100	100	100	100	100

Source: Population Census (2011; B-series Tables).

Table 3.4c City-Wise Percentage Share of Women in Each Occupational Division, 2011

Occupation	Delhi	Lucknow	Pune	Coimbatore
Legislators, senior officials and managers	13.2	9.6	13.0	11.4
Professionals	25.7	21.3	27.9	30.7
Technicians and associate professionals	29.7	34.0	37.9	37.3
Clerks	23.2	15.7	28.4	37.2
Service and sales workers	8.0	11.2	19.5	18.9
Skilled agriculture and fishery works	5.4	7.7	19.5	21.9
Craft and related works	5.4	7.3	10.3	18.1
Plant and machine operators, and assemblers	3.4	3.3	5.7	9.8
Elementary occupations	16.5	12.8	27.3	33.8
Workers not classified by occupations	17.5	21.2	33.4	43.5
Total	14.0	15.6	22.1	24.9

Source: Population Census (2011; B-series Tables).

Migrants constituted around 8 per cent of the sample population; the ratio was very high (14.8%) in Pune and ranged between 5 and 7 per cent in other cities. If we consider a much broader aspect of migrant population, that is, those not born in the city of enumeration, the proportion of such population jumps to as high as over 40 per cent in Delhi, and at least 10.5 per cent in Coimbatore (Table 3.5). However, it merits mention here that such demographic features of the sample population should not be generalised as these are necessarily not the representative of the city's population universe due to its different purposiveness.

Educational Levels

Among the sample population, literacy levels of men reached almost 100 per cent. But a sizeable proportion of women are still illiterate. The proportion of population with secondary and above level education

Table 3.5 Broad Features of Sample Households

Characteristics	Lucknow	Delhi	Pune	Coimbatore	All
Sample HHs (No.)	700	1,100	700	500	3,000
Sample population (No.)	3,338	4,755	2,653	1,798	12,544
Sex ratio (per 1,000)	855	827	801	891	838
Population in 18–45 yrs age group (%)	60.90	62.20	63.80	62.20	62.20
Social Background (%)					
SC and ST	50.80	38.20	32.40	41.80	40.80
OBC	28.60	22.10	30.10	53.10	30.00
Others	20.60	39.80	37.50	5.10	29.20
Religious Background (%)					
Hindu	87.10	82.90	77.60	84.60	83.20
Muslim	12.40	15.40	8.50	10.00	12.40
Others	0.50	1.70	13.80	5.40	4.50
Place of Birth (%)					
City of enumeration	78.22	59.45	61.67	89.49	69.22
Other city/town	7.88	13.94	14.78	5.01	11.22
Village	13.90	26.60	23.56	5.51	19.56
Migrant@ (%)	6.60	6.00	14.80	5.20	7.90
Not born in the city (%)	21.78	40.55	38.33	10.51	30.78
Literacy rate (%)	89.32	91.20	92.21	93.55	91.24

Source: Primary field survey (2014–2015).

Note: @ Following the Census definition, we have treated as migrant population to the city those persons whose last place of residence was different than the current one in the city, and residing there for less than 10 years.

is high among males as compared to females. However, educational levels of men in Coimbatore sample are comparatively much lower than those in Delhi. The proportion of graduates and postgraduates is the highest among the Delhi sample and comparatively lowest in the case of Coimbatore. Similar pattern is also observed in the Population Census data (Figure 3.1a and 3.1b). The share of persons with technical education (including degree and diploma) is again highest (16.4%) in Delhi, closely followed by Pune. Again, it is lowest in Coimbatore. Proportionately, the share of females having technical education is much less than their male counterparts across all the four cities (Table 3.6). In brief, the educational levels of the sample population are reasonably higher. This is due to the selection of such households where at least one member was actively searching a job in the urban labour market.

Broad Features of Employment and Unemployment among Sample Households

Working Population

Nearly half of the sample population was working at the time of survey. This is generally referred as WPR). It varied substantively

Table 3.6 *Educational Levels of Sample Population (7 Years and above; %)*

	Lucknow	Delhi	Pune	Coimbatore	Total
Educated (Secondary Education and above)					
Male	76.36	82.71	76.04	62.99	76.93
Female	60.88	65.06	60.37	63.64	62.73
Both	69.18	74.74	69.12	63.30	70.45
Graduate and above					
Male	36.86	41.60	30.87	24.79	35.73
Female	31.44	34.14	23.42	26.10	29.99
Both	34.35	38.23	27.58	25.42	33.11
Technical Education (both Degree and Diploma Levels)					
Male	12.56	19.02	17.93	9.35	15.95
Female	7.30	12.98	11.37	4.94	10.04
Total	10.20	16.40	15.15	7.30	13.35

Source: Primary field survey (2014–2015).

across cities, ranging between 68.6 per cent in Pune and nearly 30 per cent in Lucknow (Table 3.7). The WPRs were comparatively much lower among women but very high among the migrant population. The higher WPRs among migrant population was largely due to the proportionately smaller number of dependent population. Among social groups, the proportion of workers was comparatively low among ST/SC sample population as compared to OBCs and OCs in all the sample cities except Coimbatore. Similarly, Muslim sample population had marginally lower WPRs as compared to Hindus and other religious minorities ([ORMs] Table 3.7).

Table 3.7 Workforce Participation Rate among Sample Population (%)

Category	Lucknow	Delhi/NCR	Pune	Coimbatore	Total
Gender					
Male	47.58	59.24	71.42	66.04	59.74
Female	9.10	18.22	65.08	33.06	27.63
Social Group					
STs/SCs	28.34	40.34	62.75	51.86	41.82
OBCs	30.71	39.68	67.54	49.63	45.85
OCs	32.31	41.54	74.50	48.35	48.94
Religious Group					
Hindu	29.90	41.13	69.08	50.99	44.96
Muslim	29.23	36.80	66.52	49.16	40.55
ORMs	33.33	53.75	67.21	45.36	60.43
Migrant/Non-migrant					
Migrant	37.27	63.67	82.44	72.34	66.06
Non-migrant	29.31	39.18	66.19	49.30	43.30
Total	29.84	40.67	68.60	50.50	45.11
Sample population (No.)	3,338	4,755	2,653	1,798	12,544

Source: Primary field survey (2014–2015).

Both working and unemployed population constitute the labour force. The share of unemployed in labour force (also termed as the unemployment rate) was highest in Lucknow sample (32.5%), followed by Coimbatore, and almost equal in Delhi and Pune (about 18%; Table 3.8). Such high rates of unemployment, particularly in Lucknow and Coimbatore are due to very high rates of unemployment among female labour force. As high as 57 per cent of the female labour force reported unemployed and actively seeking work in Lucknow. High rates of unemployment among females are a well-known phenomenon despite their overall lower LFPRs (Papola & Sahu, 2012; Rustagi, 2017).

Unemployment rates are generally high among STs/SCs and Muslims in urban areas as compared to other socio-religious groups.

Table 3.8 *Unemployment Rate in Sample Population (%)*

Category	Lucknow	Delhi/NCR	Pune	Coimbatore	Total
Gender					
Male	25.50	13.47	12.33	10.92	15.67
Female	57.06	30.25	9.33	43.20	29.08
Social Group					
STs/SCs	32.16	19.32	13.76	25.43	22.51
OBCs	33.56	19.50	12.92	23.42	21.57
OCs	31.69	14.57	7.60	21.43	14.73
Religious Group					
Hindu	32.53	17.29	11.06	24.44	20.18
Muslim	31.64	19.70	9.04	22.12	20.48
ORMs	40.00	10.42	12.46	24.14	14.61
Migrant/Non-migrant					
Migrant	46.75	20.69	14.96	21.84	22.95
Non-migrant	30.81	17.14	10.20	24.39	19.48
Total	32.47	17.49	11.09	24.21	19.90

Source: Primary field survey (2014–2015).

This feature is also revealed in our sample data. The unemployment rate among our sample population is much higher as compared to NSSO estimates for urban areas, primarily due to the purposive sampling.

Characteristics of Employment

Most of the workers in our sample households were working in regular salaried jobs in all cities, ranging from 45 per cent in Lucknow to over 60 per cent in Coimbatore. Contractual employment is yet another job category accounting for nearly one-fourth of the total workers in Delhi, 19 per cent in Lucknow, 14 per cent in Pune and least 8.4 per cent in Coimbatore. The private sector is understandably a major employer of salaried workers including both regular and contractual (Table 3.9). The share of self-employed workers ranged between 20 and 28 per cent across the sample cities. The share of casual labourers was over 7.5 per cent. In brief, the private sector is a major source of employment for salaried workers employing over 54 per cent of the workers in sample households. The share varied significantly in each

Table 3.9 Distribution of Workers by the Type of their Employment (%)

Type of Employment	Lucknow	Delhi/NCR	Pune	Coimbatore	Total
Self-employed	25.90	21.25	20.60	27.97	22.94
Regular salaried public sector	18.27	15.15	6.76	6.39	11.59
Regular salaried private sector	26.51	35.32	50.44	47.69	41.68
Contractual public sector	2.71	7.50	1.26	0.99	3.61
Contractual private sector	16.47	16.13	12.75	7.49	12.65
Casual labour	9.74	4.29	7.97	9.03	7.19
Apprentice trainees	0.40	0.36	0.22	0.44	0.34
Total	100	100	100	100	100
Number of working population	996	1,934	1,820	908	5,658

Source: Primary field survey (2014–2015).

sample city with 63 per cent in Pune, 55.2 per cent in Coimbatore, 51.4 per cent in Delhi and 43 per cent in Lucknow.

For a detailed analysis of the characteristics of employment, we have collected the information of workers in the 18–45 years age group. This age group was selected specifically because of their active job search in the labour market. In all, there were 3,470 workers in the 18–45 years age group among the sample households. The information on employment includes the type of employment, length of period in current employment, the type of enterprise, location of workplace, occupation and industry of employment, and average earnings (Table 3.10).

A majority of workers in the 18–45 years age group were employed in the salaried jobs. Contractual employment has emerged as the new form of employment where workers are not directly employed by a principal employer but employed through a contractor for specific jobs. In Delhi and Lucknow samples, the proportion of contractual workers was high—32 per cent and 27 per cent, respectively, whereas the proportion of such workers was least in Pune at 15 per cent. The contractual route is being used increasingly by employers to reduce the costs of labour and also to control the labour power. The share of such workers in both public and private sectors has increased substantially

Table 3.10 *Distribution of Workers (18–45 Years) by their Job/ Work Status (%)*

Job/Work Status	Lucknow	Delhi/NCR	Pune	Coimbatore	Total
Self-employed	22.90	12.30	20.20	10.90	17.00
Regular salaried	43.60	51.70	59.20	58.37	53.32
Contractual	26.70	32.00	14.90	21.97	24.14
Casual	5.90	3.20	5.20	8.80	5.20
Apprenticeship trainee	0.80	0.90	0.40	–	0.50
Total	606	1,047	1,339	478	3,470

Source: Primary field survey (2014–2015).

over the years, particularly after the economic reforms of the early 1990s. For example, the share of contract workers in the organised manufacturing sector in India increased sharply from 13.9 per cent in 1995–1996 to 34 per cent in 2011–2012 (Goldar & Suresh, 2017). Nearly one-fifth of the workers were self-employed in Lucknow and Pune samples, and over one-tenth in Delhi and Coimbatore, respectively. Apprenticeship trainees strictly are not workers but their services are being used increasingly by the employers for the production of goods and services. The proportion of such apprenticeship trainees, however, was less than 1 per cent among the sample workers.

Gender-wise, there is not much difference in the work status of men and women. But it differs significantly among workers belonging to various social groups. The proportion of contractual and casual workers was higher among ST and SC workers as compared to those belonging to OBCs and OC social groups (Figure 3.2). On the other hand, the proportion of regular salaried workers was higher by about 6 percentage points for OBCs and OCs than STs/SCs. In other words, workers belonging to SC/ST communities have relatively poor quality of employment. This pattern has been observed at the national level as well (IHD & ISLE, 2014; Mamgain & Tiwari, 2017). Religion-wise, the work status of workers belonging to Hindu and Muslim religions is almost similar with the marginally higher proportion of self-employed workers among Muslims. However, workers belonging to other religions were proportionately more in regular salaried jobs (Figure 3.3).

Workers by their Type of Enterprises

Since our focus was on job search in the private sector, our sample is dominated by the workers employed in private firms, ranging from 68 per cent in Pune to 92 per cent in Coimbatore. Next important sector of employment is the public sector employing 14–18 per cent of workers in our sample cities except Coimbatore, where only 5 per cent of the workers were employed in the public sector (Table 3.11). We could also cover workers working in multinational firms. A highest 4.8 per cent of the workers in Delhi were working in MNC firms. In

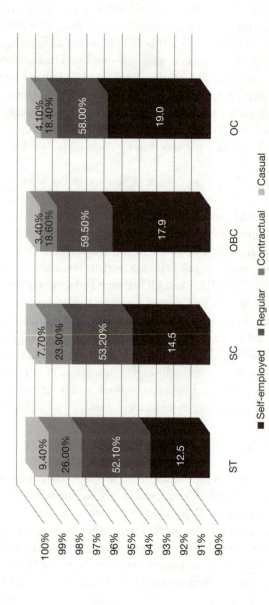

Figure 3.2 *Job/Work Status of Workers by Their Social Group*

Source: Primary field survey (2014–2015).

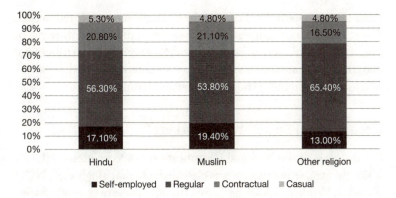

Figure 3.3 *Job/Work Status of Workers by Their Religious Group*

Source: Primary field survey (2014–2015).

Table 3.11 *Distribution of Workers (18–45 Years) by the Type of Enterprises (%)*

Type of Enterprise	Lucknow	Delhi/NCR	Pune	Coimbatore	Total
Public sector	14.50	17.80	16.00	5.00	14.80
Cooperatives	1.30	6.60	8.30	1.50	5.60
Proprietary/ Partnership firms	40.30	16.00	24.90	7.10	22.40
Private Ltd	40.10	53.10	42.60	84.90	51.20
Multinational firms	0.50	4.80	2.90	0.20	2.70
Employer HH	2.80	1.10	4.40	1.30	2.70
Others	0.50	0.80	0.80	—	0.60
Total	606	1,047	1,339	478	3,470

Source: Primary field survey (2014–2015).

Notes: Cooperatives consist of those enterprises which are registered under the Societies Registration Act/Indian Trusts Act. Private Ltd enterprises include both public limited companies and private limited companies in the private sector.

Pune sample, nearly 3 per cent of the workers were employed in such firms. In brief, our sample workers were well diversified in terms of their employers. There were no major differences in the distributional pattern of workers across various types of enterprises by their socio-religious background, gender or migration status.

Occupational Structure of Workers

On the basis of the National Classification of Occupations (NCO)-2005, the sample population was classified into nine single digit NCO divisions. Workers belonging to first two divisions are generally put on the top of the occupational hierarchies, whereas elementary occupations remain at the bottom. By using such criteria, over one-fifth of the workers in sample households were employed in the top-ladder occupations, that is, senior officials, managers and professionals. Another one-fourth of the workers were working as technicians and associate professionals. In service and sales occupations, about 21 per cent of the workers were employed. Another 12 per cent of the workers were engaged in craft and related occupations. Clerical and machine operating occupations employed about 7 per cent of the workers. The lowest number of workers was employed in elementary occupations (Table 3.12). A lower proportion of the workers in elementary occupations in our sample households as compared to population census-based occupational distribution are understandably due to our purposive sample to understand the job-search methods among the educated workforce.

The city-wise distribution of workers across their occupations differed significantly. The share of workers in two top occupations in Lucknow was quite low as compared to other cities. This also indicates the scarcity of such jobs largely associated with the fewer job opportunities in higher end occupations in Lucknow. In Delhi, the highest 37 per cent of the sample workers were working as technicians and associate professionals. This is largely associated with the location of IT and other service industries in Delhi NCR region (Table 3.12).

Table 3.12 Distribution of Workers (18–45 Years) by Their Occupations (%)

Type of Occupation	Lucknow	Delhi/NCR	Pune	Coimbatore	Total
Legislators, senior officials and managers	8.6	7.2	6.9	6.3	7.2
Professionals	6.6	17.4	17.6	16.1	15.4
Technicians and associate professionals	23.4	36.6	19.9	19.7	25.5
Clerks	6.6	10.3	5.8	6.1	7.3
Service and sales workers	24.1	15.3	23.8	21.5	21.0
Skilled agriculture and fishery works	1.0	0.5	0.2	0.4	0.5
Craft and related works	15.2	7.3	12.5	16.5	12.0
Plant and machine operators, and assemblers	8.7	3.2	6.7	7.3	6.1
Elementary occupations	5.8	2.4	6.5	6.1	5.1
All	606	1,047	1,339	478	3,470

Source: Primary field survey (2014–2015).

Is there any difference in the occupational distribution of migrant and non-migrant workers? It appears that migrant workers are proportionately more in high-end occupations such as managers, professionals, technicians and associate professionals, employing over 55 per cent of the total migrant workers. The corresponding share of non-migrant workers in these occupations was 46.6 per cent only. As compared to migrant workers, the number of non-migrant workers was proportionately more in occupations such as service and sales, craft and related works, and elementary occupations (Figure 3.4). Such pattern in occupational distribution of workers was observed distinctly in Delhi, Pune and Lucknow, but with mixed pattern in Coimbatore. Migrant workers in Coimbatore were proportionately more in service and sales related occupations, and also in plant and machine operations.

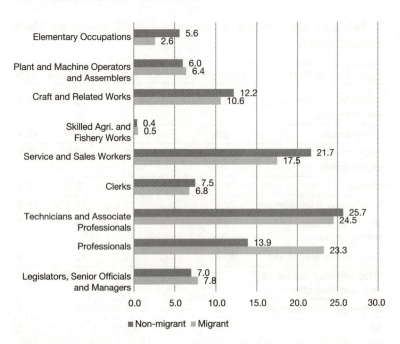

Figure 3.4 *Migrant and Non-migrant Workers by their Occupations (%)*

Occupational Pattern of Workers by their Social Group

Does the social group of workers matter in their access to various kinds of occupations? It is well known that the representation of socially disadvantaged groups such as women, STs, SCs and Muslim minorities is comparatively much lower in better paid and more coveted occupations as compared to the OCs (IHD & ISLE, 2014; Mamgain, 2017). In an analysis of the occupational pattern based on NSSO rounds on employment and unemployment, Mamgain (2017) finds high value of occupational Dissimilarity Index (DI) (0.32 in 2011–2012) between STs and Others. This shows that at least 32 per cent of the ST workers have to shift their occupations to have identical occupational characteristics with the workforce belonging to OCs. The next highest level of dissimilarity is observed in the occupations pursued by SCs with respect to 'Others'. The least dissimilarity can be seen in the occupational distribution of Muslims versus Others. The DI value was high between women and men (0.36 in 2011–2012). It has been seen that the occupational dissimilarity among SCs and Others initially increased during the pre-reform period (1983 to 1993–1994) and then declined during the post-reform period, but at a slower pace after 2004. In other words, the introduction of the economic reforms and the consequent high-growth regime not only led to the higher employment growth among SCs but also enabled them to diversify into newer occupations wherein their presence had earlier been almost negligible. This decreasing occupational dissimilarity has largely been accompanied by their growing number entering into the poor quality jobs as well as improvement in their share in high-end jobs.

The city-level sample data also confirms the dissimilarity in the occupational pattern of workers belonging to different social groups. The SCs were largely concentrated in the occupational divisions such as service and sales workers, plant and machinery operators, and elementary occupations. Among SC workers, about 41 per cent were employed in the top three occupations. The corresponding figure for OC workers was about 56 per cent and that for OBCs 47 per cent (Table 3.13). About 9 per cent of the SC workers were engaged in elementary occupations as compared to 2.5 per cent for OCs. OBCs are relatively better off than SCs in their access to top three occupations but certainly lag behind OCs on this count. STs are far better than SCs and OBCs on this count.

Extent of Occupational Segregation

We have measured occupational dissimilarity with the help of the Duncan's DI. This is defined as:

$$D = \frac{1}{2} \cdot \sum_i^n \left| \frac{S_{ij}}{S_j} - \frac{O_{ij}}{O_j} \right|$$

Table 3.13 Occupational Pattern of Workers by Their Social Group (%)

NCO	Type of Occupation	STs	SCs	OBCs	OCs
1	Legislators, senior officials and managers	5.20	6.80	6.60	8.20
2	Professionals	28.10	11.30	17.10	17.00
3	Technicians and associate professionals	17.70	23.20	23.30	30.30
4	Clerks	3.10	7.90	7.00	7.40
5	Service and sales workers	24.00	21.30	23.80	17.90
6	Skilled agriculture and fishery works	2.10	0.60	0.30	0.30
7	Craft and related works	3.10	12.00	13.40	11.30
8	Plant and machine operators, and assemblers	7.30	8.20	4.80	5.00
9	Elementary occupations	9.40	8.70	3.70	2.50
	All	96	1,155	1,036	1,183

Source: Primary field survey (2014–2015).

where S_{ij} is the number of workers in occupational category i and social group j, S_j is the total number of workers in social group j, O_{ij} is the number of workers in occupational category i and social group k ($\neq j$), and O_j is the total number of workers in social group k.

The Duncan Index, therefore, delineates the degree of similarity in the occupational structure between two groups of workers such as women and men, or ST/SC and OC workers. The value of index (D) ranges between zero and one, and is interpreted as the proportion of either gender or social group that would have to shift occupations to generate identical occupational distributions. If D is zero, it shows complete integration, which indicates that the distribution of one gender/social group across occupations is identical to that of the comparator group, and if D is one, there is a complete occupational segregation, which occurs when workers from one group are engaged in occupations that are not populated at all by the comparator group (Blau & Hendricks, 1979; Spriggs & Williams, 1996).

We have calculated this index for each pairing of our group of workers such as SCs–OCs, OBCs–OCs and women–men. For example, while comparing SCs and the members of the OC groups, the Duncan Index is simply $0.5\Sigma|S_i - O_i|$, where S_i is the proportion of occupation i among SCs and O_i is the proportion of occupation i among OCs. The Duncan Index has also been calculated for each pairing listed above at the one-digit classification of occupation. This has been done to capture the maximum variations in the occupational distributions across two groups of workers. Due to the small number of workers, we have avoided measuring the occupational segregation at NCO 2-digit level of occupations. The values of DI are presented in Table 3.14.

It emerges that the occupational DI between women and men is highest in Lucknow, followed by Delhi, Coimbatore and least in Pune. This shows that at least 36 per cent of the women in Lucknow have to shift their occupations to have identical occupational characteristics with the male workforce. As regards the occupational segregation among social groups, the highest level of dissimilarity is observed in the occupations pursued by the SCs in comparison to those falling in the category of OCs. This is observed across our sample cities, but the value of DI is highest (0.24) in Lucknow and Coimbatore. This is mainly due to their higher concentration in the mid and bottom-ranking occupations. The next highest level of dissimilarity is observed

Table 3.14 *Duncan Index of Occupational Segregation*

City	SCs–OCs	OBCs–OCs	Women–Men
Lucknow	0.246	0.199	0.364
Delhi	0.178	0.116	0.303
Pune	0.167	0.129	0.069
Coimbatore	0.241	0.210	0.261
Total	0.143	0.093	0.147

Source: Primary field survey (2014–2015).

in the occupations pursued by the OBCs with respect to the SCs-OCs across all the cities, yet the highest is in Coimbatore (0.21; Table 3.14).

In brief, the occupational segregation also indicates the differing access of workers belonging to different genders and social groups to various types of occupations. This may be due to the differences in their human capital (endowments) determining access to various kinds of occupations. Studies have shown that endowments such as education and experience serve as important factors for the occupational diversification. However, the access to different occupations is limited by the discrimination and resultant segregation in the labour market-based on caste and gender even after controlling for endowment factors (Madheswaran & Attewell, 2010; Mamgain, 2017). Madheswaran (2017) shows that in urban labour market, job discrimination is much higher than wage discrimination.

Conclusion

The sample cities differ in select demographic indicators such as the size of population, sex ratio, share of SCs/STs and other marginalised population, educated population and participation in work, particularly that of women. Generally, as compared to the rural areas, the WPRs of females in the urban areas are lower, which according to the Census data ranged between nearly 20 per cent in Coimbatore and 10.6 per cent in Delhi in 2011. Unlike the rural areas, the proportion of marginal workers is comparatively low in urban areas. This is due to the availability of work in the urban areas for a relatively longer duration. However, this may not be true for all cities. For example, the proportion of marginal workers is highest in Lucknow constituting over 8 per cent of the city's population. This share is much lower in other cities indicating the lack of stable employment opportunities in Lucknow.

Like the broad national pattern, our sample survey results show a high rate of unemployment, particularly among women in Lucknow and Coimbatore. Such high rates of unemployment are partly attributed to our sample selection process as we focused more on those households whose members are actively engaged in job search in the urban labour markets. Nevertheless, these rates indicate the demand-side situation of employment in urban labour markets, particularly in cities such as Lucknow and Coimbatore.

A majority of sample workers in the 18–45 years age group were employed in salaried jobs. Contractual employment has emerged as the new form of employment where workers are not directly employed by a principal employer but through contractor for specific jobs. The proportion of such workers among total workers was high in Delhi and Lucknow. This method is increasingly being used by the employers to reduce the labour costs as also control labour power. The proportion of contractual and casual workers was higher among ST and SC workers as compared to those belonging to OBCs and OCs. Studies show how the share of such workers in both public and private sectors has increased substantially over the years, particularly after the economic reforms of the early 1990s. This has seriously eroded the collective bargaining power of workers in the recent years. Such trends also show how workers belonging to SC/ST communities are relatively disadvantaged in their access to quality jobs.

Since our focus was on job search in the private sector, our sample is dominated by the workers working in private firms, ranging from 68 per cent in Pune to 92 per cent in Coimbatore. We could also cover about 4.8 per cent of the workers in Delhi who were working in MNC firms. In Pune sample, nearly 3 per cent of the workers were employed in such firms. There were no major differences in the distributional pattern of workers across various types of enterprises by their socio-religious background, gender or migration status.

The information on the occupations of workers shows varying patterns across gender and social groups of workers. The chapter shows how the occupational DI between women and men is highest in

Lucknow, followed by Delhi, Coimbatore and least in Pune. Such dis-similarity is observed in the occupations pursued by SCs in comparison to OCs. This is mainly due to the higher concentration of SC workers in the mid and bottom-ranking occupations. The next highest level of dissimilarity is observed in the occupations pursued by OBCs with respect to OCs across all the cities, yet highest in Coimbatore (0.21).

The nature and forms of employment significantly differed among our sample cities. The varying degree of the occupational segregation shows differing access of workers belonging to different genders and social groups to various types of occupations. This may be due to the differences in their human capital (endowments) determining access to various kinds of occupations and resultant occupational diversification. However, the access to different occupations is limited to a certain extent due to the discrimination and resultant segregation in the labour market based on caste and gender even after controlling for endowment factors such as education and experience.

CHAPTER 4

Job Search Methods and Access to Jobs

Information, Job Search and Labour Market

Job search is the process by which a job seeker gathers information about employment opportunities, associated wages and conditions that are on the offer by prospective employers. It helps a job seeker to decide whether or not to seek and accept an offered employment. Such job search is an important activity in the labour market that is typically carried out by both employed and unemployed persons. Thus, the role of information and its access to both job seekers and employers is crucial for the smooth functioning of the labour market and is well recognised in neoclassical economics. The neoclassical economic theory would suggest that more the information the employer can gather about potential workers before the hiring decision, more accurate will their decisions be. This implies that in order to reduce risks, employers would prefer to hire workers about whom they have more information (Spence, 1973).

Stigler (1961, 1962), in his seminal work, put the role of information at centre stage in the labour market processes. He discussed the problems faced by a young job seeker in the labour market thus:

The young person entering the labour market for the first time has an immense number of potential employers, scarce as they seem the first day. . . . He faces the problem of how to acquire information on wage rates, stability of employment, conditions of employment, and other determinants of job choice, and how to keep the information current. . . . (Stigler, 1962)

Thus, the youth face enormous updated informational challenge at the entry level in the labour market. Stigler (1962) has further argued that the informational challenge is faced by both employers and job seekers. In the context of wage search, it has been mentioned, '. . . a worker will search for wage offers (and an employer will search for wage demands) until the expected marginal return equals the marginal cost of search.'

In order to get better job or suitable employer, job seekers in the labour market give indication about their strengths, which has been discussed in Michael Spence's (1973) theory of job market signalling. The information attributes which determine productivity (may be perfect or imperfect) from job seekers are transmitted to employers as signals. The role of information about the applicant in the labour market has been very important for an employer to make a decision about the former. Spence (1973) mentions that the exchange in the labour market has been an 'endogenous market process whereby employers require (and individuals transmit) information about the potential employee which ultimately determines the implicit cost involved in hiring, the offered wages, and in the end the allocation of jobs to people, and to jobs in the market'. The signalling theory further predicts two attributes of job applicants: indices and signal. The former is unalterable (such as gender, social group, race and region), whereas the latter that includes observable characteristics such as education, skills and experience could be altered by the applicant through invest-ment. Thus, a job seeker incurs search cost by investing in improving his/her alterable attributes to give signals to the prospective employer (see Figure 4.1).

Thus, the information challenge in the labour market is faced by both job seekers and employers, and simultaneously information about

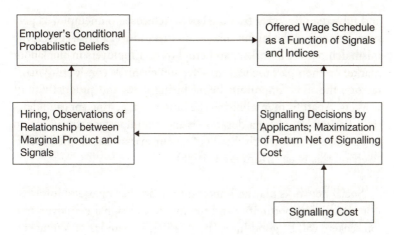

Figure 4.1 *Informational Feedback in the Job Market*
Source: Spence (1973).

one's productivity as transmitted by job seekers in the form of signals. However, in between these two things what is of more significance is the channel of information dispersion, which is required for job search as well as employee search. Rees (1966) has discussed different channels of the labour market information that can be distinguished between formal and informal categories. In the Indian context, the formal category includes the state employment services through the employment office in each district, private fee-charging employment agencies, newspaper advertisements, web portals, educational institutions' placement cells, job fairs, etc. The informal category includes family members, relatives/friends, other social networks, referrals from employees as well as other employers and miscellaneous sources, and walk-ins or hiring at the gate. Channels of information can be further grouped as traditional and modern or innovative channels of recruiting and posting job by employers and job seekers, respectively. One of the most important factors in getting employment or further suitability of job search method is the information network. A job search method with better information network would be helpful in improving the probability of job offer and thus will be the widely used method. Thus, an efficient job search method may reduce the labour market friction and subsequently lower frictional or search costs to unemployed persons. Friction in the labour market, as Pissarides (1985) argues, is the mismatch between workers and employers. Employers in the labour market on their part use various selection channels considering many factors, the most important being hiring costs and productivity of workers. Apart from minimising the hiring cost, getting apt candidates that stay in job for longer duration is another important consideration of employers. The search theory of labour market has studied extensively on this issue (Mortensen, 1986).

Social networks play an important role in sharing useful information about job opportunities and employers, and 'signal' employers that job seekers will be good hires (Bian, 1997; Fernandez & Weinberg, 1997; O'Connor, 2013; Portes, 1998). For example, among various channels of job search, the most effective is searching job through friends and relatives. One of the reasons for friends and relatives as an effective mode of job search is that it provides information to the job seeker about the nature of work and firm. So with authentic information about the employer and the nature of work, the chance of getting suitable job increases. Social networks are also very important in helping employers find prospective employees. The role of social contact in the labour market has been extensively addressed in the literature during the last four decades (Granovetter, 1974, 1995; Marsden & Gorman, 2001; Montgomery, 1991), which shows how social network connections helped in finding about half of the jobs. O'Connor (2013) shows how job search depends on the quality of contact that a job seeker approaches. 'Job seekers with high status contacts are generally in a better position to find jobs rather than those who rely on female, unemployed, less educated or unfamiliar contacts (p. 601).'

In India, a number of studies have demonstrated the role of social networks in getting access to employment in urban areas (Papola, 1981; Upadhya, 2007). Social networks are found to be important in migration decisions to cities (Banerjee & Knight, 1985; Mitra, 2006), which strictly function not only on caste-class lines but also on location-specific co-villagers. In contrast, Holström (1984), Panini (1996) and others suggest that employment in many Indian industries has been monopolised by the members of certain castes, thereby restricting the entry of other groups such as SCs/STs. Munshi and Rosenzweig (2005) find sub-caste or jati as the powerful boundary for labour market networks, which help them to garner proportionately larger representation in employment in various industries. The importance of social networks in job access has rather strengthened despite IT-led improved access to information about jobs and employers through web portals, placement agencies, social network platforms, etc., which was earlier not accessible to a large section of job seekers. More recently, Murti and Paul (2016) have found how around 83 per cent of the sample firms used social networks for their recruitment exercise. Such social networks along with the prevalence of discrimination in labour market by employers in their hiring decisions reduce the chances of job information and employment access to socially marginalised groups, namely SCs, STs and Muslims (Mamgain, 2017; Thorat & Newman, 2010).

In brief, the argument that information asymmetries hinder the functioning of labour market, leading to low productivity and low earnings, is gradually easing out with the extensive use of IT in job signalling and hiring. Nonetheless, social network contacts are still a major source of job information and job access to job seekers. The access to jobs and earnings are significantly influenced by the nature of such contacts. Such overdependence on social networks in the labour market is primarily due to the lack of active policies which facilitate access to information to both job seekers and employers. This perpetuates inequality in the efficient allocations of resources in the labour market.

While commenting on the role of information in the labour market and concerns for equity, Papola (2005) notes:

> The public sector employment exchanges have been an important institution in the labour market to help employers and job seekers in finding a suitable job with a strong focus on social equity during its golden period of 1970 and 1980s. These have almost lost their

relevance with the changing time. The current market based labour market intermediaries purely function on a market principle where equity becomes a casualty.

Employers are increasingly depending on private manpower companies which provide them workers who are not enrolled as their employees. Little is known about various mechanisms of job search, job postings by employers, processes of hiring, subsequent exclusion/inclusion of applicants belonging to various social and religious backgrounds, and differing terms and conditions of employment and wages. The discriminatory process can extend beyond access to information to processes of selection in which attributes have little relevance for the performance of the job but tend to favour candidates with better social and economic endowment (Upadhya, 2007).

As mentioned earlier, job seekers can be divided into two groups, namely unemployed (off-the-job search) and employed (on-the-job search). According to the job search theory, the intensity of job search is higher among the unemployed as they not only use more job search methods but also devote longer hours of search, resulting in more effective job search (Holzer, 1987). At the same time, those who are working may have a higher level of expectation as their foregone earnings due to time spent on job search have been zero. Thus, they may be selective in job search and are often termed as 'passive' job seekers. Contrary to this, some studies have observed search activity among the employed more effective than the unemployed simply due to low search cost (Blau & Robins, 1990).

Against this background, this chapter analyses the characteristics of job seekers (in the 18–45 years age group) in the Indian urban labour market in the succeeding section. Apart from the two common categories of job seekers—unemployed and employed—there exists yet another category of job seekers comprising students who are actively searching jobs and plan to join labour market immediately after completing their education. The propensity of job search and reasons for job search among employed job seekers are also discussed. Section 'Job Information and Job Search Methods among Employed

Persons' analyses the sources of job information that the employed persons used for finding their current job with a focus on gender and social group. Section 'Job Information and Intensity of Job Search among Unemployed Persons' analyses the job search methods among unemployed persons as well as final-year students and the intensity of job search among them. The role of social networks in job search is analysed in Section 'Likelihood of Using Social Networks in Job Search' with a focus on employed persons in finding their current job. Section 'Types of Occupations Searched' describes the jobs that are being searched by employed and unemployed persons. It shows how most of the workers are striving for upward occupational mobility. Section 'Application Realisation Rate and Reasons for Not Being Selected—Unemployed Persons' analyses the application realisation rates for them. The last section dwells on the important conclusions deduced in the chapter.

Characteristics of Job Seekers

The characteristics of unemployed and employed job seekers in the 18–45 years age group are described across five different attributes, namely gender, education level, social groups, religion and migrant status (Table 4.1). Among the unemployed persons, over half of them are male and nearly three-fourths are graduates and postgraduates. Almost 15 per cent of the sample unemployed persons are graduates and postgraduates in technical and professional educational streams. Most of them are in the 18–29 years age group. This reconfirms the general trend of high unemployment rate among youths (Mamgain & Tiwari, 2016). About 43 per cent of the unemployed persons in the sample are SCs and another 34 per cent OBCs. It merits clarification here that such trends in social composition of job seekers are due to purposive sampling aimed at understanding the job search among SCs and other graduates in the urban labour market. Interestingly, if we see the unemployment rate among sample households belonging to different social groups, it was higher for SCs and OBCs (over 14%) as compared to 9.8 per cent for Others, thereby indicating the difficulty of SCs and OBCs in getting jobs in the urban labour market in

Table 4.1 *Characteristics of Job Seekers (18–45 Years; %)*

Characteristics	*Unemployed and Actively Searching Job*	*Employed Persons but Also Searching New Job*
Gender		
Male	54.0	66.7
Female	46.0	33.3
Social Group		
STs	1.7	3.0
SCs	42.6	33.8
OBCs	33.6	27.6
OCs	22.1	35.6
Religious Group		
Hindu	84.1	82.7
Muslim	11.7	10.7
ORMs	4.2	6.6
Migration Status		
Migrant	14.1	18.1
Non-migrant	85.9	81.9
Educational Level		
Below high school	1.7	12.8
High school and higher secondary school	25.9	35.1
Graduate and above (general)	27.5	37.0
Graduate and above (professional and technical)	14.9	15.1
Total	100.0	100.00
No. of persons	1,370	2,262

Source: Primary field survey (2014–2015) for this study.

comparison to Others. Muslims constituted about 12 per cent of the unemployed in our sample. Unemployed migrants constituted over 14 per cent of all unemployed persons (Table 4.1).

Among employed persons in the 18–45 years age group, about two-thirds were searching for another job. Nearly two-thirds among them were males and over half were graduates and postgraduates, including 15 per cent graduates and postgraduates in technical and professional education. About one-third of the employed job seekers were SCs and a highest 36 per cent were OCs. Religion-wise, job seekers were predominantly Hindus. Muslims and other religious minorities constituted about 17 per cent of the employed job seekers. About 18 per cent of the employed job seekers were migrants (Table 4.1). In brief, a comparative analysis of the characteristics of unemployed and employed job seekers in our sample broadly shows a similar pattern, that is, proportionately higher number of males, youth and graduates. A higher proportion of SCs and graduates among job seekers is mainly due to the purposive sample design aimed at the comparative analysis of job seekers belonging to various social groups.

Propensity of Job Search among Employed Persons

Among the currently employed persons, a majority of them were searching for a new job. Such propensity of job search is significantly high among women, SCs, migrant and graduate workers (Table 4.2). City-wise, the propensity of job search among employed persons ranged between the highest 73 per cent in Pune and 43 per cent in Coimbatore. It indicates the quest for finding a remunerative and decent employment, and the lack of such opportunities in the labour market. We shall analyse the reasons for searching new jobs by employed persons in the next section.

Reasons for Job Search among Employed Job Seekers

Theoretically, the reasons for new job search by an individual may be guided purely by the economic considerations or a mix of economic

Table 4.2 *Percentage of Employed Persons Actively Searching Another Job*

	Lucknow	Delhi/NCR	Pune	Coimbatore	Total
Gender					
Male	64.8	66.4	70.7	41.5	63.6
Female	77.5	76.3	76.0	47.5	73.4
Social Group					
ST	83.3	57.9	73.9	80.0	71.6
SC	62.5	74.4	72.5	50.3	67.0
OBC	71.6	67.8	70.5	37.2	61.8
OC	69.4	65.6	74.9	38.1	70.0
Migrant/Non-migrant					
Migrant	77.3	70.6	77.8	31.8	72.2
Non-migrant	65.4	68.6	71.6	44.0	65.5
Educational Level					
Up to middle	31.5	22.2	72.0	33.3	57.5
High school and higher secondary	68.1	57.9	72.3	44.4	63.9
Graduate and above (general)	71.7	79.1	72.3	43.8	71.2
Graduate and above (technical and professional)	72.1	65.5	78.4	58.3	70.5
Total	66.7	68.9	73.0	42.8	66.6
No. of persons	395	709	962	196	2,262

Source: Primary field survey (2014–2015).

and non-economic factors. For example, a worker may search another job simply due to the discrimination and harassment at her workplace or undue work pressure. The reasons for job change thus can be broadly classified under four categories, namely income related, aspirational like career prospects, work pressure and treatment at workplace. Reasons such as no scope to learn, no prospects of promotion, low job profile and fear of firm's closure can be grouped under the category of 'career prospects'. Work pressure and distance from home can be broadly grouped into the category of 'work pressure'. Reasons such as discrimination and harassment at workplace may be grouped under 'harassment/discrimination at workplace'. In response to a question on the most important reason for job search by employed job seekers, some interesting features are worth to mention.

The first and the foremost reason for searching new job by employed persons turns to be low income from their current employment in a majority of cases. Such results are on the expected line, particularly when wages in the private sector have not increased in proportion to the wage growth in the public sector. About 17 per cent of the employees were searching new jobs mainly due to the weak career progression in their current employment. Another 10 per cent were looking out due to the work pressure and long commuting distance to work. Harassment and discrimination at workplace were also reported as main reasons for new job search by over 4 per cent of our sample employees. The discrimination is reported in the form of work allocation, harassment at workplace and mixing with other employees (Table 4.3a and 4.3b).

City-wise, a majority of workers tended to search for a new job due to their low income, although at a varying scale—around 81 per cent of the workers in Coimbatore and Lucknow, 71 per cent in Delhi and least 62 per cent in Pune. The concerns for career progression are proportionately high among job seekers in Pune as compared to the remaining three cities. Longer distances to reach workplace also formed an important reason for a job search at nearer places in cities such as Delhi, Pune and Coimbatore. Thus, the concerns for career advancement as reasons for job search were least among those searching jobs in Coimbatore and Lucknow. Although the proportion of workers searching jobs due to their concerns about prevailing discrimination, harassment and overall working environment is low, it is almost four times higher in Pune, and double in Delhi as compared to Coimbatore and Lucknow. Such patterns also show the city contexts,

Table 4.3a City-Wise Main Reason for Job Search among Employed Job Seekers (%)

Reason	Lucknow	Delhi/NCR	Pune	Coimbatore	Total
Low income	81.0	70.8	61.7	81.6	69.7
Poor career prospects	11.9	16.2	20.3	8.2	16.5
Work pressure	5.3	9.9	12.2	8.7	10.0
Harassment/discrimination	1.8	3.1	5.8	1.5	3.9
Total	100.0	100.0	100.0	100.0	100.0
No. of persons	395	709	962	196	2,262

Source: Primary field survey (2014–2015).

where workers in cities such as Lucknow and Coimbatore have generally low-income levels as their primary concerns, and are thus seeking higher income jobs. However, the opportunities for such jobs are limited, particularly in Lucknow. Career advancement concerns are more visible among job seekers in Pune and Delhi (Table 4.3a). These cities also provide a variety of employment opportunities in the private sector.

Reasons for job change do not differ much among men and women job seekers. Women were generally reluctant to report harassment at their workplace more vociferously. However, those few women reporting harassment at workplace were of the opinion that most of them face various forms of discrimination in private sector employment. Such observations are in consonance with the earlier findings of gender discrimination in the labour market (Rustagi, 2017).

The proportion of employed SC/ST and OBC job seekers searching new jobs due to low income was higher than other social groups (OCs) or high castes (Table 4.3b). The quest for career progression as a reason for job search was proportionately more among OCs and lowest among SCs/STs. Poor office and work environment in terms of discrimination and harassment surprisingly turns to be proportionately

Table 4.3b *Main Reason for Job Search among Employed Job Seekers by Their Social Group and Migration Status*

Reason	Social Group			Migration Status	
	SCs/STs	OBCs	OCs	Migrant	Non-migrant
Low income	72.3	72.1	65.1	64.8	70.7
Poor career prospects	14.8	15.7	19.0	22.0	15.3
Work pressure	9.5	9.0	11.2	11.6	9.6
Harassment/discrimination	3.5	3.2	4.8	1.6	4.4
No. of persons	832	625	805	409	1,853

Source: Primary field survey (2014–2015).

higher as a reason of job search for OCs as compared to SCs/STs and OBCs. In other words, it seems that a major concern among a large majority of SC workers is their low-income earnings, whereas for OC workers, concerns such as career progression and working environment are also more important for their job change along with higher income jobs.

Similarly, low income is a main reason for jobs search among migrant and non-migrant job seekers. However, a significant percentage of migrant workers (22.0%) were also searching jobs for their career progression (Table 4.3b). Such a proportion of job seekers was much lower (15%) among non-migrants. This pattern is not very surprising as migrant workers were also comparatively better educated and had to struggle for their upward mobility in the urban labour market.

In response to a question on the second important reason for job, over half of the 78 per cent of the sample respondents gave career progression their answer. Over one-fourth of the employed persons said that they were also searching jobs due to the heavy work pressure while another 15 per cent said it was due to the low income from their current employment. About 8 per cent of the workers stated discrimination and harassment as the second important reason for their job search (Table 4.4). A highest one-tenth of the SCs/STs and OBCs

Table 4.4 *Social Group-Wise Second Main Reason of Job Search*

Reason	STs/SCs	OBCs	OCs	Total
Low income	15.7	16.1	14.9	15.5
Poor career prospects	49.1	48.8	50.4	49.5
Work pressure	25.1	26.2	29.0	26.8
Harassment/discrimination	10.2	8.9	5.8	8.2
Total	100	100	100	100
Observation	650	473	639	1,762

Source: Primary field survey (2014–2015).

explicitly mentioned harassment at workplace as the next main reason for their job search after low salary. The corresponding figure for OCs was much low (also see Tables 4A.1 and 4A.2). In brief, while low income in the present job was the primary concern of a majority of workers and thus, first and the foremost reason for their job search, concerns such as career progression and better workplace environment are also equally important, though on a varying scale among other reasons for job search.

Job Information and Job Search Methods among Employed Persons

In this section, we analyse the sources of job information that employed persons used in finding their current employment. The purpose is to examine how a source of job information helps in getting access to employment in the labour market. It would also examine how the source of information determines the access to quality job in terms of its nature and income. Equally important would be to analyse the nature and access of job information to job seekers belonging to various socio-economic groups. It is generally believed that the information about job opportunities is relatively weak and informal in its nature in the case of migrant workers to cities, women, marginalised communities and those with low educational attainments. It is argued that the free flow of information is hampered to job seekers in segmented labour markets, resulting in inequality in productivity and wage earnings (Kannappan, 1977, 1985; Papola, 1981).

We have enlisted different sources of job information for job seekers into 19 categories (including others that are not defined). These have been regrouped into 12 categories. Ideally speaking, there may be more than one source of job information for a job seeker. However, we have restricted ourselves to understand the main source of job information for them while finding their current as well as first job.

Let us first analyse the source of information for the current employment for our sample respondents. The most prominent source of job information is informal social networks, which include friends, relatives, family members, caste networks, etc. The importance of social networks in providing access to labour market information is well documented in the earlier studies as well (Harris, Kannan, & Rodgers, 1990; Munshi & Rosenzweig, 2006). Newspaper advertisements along with web portals were the sources of information for nearly 22 per cent persons. For about 4.63 per cent of the workers, employee referral was the source of job information. About 5 per cent said that they had directly approached the employers. Unlike in the past, employment exchanges are no more a major source of job information. In brief, social contacts/networks emerged as the most important source of job information for a majority of employed persons (Table 4.5). These included family members, friends, relatives, caste/community networks, co-villagers, migrants, employee referrals, etc.

This pattern in the use of different sources of job information is similar among different cities. For instance, family connection as a source of job information was relatively stronger in Lucknow and Coimbatore as compared to Delhi and Pune. Interestingly, in Coimbatore, friends/acquaintances network seems to be more effective in getting a job as compared to other three cities. Newspaper advertisements have been cited by a sizeable number of persons in all cities except Coimbatore. Web portals have emerged as an

Table 4.5 City-Wise Source of Information for Current Employment

Source of Job Information	Lucknow	Delhi	Pune	Coimbatore	Total
Family connections	22.92	13.61	20.50	24.45	19.36
Friends/acquaintances	44.31	43.05	41.61	60.92	45.12
Employee referral	4.92	5.15	5.54	0.44	4.63
Newspaper advertisements	13.92	14.38	19.06	8.52	15.33
Web portal	3.40	13.31	5.77	0.87	6.98
Placement agencies/Staffing companies	0.51	0.78	0.46	0.22	0.53
School/college	0.51	0.78	0.08	0.66	0.44
Campus placement	0.17	1.85	0.91	0.22	0.97
Directly approaching employers	8.32	6.12	4.40	2.84	5.39
Contractor/middleman	0.68	0.19	1.59	0.44	0.85
Employment exchanges	0.00	0.10	0.08	0.22	0.09
Others	0.34	0.68	0.00	0.22	0.29
Total	100	100	100	100	100
No. of persons	589	1,029	1,317	458	3,393

Source: Primary field survey (2014–2015).

important source of job information and the highest 13.3 per cent of the employed persons in the Delhi sample used this source for finding their current job.

Whether sources of job information vary for men and women workers in the labour market? Broadly speaking, social networks are the main source of job information for both men and women. However, friends/acquaintances as a main source of job information were of lesser importance for women workers as compared to their male counterparts. For over 18 per cent women, newspapers were the main source of their job information, whereas about 14 per cent men used this source of information. The proportion of women directly approaching the employer for job was almost double than men (Table 4.6). Such behaviour of job search information has also

Table 4.6 *Source of Information for Current Employment by Gender and Social Group*

Source of Job Information	Gender		Social Group			
	Male	Female	STs	SCs	OBCs	OCs
Family connections	19.34	19.41	8.42	20.91	19.82	18.33
Friends/acquaintances	46.83	41.17	30.53	46.40	47.57	42.92
Employee referral	4.90	4.00	16.84	3.87	5.35	3.74
Newspaper advertisement	14.02	18.34	34.74	14.59	12.88	16.59
Web portal	7.73	5.27	5.26	5.10	6.64	9.30
Placement agencies/ staffing companies	0.55	0.49	0.00	0.26	0.59	0.78
School/college	0.34	0.68	0.00	0.53	0.50	0.35
Campus placement	1.06	0.78	1.05	0.62	0.59	1.65
Directly approaching to employers	4.22	8.10	1.05	6.15	5.15	5.21
Contractor/middleman	0.72	1.17	2.11	0.97	0.59	0.87
Employment exchanges	0.13	0.00	0.00	0.18	0.10	0.00
Others	0.17	0.59	0.00	0.44	0.20	0.26
Total	100	100	100	100	100	100
No. of persons	2,368	1,025	95	1,138	1,009	1,151

Source: Primary field survey (2014–2015).

been reported by the earlier studies. City-wise, there is a significant difference in the sources of job information for both employed men and women (Tables 4.6, 4A.3 and 4A.4). For example, only one-third of the women respondents got job information from their friends/ acquaintances social network in Lucknow and Delhi as compared to 57.4 per cent in Coimbatore and 43 per cent in Pune. Also, the proportion of women directly approaching employers for job information was higher in Lucknow and Delhi as compared to Pune and Coimbatore.

The predominance of social networks as sources of job information is true for workers belonging to various social groups albeit with relatively lesser dependence on such sources among OCs. There is a significant variation in friend/acquaintance as a source of job information among workers belonging to various social groups. Proportionately, more OC workers used newspaper advertisements and web portals as compared to SCs and OBCs. Campus placement cells were the main source of job information for about 2 per cent of the OC workers as compared to about 0.6 per cent for SCs and OBCs. It merits mention here that though job information through college placement cells may be accessible to all, but the cut-off marks for such placements are generally high wherein SCs and OBCs remain at a disadvantageous position due to their educational background (Chakravarty & Somanathan, 2008).

In brief, the dependence on social networks for job information is comparatively more among SCs and OBCs as compared to OCs. This is in contrast to the earlier studies which showed how due to weak social networks, SC job seekers in urban labour market suffer from higher unemployment incidence (Banerjee, 1983; Harris, Kannan, & Rodgers, 1990). However, this has been observed here in the case of STs who are largely dependent on other sources of job information rather than social networks.

Across occupational groups, there exists a significant diversity in sources of job information for workers working therein. For occupations at the bottom of occupational hierarchies such as craft and related works, plant and machine operators, and elementary occupations, an overwhelming majority of workers receive job information through their social networks. For those working in elementary occupations, about 13 per cent received job information through contractors/middlemen. Unlike this pattern, the dependence for job information is relatively less on social networks and other informal channels for workers working in top occupational ladders, for example, senior managerial and professional positions (NCO 1 and NCO 2). About 40 per cent of the workers in these two top occupational groups received job information through formal channels such as newspapers, print media and web portals. Employee referral was also an important channel of job information for managerial, professional, technical, clerical and sales-related occupations, providing such information to 4–7 per cent of the workers therein. About 4 per cent of the workers working in professional occupations and another 2.5 per cent in managerial occupations received job information through their college placement cells (Table 4.7). The presence of this source of job information is almost nil for workers employed in other occupational groups. This also shows

Table 4.7 *Occupation-Wise Pattern in Job Search Information (%)*

Source of Job Information	NCO 1-Digit								
	1	2	3	4	5	6	7	8	9
Family connections	11.1	12.8	14.1	22.8	27.6	25.0	24.8	17.2	28.7
Friends/acquaintances	32.8	30.2	44.0	39.8	51.3	50.0	58.5	57.4	50.6
Employee referral	4.1	4.8	4.9	7.1	5.3	0.0	3.0	3.4	2.9
Newspaper advertisement	22.5	22.7	19.0	19.7	10.2	16.7	8.0	9.8	1.7
Web portal	18.4	17.9	7.5	5.9	1.4	8.3	1.0	0.5	0.6
Placement agencies/ staffing companies	0.8	1.3	0.6	1.2	0.1	0.0	0.0	0.0	0.0
School/College	0.4	1.0	0.7	0.4	0.0	0.0	0.3	0.5	0.0
Campus placement	2.5	3.6	0.6	0.0	0.0	0.0	0.8	0.0	0.0
Directly approaching to employers	6.6	5.5	7.9	2.8	3.8	0.0	2.5	10.3	2.3
Contractor/middleman	0.4	0.0	0.0	0.0	0.3	0.0	0.8	0.0	13.2
Employment exchanges	0.4	0.0	0.0	0.4	0.0	0.0	0.0	0.5	0.0
Others	0.0	0.2	0.7	0.0	0.0	0.0	0.5	0.5	0.0
Total	100	100	100	100	100	100	100	100	100
No. of persons	244	524	877	254	704	12	400	204	174

Source: Primary field survey (2014–2015).

Notes: 1. Legislators, senior officials and managers; 2. Professionals; 3. Technicians and associate professionals; 4. Clerks; 5. Service and sales workers; 6. Skilled agriculture and fishery works; 7. Craft and related works; 8. Plant and machine operators, and assemblers; 9. elementary occupations.

the limited role of college placement cells in providing job information and placement assistance to their graduates.

As regards the social connections of those using employee referrals in job search, almost 58 per cent of the respondents reported having been referred by their friends, followed by 18 per cent referred by relatives excluding family member, 16 per cent each through village acquaintances and other acquaintances, and less than 4 per cent had family members in among employee referrals. Such trends in the social connections of employee referrals are quite contrary to the findings by Dhillon, Iversen and Torsvik (2013), who found almost 80 per cent of the workplace referrals with the help of relatives and members of the same household. This was mainly for blue-collar unskilled jobs. Contrary to this, our sample consists of well-educated and skilled workers who largely use their social network of friends already working in the industry.

Job Information and Intensity of Job Search among Unemployed Persons

As stated earlier in Table 4.1, there were 1,370 unemployed persons in the 18–45 years age group, representing 17.4 per cent of the sample population in that age group. Nearly half among them were had been unemployed for more than a year. This figure included both men and women. City-wise, a longer spell of unemployment was in Lucknow, closely followed by Pune (51.2%), Coimbatore (45.7%) and Delhi (39.2%). About three-fourths of the unemployed were not registered with any formal employment service agencies such as government employment exchanges and private placement agencies. This is also indicative of the limitations of such employment services in offering jobs to the unemployed.

Intensity of Job Search among Unemployed

We asked each unemployed person a question about his/her job search method and number of times each method had been used during last six months. Although such information may be hampered by memory lapse affecting accuracy, nevertheless it throws some interesting features about the intensity of job search among unemployed persons. An overwhelming majority of unemployed persons used internet job portals such as Naukari.com and DevNet, social sites such as LinkedIn and Facebook, websites, and print and electronic media for their job search. The other dominant mode of job search is social network comprising friends/relatives (Table 4.8a).

Apart from these three dominant modes of job search, employee referrals are used by every third unemployed person. Another 13.3 per cent also used college campus placement cells for their job search. The role of private placement agencies as labour market intermediaries has grown in the recent years as about one-fifth of the unemployed persons used this method of job search as well. Job fairs are also used by about 14 per cent of the unemployed persons while looking for jobs. In other words, various new methods of job search that are greatly facilitated by IT have emerged over the years. Thus, the dependence on traditional labour market information such as public employment exchanges, newspaper advertisements and contract/middlemen has considerably reduced over the years, particularly for educated unemployed. Less than one-fifth of the unemployed persons used this service for their job search (Table 4.8a). A large majority of unemployed persons are aware about the different sources of job information, but most of them used print and electronic media, e-job portals and social networks of friends for job vacancies.

Now let us look at the frequency with which the unemployed persons used a given source for their job search. Such intensity is the highest in the case of formal sources of job information such as print media and web portals. A highest 32 per cent of those using web portals for job search used it more than five times in the past six months. The intensity of use of other job search methods was limited, as a large majority of those using such methods used the same up to two times (Table 4.8a). For example, three-fourths of those using employee referrals in their job search used the method up to two times only while

Table 4.8a Intensity of Use of Job Search Methods among Unemployed Persons (during Last Six Months)

Method of Job Search	% of Unemployed Using the Method[a]	Number of Times Used for Applying for Jobs (Intensity of Use) (%)			Not Aware About the Source	Intensity Score[b]
		Up to 2	3–5	> 5 Times		
Advertisements in newspapers and other print media	74.4	43.3	36.3	20.4	4.4	2.95
Free electronic portals including websites	85.1	29.4	38.3	32.3	6.9	3.34
Government employment exchanges	18.3	79.1	13.3	7.7	14.7	0.37
Private placement agencies	21.5	69.9	27.6	2.5	18.6	0.54
College campus placement cells	17.3	88.6	11.5	0.0	11.5	0.35
HR firms/Staffing companies	4.6	62.2	32.2	5.6	53.7	0.13
Job fairs	13.8	85.6	14.4	0.0	18.7	0.25
Employee referrals	35.4	74.1	21.4	4.6	7.4	0.71
Relatives/friends	61.6	68.3	25.7	6.0	4.9	1.54
Family connections	32.5	78.4	20.2	1.4	4.4	0.65
Caste/community contacts	12.6	84.6	15.4	0.0	8.2	0.23
Directly approaching to employers	32.3	68.2	25.9	6.0	6.9	0.81
Contactor/middleman	6.1	77.3	16.0	6.7	7.4	0.12
Others	1.4	78.6	14.3	7.1	21.1	0.03

Source: Primary field survey (2014–2015).

Notes: [a]Based on the use of a given source by unemployed persons. This may not add to 100; [b]Intensity score of a given source of job information is calculated as follows: (spread of use × mean number of times used) %100. Spread of use refers to the percentage of unemployed using a given source of job information.

applying for a job. Similar has been the intensity in the case of other informal social networks such as relatives/friends, family connections and caste/community contacts. In other words, the informal sources of job information in most of the cases are used less frequently for job applications. This is due to the fact that job information available through such sources is on a limited scale. However, such informal job information channels are quite effective in getting access to jobs in the urban labour market as observed in the earlier sections in this chapter.

Intensity of Job Search among Final-Year Students

We also collected information from 2,815 final year students across our sample cities, mostly from graduate-level courses. About 58 per cent of them wanted to join the labour market after completing their education and said that they were actively searching jobs while pursuing their studies. Another 31 per cent wanted to pursue higher education. Like our unemployed respondents, we asked our sample students, who were actively searching jobs, questions pertaining to the different methods of their job search during last four months. The pattern of the use of job search information varies among such students as compared to the unemployed persons. For example, most of them use formal methods of job search like internet job portals more intensively and are less dependent on social networks for job information (Table 4.8b).

It clearly emerges that job information asymmetries in the labour market reduce the intensity of job searches by job seekers. The use of IT has contributed in reducing such asymmetries, thereby making access of job information easier to educated job seekers, irrespective of their age, gender, caste and ethnicity to a certain extent. It is seen how free access to job information to job seekers through print/electronic media and job portals increases the intensity of job searches. This also widens the choices of employers while searching for suitable job applicants. On the other hand, although social networks as sources of job information are used by a majority of job seekers, the intensity of their use is rather limited. Due to this fact, the employers may find difficulty in job matching and getting workers suitable to their needs.

Table 4.8b Intensity of Use of Job Search Methods among Final-Year Students (during Last Four Months)

Method of Job search	% of Unemployed Using the Method[a]	Number of Times Used for Applying for Jobs (Intensity of Use) (%)			Not Aware about the Source	Intensity Score[b]
		Up to 2	3–5	> 5		
Advertisements in newspapers and other print media	53.9	57.3	35.7	7.0	1.9	1.89
Free electronic portals	73.2	48.9	35.2	15.9	2.4	2.20
Government employment exchanges	10.0	89.7	10.3	0.0	7.2	0.16
Private placement agencies	8.9	84.8	15.2	0.0	8.6	0.16
College campus placement cells	37.5	79.9	20.1	0.0	1.6	0.83
HR firms	3.8	87.4	12.6	0.0	24.0	0.09
Job fairs	11.2	85.1	14.9	0.0	9.2	0.25
Employee referrals	17.7	90.1	9.9	0.0	5.3	0.33
Relatives/friends	35.1	83.3	16.7	0.0	2.7	0.70
Family connections	13.4	91.6	8.4	0.0	1.5	0.25
Directly approaching to employers	11.5	77.5	16.7	5.9	2.9	0.29

Source: Primary field survey (2014–2015).

Notes: Total number of final year students was 2,815. About 1,983 were actively searching jobs. This information pertains to 1,983 students who were actively searching jobs; [a]Based on the use of a given source by unemployed persons. This may not add to 100; [b]Intensity score of a given source of job information is calculated as follows: (spread of use × mean number of times used) %100. Spread of use refers to the percentage of unemployed using a given source of job information.

Likelihood of Using Social Networks in Job Search

From the above analysis, it clearly emerges that informal social networks as a source of job information dominate the urban labour market. Open access to job information on a wide scale is yet to see the way in Indian urban labour market despite a phenomenal rise in IT in recent years. Employers are still using social networks of workers to disseminate job information, mainly for low-end jobs. This is mainly to reduce the cost of recruitments and to control the new hire through their social contact. A study by Munshi and Rosenzweig (2006) observed referrals as important source of job information and recruitment as about 70 per cent of the blue-collar jobs, and 44 per cent of the white-collar jobs were found through referrals in Mumbai. It is, therefore, important to understand the factors influencing the use of social networks for job search in the urban labour market. The likelihood of using social networks for getting job information in urban labour market may be influenced by the characteristics of job seekers, namely age, gender, social group, migration, education, occupation, income and place of residence, etc. For this, we applied logistic regression to estimate the effect of these variables on the decision of job seekers to use social network as a source of job information for employed job seekers.

Logistic Regression Results and Analysis

Table 4.9 reveals interesting results of logistic regression. The probability of using social networks as a source of job information tends to reduce, significantly, with every increase in the numbers of years of education of job seekers. The odds ratio shows that one year increase in education reduces the odds in the favour of using social network as job search method by around 11 per cent. It thus indicates that job seekers with a high level of education do not employ social network as job search method as intensively as compared to job seekers with low level of education. Similarly, the likelihood of using social networks

Table 4.9 *Decision to Use Social Network as Job Search Method by Employed Persons in Finding Their Current Job*

Social Network	Coefficient	Odds Ratio	Standard Error	Z	P>|Z|
Constant	1.3101	3.7067	0.4155	3.15	0.002
Education	–0.1084	0.8972	0.0145	–7.46	0.000
Income	–0.0000	0.9999	0.0000	–6.20	0.000
Age	0.0051	1.0051	0.0064	0.81	0.421
Gender	0.2327	1.2620	0.0893	2.60	0.009
Migrant	–0.1867	0.8296	0.0846	–2.21	0.027
SC	0.9419	2.5650	0.2419	3.89	0.000
OBC	1.0146	2.7583	0.2434	4.17	0.000
OC	1.1343	3.1090	0.2407	4.71	0.000
Occupation I	–0.5597	0.5713	0.2096	–2.67	0.008
Occupation II	0.1057	1.1115	0.2096	0.50	0.614
Occupation III	0.2147	1.2395	0.2197	0.98	0.328
Delhi	–0.0115	0.9885	0.1194	–0.10	0.923
Pune	–0.1327	0.8756	0.1235	–1.07	0.283
Coimbatore	1.0658	2.9033	0.1684	6.33	0.000
Total Observations			3,232		
LR chi2(14)			517.05		
Pseudo R2			0.1222		

Source: Primary field survey (2014–2015).

Notes: Education is measured as the number of years of education; income reflects per capita monthly income of workers; age in number of years. Except these three variables, other variables are categorical. For gender, social group and occupation dummies are used as females, STs and occupation IV (elementary occupations), respectively. Lucknow is used for city dummy.

declines significantly for higher income jobs. The variable 'age', however, does not have any significant impact upon the likelihood of using social network for job search in the urban labour market.

It is seen that the coefficient of gender dummy is significantly different from zero and the odd ratio in the favour of men using social network is higher by about 26.2 per cent as compared to women. The dummy variable capturing migration shows that if the job seeker is a migrant, it reduces the odds in the favour of using social network as job search method as compared to non-migrant job seeker. This implies that the migrants have less social fabric to explore jobs in the urban labour market. This result is in contrast with some earlier studies on rural to urban migration which revealed how informal social networks helped majority of migrants to get employment in the urban areas (Papola, 1981; Oberai, 1987)

Chances of using social network as a source of job information are significantly influenced by the social belonging of job seekers. The three social group dummies are statistically significant from zero and they increase the odds which favour the choice of employing social network as job search method by job seekers compared to the omitted category, STs. These results clearly show how the likelihood of using social network for job information by job seekers is highest for those belonging to OSG as compared to the lower caste-group (say, ST and SC).

One-digit NCOs are regrouped into four groups: Occupation I, Occupation II, Occupation III and Occupation IV. Occupation I includes three top most occupations in occupational hierarchy, namely legislators, senior officials and managers (NCO 1), professional (NCO 2) and technician (NCO 3); Occupation II comprises clerks (NCO 4), service and sales workers (NCO 5); Occupation III includes skilled agriculture and fishery works (NCO 6); craft and related works (NCO 7); and machine operators and assemblers (NCO 8), and finally Occupation IV (omitted category) comprises elementary occupations (NCO 9).

The chances of using social network for job search significantly differ with the type of occupation being searched. The declining values of odds ratios with rising occupational hierarchies reconfirm that the chances of workers using social networks for top-end occupations are significantly lower than those in lower occupational hierarchies in the urban labour market. This finding is in conformity with the earlier studies showing social networks as an important channel to seek entry into low-end occupations, which often results in segregations in the labour market of various types (L. K. Deshpande & Deshpande, 1979; Kannappan, 1985; Papola, 1981).

Finally, the effect of location or city on the decision to use social network as job search method is measured through the usage of location dummies. The coefficients on dummies—Delhi and Pune—are not found to be different from zero. However, Coimbatore is significantly different from zero, which indicates that as compared to Lucknow, social network has been used in a greater degree to search a job in Coimbatore. In other words, the use of social networks in Delhi, Pune and Lucknow is almost identical, whereas the same is significantly different and higher in Coimbatore.

In brief, social networks are significant in providing job information and access to jobs in urban labour market, particularly for low-end occupations fetching low income to job seekers.

Types of Occupations Searched

Employed Job Seekers

As observed earlier, a majority of employed persons were searching another job due to a variety of reasons. It would be interesting to see what type of jobs they were searching— whether they were looking for jobs broadly in their present area of work (i.e., occupational group) or searching for other occupational categories? An overwhelming majority of those working in top two occupational groups, that is, managers (NCO 1) and professionals (NCO 2), tended to search jobs in the same occupational groups. Those working in the mid-level occupational groups such as clerical, and sales and service jobs, about 42–48 per cent were searching jobs in other occupational groups, mostly for top three occupational groups, that is, NCOs 1, 2 and 3 respectively. A sizeable number of persons working in plant and machine operating occupations, and elementary occupations were looking for jobs as sales and service workers, technicians and crafts workers. In other words, most of the job seekers were attempting upward occupational mobility (Table 4.10). Such pattern of job search also indicates the educational mismatches in labour market where a sizeable number of job seekers, despite having educational qualifications for higher order occupations, are hoarded in other occupational categories not requiring such high levels of education. This is generally being termed now as the problem of overeducated in labour market (ILO, 2014).

Table 4.10 *Type of Job Being Searched by Employed Job Seekers by Their Present Occupation (%)*

Current Occupation	Type of Occupation Being Searched (NCO 1-Digit)									No. of Persons
	1	2	3	4	5	7	8	9	Total	
Legislators, senior officials and managers	81.4	10.1	3.9	2.3	1.6	0.0	0.0	0.8	100	129
Professionals	2.4	90.8	3.8	1.6	0.8	0.5	0.0	0.0	100	369
Technicians and associate professionals	6.6	7.9	73.3	9.3	1.8	0.3	0.8	0.0	100	610
Clerks	4.1	13.8	19.0	59.0	1.5	1.0	1.5	0.0	100	195
Service and sales workers	1.4	7.1	18.6	16.5	49.9	4.7	0.9	0.9	100	425
Craft and related works	0.0	5.1	10.1	5.8	6.9	69.7	1.8	0.7	100	277
Plant and machine operators, and assemblers	0.7	1.4	7.1	7.8	12.1	5.0	66.0	0.0	100	141
Elementary occupations	0.0	0.9	17.2	14.7	29.3	9.5	0.9	27.6	100	116
Total	7.6	21.0	29.4	12.4	13.6	9.9	4.5	1.6	100	2,262

Source: Primary field survey (2014–2015).

Notes: 1. Legislators, senior officials and managers, 2. Professionals, 3. Technicians and associate professionals, 4. Clerks, 5. Service and sales workers, 6. Skilled agriculture and fishery works, 7. Craft and related works, 8. Plant and machine operators, and assemblers, 9. Elementary occupations.

Unemployed Persons

Since most of the unemployed persons were graduate and above, the highest 39 per cent were searching jobs in the occupational category of technicians and associate professionals such as technicians in science and engineering, and teaching associates. Another one-fifth of the persons were looking for jobs in the occupational group of professionals in the areas of science and engineering, teaching, business, law and other social sciences. Since, entry into the top occupational group, that is, managers and senior officials is generally associated with fairly long experience, the proportion of unemployed seeking jobs in such occupations is very low. Another one-fifth of the unemployed were seeking jobs in clerical occupations (Table 4.11a). Such a broad pattern in occupational choices among unemployed is seen in all the sample cities. However, in Lucknow and Delhi, a substantive number of workers are also searching jobs in clerical occupations.

Table 4.11a City-Wise Type of Occupation Being Searched by Unemployed Persons (%)

Occupation (NCO 1-Digit)	Lucknow	Delhi	Pune	Coimbatore	Total
Legislators, senior officials and managers	5.11	4.27	1.60	1.70	3.07
Professionals	16.56	17.30	28.00	21.77	21.89
Technicians and associate professionals	34.76	40.76	38.93	40.82	38.57
Clerks	26.99	29.15	13.20	17.01	20.66
Service and sales workers	9.20	4.50	7.73	10.88	7.88
Craft and related works	3.68	2.84	6.40	7.48	5.12
Plant and machine operators, and assemblers	2.04	1.18	1.20	0.00	1.23
Elementary occupations	1.64	0.00	2.93	0.34	1.59
Total	100.00	100.00	100.00	100.00	100.00
No. of persons	424	345	217	250	1,236

Source: Primary field survey (2014–2015).

Gender-wise, no substantial differences exist in the occupational choices except that a larger proportion of women were seeking jobs in the occupational groups of technicians and associate professionals, and clerks (Table 4.11b). There are significant differences in the pattern of jobs being searched among unemployed persons belonging to different social groups. For example, the highest 28 per cent of OCs were searching jobs related to the occupational group 'professionals'. The corresponding share among STs was only 5.3 per cent and that among SCs, about 18.7 per cent. Unlike OCs, a larger percentage of both ST and SC unemployed persons were looking for jobs in occupational groups such as clerks, sales and service jobs, and crafts and related jobs (Table 4.11b). In other words, job aspirations are generally high among unemployed persons from OC social group. This is partly related to better educational attainments among them and partly to their aspirations.

Table 4.11b *Type of Occupation Being Searched by Unemployed Persons by Their Gender and Social Group (%)*

Occupation (NCO 1-Digit)	Gender		Social Group			
	Men	Women	STs	SCs	OBCs	OCs
Legislators, senior officials and managers	4.00	1.99	0.00	2.85	2.52	4.61
Professionals	23.55	19.98	5.26	18.69	23.03	28.07
Technicians and associate professionals	34.60	43.16	31.58	38.99	38.80	38.38
Clerks	19.16	22.41	22.81	22.03	20.19	18.64
Service and sales workers	8.77	6.84	10.53	8.79	8.83	4.61
Craft and related works	6.20	3.86	22.81	5.45	4.26	3.51
Plant and machine operators, and assemblers	1.81	0.55	1.75	1.49	1.42	0.44
Elementary occupations	1.91	1.21	5.26	1.73	0.95	1.75
Total	100.00	100.00	100.00	100.00	100.00	100.00
No. of persons	675	561	24	524	418	270

Source: Primary field survey (2014–2015).

Application Realisation Rate and Reasons for Not Being Selected—Unemployed Persons

While using different sources of job information, it was seen that nearly two-thirds of the unemployed persons got the chance to appear in a job interview during last six months. In other words, about one-third of the unemployed did not get even a single chance to appear for job interviews. Over one-third of the unemployed persons got a single chance for a job interview during the reference period and less than one in five appeared for an interview at least twice in the reference period. Thus, there were very few unemployed persons who appeared for job interviews on more than three occasions. This shows the tight job market situation in urban areas where even the chances of getting job interview calls were quite low for a majority of the unemployed persons (Table 4.12a).

Does such a tight job market situation differ along caste and gender groups among unemployed persons? It is seen that the proportion of SCs/STs not able to get a single chance for job interviews was much higher than OBCs and OCs. Similar has been the case of unemployed females as compared to their male counterparts. Likewise, maximum

Table 4.12a *Number of Times Appeared for Interview (during Last Six Months)*

Number of Times	Gender (%)		Social Group (%)			Total (%)
	Male	Female	SCs/STs	OBCs	OCs	
0	31.43	36.78	37.13	32.86	29.01	33.86
1	33.90	39.07	35.01	38.55	35.38	36.25
2	20.61	16.32	17.17	19.80	20.66	18.66
3	5.89	2.76	3.85	3.74	6.37	4.47
4 and above	8.16	5.07	6.84	5.05	8.58	6.76
Total	100	100	100	100	100	100
No. of persons	675	561	548	418	270	1,236

Source: Primary field survey (2014–2015).

number of unemployed belonging to different social groups got one chance to appear for a job interview. The proportion of those who appeared more than three times for job interviews was highest for OCs (14%) as compared to OBCs (8.8%) and SCs (10.7%; Table 4.12a). These patterns thus show that the job market is comparatively tighter for SCs/STs than OCs. Reasons for such a tight labour market for SCs/STs may be associated with their poor endowments such as education, skills and location, but also partly due to the discrimination in the labour market (Madheswaran & Attewell, 2010). A correspondence study by Madheswaran and Attewell (2010) shows how the chances of getting job interview offers are significantly low for Muslims and SCs in the urban labour market despite having the same or higher level of education than those applicants from other socio-religious groups.

Across the sample cities, it appears that the urban labour market was very tight in Lucknow as well as Delhi. Nearly half of the unemployed persons in Lucknow and about 39 per cent in Delhi did not get any chance to appear for a job interview. Coimbatore and Pune cities are comparatively far better in this regard. The proportion of persons getting three or more chances for job interviews was much higher in Delhi and Pune (about 16% each) than Coimbatore (5%) and Lucknow (8.8%; Table 4.12b).

Table 4.12b City-Wise Number of Times Appeared for Interview (during Last Six Months; %)

Number of Times	Lucknow	Delhi/NCR	Pune	Coimbatore
0	48.8	39.1	17.1	15.6
1	28.3	27.1	38.3	60.6
2	14.2	17.3	29.0	18.7
3	5.0	5.1	5.1	2.4
4 and above	3.8	11.3	10.6	2.6
Total	100	100	100	100
No. of observations	424	345	217	250

Source: Primary field survey (2014–2015).

Are the chances of appearing for an interview associated with the educational levels of the unemployed? It emerged that as compared to graduates, a larger proportion of unemployed with secondary and postgraduate-level education had at least one chance to appear for job interviews during the last six months (Table 4.12c). However, the chances of getting more than one interview call is much higher among graduates and postgraduate unemployed persons, thereby indicating the availability of relatively higher job opportunities for such persons in the urban labour market as compared to those with lower educational levels. This does not mean that the unemployment rate would be lower among graduates. The NSSO data show a higher rate of unemployment among graduates and postgraduates, particularly among technical degree graduates as compared to those with the lower levels of education (Mamgain & Tiwari, 2016).

Application Realisation Rates for Final-Year Students

As in the case of unemployed persons, nearly one-third of the job-searching students did not get a single call for a job interview during the reference period. The remaining got one to two chances. The

Table 4.12c *Number of Times Appeared for Interview (during Last Six Months) by the Educational Level (%)*

Number of Times	Secondary and Senior Secondary	Graduate	Postgraduate
0	31.6	36.5	31.1
1	41.5	33.7	32.7
2	18.9	17.4	22.1
3	2.3	5.3	6.4
4 and above	5.6	7.2	7.7
Total	100	100	100
No. of persons	386	644	190

Source: Primary field survey (2014–2015).

proportion of female students not getting a single chance of a job interview was substantively higher than their male counterparts. Likewise females, the proportion of job seeking students not appearing in a single job interview was highest among SC students. The proportion of students appearing in three or more job interviews was comparatively higher among OCs and male students (Table 4.13a).

The situation was, however, somewhat different across the sample cities. A highest 52 per cent of the final year job-seeking students did not get a single chance for a job interview in Delhi. Next was Lucknow. In Coimbatore and Pune cities, about 80–90 per cent of the final year students appeared for job interviews. A substantive proportion of job-seeking students had two chances for appearing for job interviews in all the cities except Delhi (Table 4.13b). Explanation for exceptionally higher proportion of students reporting zero call for job interviews in Delhi and, to some extent, Lucknow may be due to a substantive number of general graduates and postgraduates such as BA/BSC and MA/BSC (about 30%), who are comparatively less in demand. Pune and Coimbatore emerge to be comparatively better in terms of job opportunities.

Table 4.13a *Number of Times Appeared for Interview (during Last Six Months)—Final-Year Students by Their Gender and Social Group*

Number of Times	Gender		Social Group				Total
	Male	Female	STs	SCs	OBCs	OCs	
0	29.7	36.0	27.8	37.2	30.7	31.9	32.4
1	22.4	26.1	18.1	28.2	23.9	22.6	24.0
2	24.5	20.9	33.3	20.3	27.0	20.6	22.9
3	9.0	7.4	11.1	8.2	7.6	8.9	8.3
4 and above	14.3	9.7	9.8	6	10.8	15.9	12.2
Total	100	100	100	100	100	100	100
No. of persons	1,116	865	72	379	619	911	1,981

Source: Primary field survey (2014–2015).

Table 4.13b *City-wise Number of Times Appeared for Interview (during Last Six Months)—Final-Year Students*

Number of Times	Lucknow	Delhi/NCR	Pune	Coimbatore
0	26.9	51.9	17.9	10.7
1	21.6	22.9	16.1	39.9
2	25.7	11.1	38.0	30.9
3	8.6	4.9	16.7	7.7
4 and above	17.1	9.2	11.3	10.7
Total	100	100	100	100
No. of persons	606	748	329	298

Source: Primary field survey (2014–2015).

To sum up, the urban labour market showed a tight position for job opportunities for the unemployed as a sizeable number of them could not get even a single opportunity for job interviews during the past four months. This situation was more worrisome in Lucknow and, to some extent, in Delhi/NCR, and that too for SCs/STs and highly educated persons.

Reasons for Not Being Selected in the Last Job Interview

As stated earlier, about 70 per cent of the unemployed persons had at least one opportunity to appear for a job interview during the last six months. Their perceptions about not being selected in the interview were recorded in the Likert scale in Table 4.14.

Over one-third of the unemployed who appeared for interviews strongly felt that their demanding higher salary had deterred employers from selecting them for observation. Another one-fifth also felt the same to some extent. Proportionately, more SC and OBC unemployed (54% and 63%, respectively) as compared to OCs (46.5%) felt that their demand for higher salary than that was offered led to

Table 4.14 Reasons for Not Being Selected in Last Interview— Unemployed Persons

Reason	Strongly Feel	Feel to Some Extent	Do not Feel so	Cannot Say
Demanded higher salary	34.5	21.0	39.5	4.9
Performance was not satisfactory	17.2	27.1	48.3	7.5
Experience was not suitable to employer	22.8	28.7	40.8	7.7
Lack of skills	23.9	20.9	50.0	5.2
No prior experience of work	24.5	29.2	41.2	5.1
Not comfortable in local language of the city	9.9	11.4	73.5	5.2
Poor in English language	18.0	29.7	47.9	4.4
Long distance to the place of work	18.8	14.2	59.7	7.3
Employer probably prefers his/her own caste/religion candidates	15.7	16.2	53.3	14.8
Employer prefers his/her own region's candidates	14.3	16.5	53.1	15.7
No relative/friend in the company/firm to support my candidature	20.0	23.3	48.0	8.8
Job profile being offered was not acceptable to me	11.9	14.1	64.2	9.8

Source: Primary field survey (2014–2015).
Note: The row percentages add to 100.

their rejection. This also reflects the aspirations of higher salary by the unemployed and rigidities on the part of employers in offering such salaries. In other words, employers have enough number of job seekers who are prepared to offer their services at much lower levels. Mismatches in the labour market in terms of required experience and skills is also reflected from the responses of the unemployed. About half of the unemployed felt that they lacked the experience and skills suitable to employers' requirements. About 30 per cent of the unemployed felt that the employer preferences for their own caste as well as region candidates may be the possible reason for their rejection in interviews. Caste group-wise, about one-third of SCs and OBCs, and one-fourth of OCs felt that employers' preferences for their own caste candidates led to their rejection. A fairly large percentage of unemployed feel that they could not get selected due to the absence of their social network connections in the enterprise. This again reinforces the importance of social networks in job information and job offers to job seekers. A majority of unemployed respondents felt that the caste and social background did not matter in employers' decisions while hiring their employees, and thus may not be the cause of their rejection in an interview. However, a significant number of unemployed feel caste/religion-based preferences by employers as one of the reasons for their rejection (Table 4.14). This can be seen as a positive trend in the labour market as even a large proportion of unemployed SCs and STs did not think that caste or religion preferences by the employers led to their rejection in job interviews. Rather the issues which concerned a large majority of unemployed were related to the lack of experience and soft skills like fluency in English language which are much in demand in the labour market.

Summing Up

Job search is a widespread activity that is not limited to the unemployed persons only in the labour market. A sizeable number (73%) of those working in different occupations also search jobs with substantive differences in job search intensity across their gender, social group and the location of city. Most of them are in their 30s and 40s, and were searching other jobs due to a variety of reasons. The predominant one, however, relates to the quest for higher income, followed by career progression and workplace environment.

This chapter finds informational asymmetries in the urban labour market despite the rapid penetration of IT. Social network contacts still remain the major source of job information and job access to job seekers, particularly for low-end occupations such as sales, service, operators and elementary occupations. The access to jobs and earnings are significantly influenced by the nature of such informal networks contacts in urban labour market. We find employee referrals gradually becoming an important source of job information and entry in enterprises. Such referrals are again a different form of informal social network that are used both by employers and employees to get trusted job applicants with low cost of recruitment yet high moral authorities on such job applicants. Based on the source of job information for the current job of employed persons, we find the likelihood of using social network for job search significantly high among less educated, men, migrant workers, OCs and those employed in low-end occupations fetching low income to job seekers. In the case of unemployed persons, a large majority of them used formal methods such as print and electronic media, free web portals, and social sites such as LinkedIn and Facebook more intensively. However, they also use informal social network of relatives and friends for their job search but not as intensively. This could be due to the limitations of social networks in providing a wide range of job information to job seekers more frequently. The role of labour market intermediaries such as public employment exchanges and private placement agencies is limited in extending employment services to unemployed persons in urban labour market. However, new forms of job information and recruitment such as campus placement cells of educational institutions, job fairs and social sites are emerging fast in the urban labour market landscape. However, such methods are yet limited and have to go a long distance to become widespread.

The methods of job search differ significantly for various types of occupations, particularly among those persons who are employed and are yet actively searching another job. Most of those employed in managerial, professional and technical occupations tend to search jobs in the same occupational groups, whereas others working at lower occupational ladders tend to apply for mid-level occupations such as sales and service jobs in larger proportion. This obviously indicates the efforts by job seekers towards upward occupational mobility. This pattern is observed for men and women as well as those belonging to different social groups.

Most of the unemployed are actively searching jobs and received at least one interview call during the last six months prior to the survey. However, the rate of such interview calls was lower in Lucknow and Delhi, and also for SCs/STs and OBCs. It was also true for graduates and postgraduates as compared to those with the lower levels of education, indicating the unwillingness of the former group of job seekers to be available for all kinds of jobs. This also shows the comparatively tight labour markets for highly educated unemployed.

In brief, job seekers use a variety of methods to find jobs in the labour market. In this entire process, the type and access to job information, and its use play a significant role in job signalling, job matching and employment outcomes. The access to such information varies significantly across different groups of job seekers based on their education, social background, gender and location. Social networks still play a dominant role in the dissemination of job information and access to jobs, and thus have their own advantages and disadvantages, particularly for employers. The advantages include lower search costs and moral pressures on hires, whereas disadvantages may include reduced alternatives for finding more competitive workers at the wages on offer.

Annexure 4A

Table 4A.1 *Gender-Wise Reasons for Job Search*

Reason of Job Search	Male	Female	Total
Low salary	68.06	66.81	67.63
Distance from home	7.82	8.59	8.08
No scope to learn	8.71	7.43	8.27
No further promotion	5.81	6.49	6.05
Non-cooperative colleague	0.78	1.05	0.87
Work pressure	2.79	2.41	2.66
Discrimination in work allocation	0.73	1.05	0.84

Reason of Job Search	Male	Female	Total
Discrimination in mixing	0.56	0.63	0.58
Low job profile	2.12	1.88	2.04
Firm closure fear	0.67	1.05	0.80
Employer harassment	0.61	0.63	0.62
Employee harassment	0.06	0.00	0.04
Others	1.28	1.99	1.53
Total	100	100	100

Source: Primary field survey (2014–2015).

Table 4A.2 *Religion-Wise Reasons for Job Search*

Reason of Job Search	Hindu	Muslims	ORMs	Total
Low salary	66.76	73.12	69.67	67.63
Distance from home	8.51	2.51	10.90	8.08
No scope to learn	8.24	8.96	7.58	8.27
No further promotion	5.98	6.81	5.69	6.05
Non-cooperative colleague	0.93	1.08	0.00	0.87
Work pressure	2.84	1.79	1.90	2.66
Discrimination in work allocation	0.98	0.36	0.00	0.84
Discrimination in mixing	0.62	0.00	0.95	0.58
Low job profile	1.91	4.30	0.47	2.04
Firm closure	0.89	0.72	0.00	0.80
Employer harassment	0.62	0.00	1.42	0.62
Employee harassment	0.04	0.00	0.00	0.04
Others	1.68	0.36	1.42	1.53
Total	100	100	100	100

Source: Primary field survey (2014–2015).

Table 4A.3 City-Wise Source of Information for Current Employment of Employed Persons by Their Gender—Males

Source of Job Information	Lucknow	Delhi/NCR	Pune	Coimbatore	Total
Family connections	23.6	13.6	20.1	24.4	19.3
Friends/acquaintances	46.5	45.9	40.8	61.9	46.8
Employment exchanges	0.0	0.1	0.1	0.3	0.1
Newspaper advertisements	12.6	13.3	18.7	7.8	14.0
Web portal	2.8	15.1	6.7	0.8	7.7
Directly approaching to employers	7.6	3.7	3.4	2.5	4.2
Employee referral	5.0	5.0	7.0	0.3	4.9
Placement agencies/staffing companies	0.4	0.8	0.5	0.3	0.5
School/college	0.2	0.4	0.1	0.8	0.3
Campus placement	0.2	1.8	1.2	0.3	1.1
Contractor/middleman	0.8	0.3	1.3	0.3	0.7
Others	0.4	0.1	0.0	0.3	0.2
Total	100.0	100.0	100.0	100.0	100.0
No. of persons	501	767	743	357	2,368

Source: Primary field survey (2014–2015).

Table 4A.4 City-Wise Source of Information for Current Employment of Employed Persons by Their Gender–Females

Source of Job Information	Lucknow	Delhi/NCR	Pune	Coimbatore	Total
Family connections	19.3	13.7	21.1	24.8	19.4
Friends/acquaintances	31.8	34.7	42.7	57.4	41.2
Employment exchanges	0	0	0	0	0
Newspaper advertisements	21.6	17.6	19.5	10.9	18.3
Web portal	6.8	8.0	4.5	1.0	5.3

Source of Job Information	Lucknow	Delhi/NCR	Pune	Coimbatore	
Directly approaching to employers	12.5	13.4	5.7	4.0	8.1
Employee referral	4.5	5.7	3.7	1.0	4.0
Placement agencies/ staffing companies	1.1	0.8	0.3	0.0	0.5
School/college	2.3	1.9	0.0	0.0	0.7
Campus placement	0.0	1.9	0.5	0.0	0.8
Contractor/middleman	0.0	0.0	1.9	1.0	1.2
Others	0.0	2.3	0.0	0.0	0.6
Total	100.0	100.0	100.0	100.0	100.0
No. of persons	88	262	574	101	1,025

Source: Primary field survey (2014–2015).

CHAPTER 5

Job Mobility in Urban Labour Market

Introduction

Notwithstanding the fair amount of research on job mobility in the developed countries, there is a dearth of research on job mobility in lower-middle income countries like India. In the past couple of decades, few studies have attempted to understand the nature and pattern of job mobility. According to them, job mobility is '...the ability of the worker to move up the scale of occupations inside an enterprise or from one enterprise to another within the same industry or even across industries...' (Acharya & Jose, 1991, p. 1). With the changing context over the years, the concept of job mobility has been extended to include three kinds of mobility, namely job-to-job mobility, occupational mobility and employment mobility. Job-to-job mobility is the movement of employees between employers; occupational mobility is the change of occupational status, for example, change of job profile and job content; employment mobility is the transition between different types of contracts, and in and out of employment (Anderson, Haahr, Hansen, & Holm-Pedersen, 2008). Job mobility could thus imply adaptability, flexibility and adjustability in the labour market (Acharya & Jose, 1991; L. K. Deshpande & Deshpande, 1990; Jefferys & Moss, 1954; Papola & Subramanian, 1975).

Further, job mobility can be vertical or horizontal in nature. The former occurs when a worker's job profile and job content changes. It is associated with the additional authority and increased remuneration, and can take place within the same firm or within the same occupation, as well as across industries and occupational sub-groups. The latter, on the other hand, occurs when an employee with a given set of skills and occupation moves across industry groups (interfirm/interindustry job mobility; Anderson, Haahr, Hansen, & Holm-Pedersen, 2008). Vertical and horizontal job mobility are, however, largely restricted to the manufacturing and high productive service sectors.[1] These types of job mobility are generally found in the organised sector (or organised labour market) of developed countries (Anderson, Haahr, Hansen, & Holm-Pedersen, 2008).

In the context of a developing economy like India where a large proportion of workers are self-employed, they remain outside the purview of the typical wage model of the labour market. Job mobility for them could be in various forms, namely change in the status of employment from self-employment to wage employment, change from home-based activity to unit-based enterprise, change in occupation and change in the industry of work. A substantial proportion of job mobility in India is involuntary in nature and is driven to a large extent by situations of extreme poverty, disasters/crises or loss of sources of livelihoods (Hnatkovska, Lahiri, & Paul, 2010; Khandker, 1992). Thus, job mobility could also be from rural to urban areas, in the form of migration, where there is movement of workers across the geographical regions in search of productive employment (Mamgain, 2004).

In general, job mobility takes place for two reasons: the first relates to the changing economic and labour market policies; the second relates to the individual or personal and household characteristics. It is often assumed that the economic restructuring process would lead to higher job mobility and the nature of this mobility could be either upward or downward. The growth of modern or technology-based

---

[1] High productive sectors are finance, banking, business services, telecommunications, IT and public administration.

industries through the restructuring process would lead to the creation of high-skilled jobs. However, the technological change would
also make some skills redundant, leading to loss of jobs, and in the
absence of demand for such skills, workers would be faced with the
threat of downward job mobility. If active labour market policies such
as training, retraining and skill development are not in place, then such
a restructuring process might tend to lead workers towards downward
mobility. Given the economic development and the opportunities,
mobility in some sense depends on the individual or personal and
household characteristics of the worker, and how well they are able
to exploit the situation to their advantage.

Given this context, this chapter examines the nature of job mobility
in the Indian urban labour market. The chapter is structured into six
sections. The next section provides a brief review of the literature on
job mobility in the Indian context. Section 'Concept, Methodology
and Data' describes the concept of job mobility that has been used for
the analysis and methodology of our empirical investigation, and presents the variables and data sources used for the analysis. Section 'Job
Mobility in the Urban Labour Market' analyses the nature and pattern
of job mobility and characteristics of those who move their jobs. In
Section 'Determinants of Job Mobility', we analyse the determinants
of job mobility. Section 'Impact of Job Mobility on Income Levels'
measures the impact of job mobility on the income of workers. The
last section concludes the chapter.

Related Literature

A number of studies have been undertaken to understand the job and
occupational mobility among workers in urban India (Acharya &
Jose, 1991; Harris, Kannan, & Rodgers, 1990; Khandker, 1992; L.
K. Deshpande & Deshpande, 1990; Mitra, 2006; Pais, 2006; Papola,
1981; Papola & Subramanian, 1975). The studies on job mobility
in the 1970s show that there was a 'higher degree of malleability of
occupations' in the labour market, and a large number of occupations

required 'generic skills' and not 'specific skills' (L. K. Deshpande & Deshpande, 1990; Papola & Subramanian, 1975). They also noted that job changes routinely involved occupational change and industry change, which also led them to conclude that the Indian labour market was 'not compartmentalised' by occupation and industry.

The studies in the 1990s examined labour mobility within the organised manufacturing sector (L. K. Deshpande & Deshpande, 1990) and mobility of workers in the unorganised sector (Acharya & Jose, 1991) in the city of Bombay. Both these studies found that job mobility leads to improved incomes for workers or upward mobility, that is, from non-manufacturing to manufacturing employment (L. K. Deshpande & Deshpande, 1990); from unskilled to skilled jobs; and from irregular to regular jobs (Acharya & Jose, 1991). These urban studies found that more than half of the workforce had changed jobs at least once in their careers.

However, Harris, Kannan and Rodgers (1990) in their study of urban labour market in Coimbatore argued that mobility could not be examined by segmenting labour markets into formal and informal sectors and by looking into occupations or other similar indicators. Rather, mobility is to be captured by looking into the shift from the most vulnerable statuses of labour across occupations. Using a comprehensive classification of labour statuses, they observed that the incidence of mobility is high among casual wage workers (unprotected irregular) and unprotected regular workers. They find an inverse relationship between mobility and regularity (and protection) of first job.

A study on leather accessories in Dharavi, Mumbai, showed that over 91 per cent of the workers in the industry changed their jobs in their careers (Pais, 2006). This estimate was much higher compared to other studies in Mumbai (Acharya & Jose, 1991) which found mobility among workers in the low-income households to be 81.9 per cent for males and 56.4 per cent for females. Papola and Subramanian (1975) found that in Ahmedabad about 47.5 per cent of their sample workers in informal sector changed jobs.

Mitra's study (2006) on the slum-dwellers of Delhi also observed high degree of mobility among workers during the period of their first job in the city and the current job. Using the status of employment, he found that among those who were employed at the time of survey in regular salaried workers, over 51 per cent moved to this status from casual wage employment and another one-fourth were self-employed in the past. In the case of those working as casual wage labour, over 62 per cent were in the same employment category in the past as well. In the case of self-employed, over half of them shifted from casual wage employment and another 30 per cent had the same employment status. In some sense, the movement from casual wage labour to self-employment and vice versa seems to be a major form of mobility among workers in low-income households.

Apart from change in the work status, job mobility has also been analysed by looking at the change in occupations. Mitra (2006) observes a sizeable degree of mobility across occupations, particularly relating to manufacturing, sales and trade. Harris, Kannan and Rodgers (1990) also find occupational mobility to be quite high among women wherein nearly three-fourths of the women workers were employed in five occupations in Coimbatore. Downward job mobility among workers, particularly those affected by technological restructuring and longer spells of unemployment, has also been documented in some of the studies (Harris, Kannan, & Rodgers, 1990; Khandker, 1992; Mitra, 2006). This has resulted in decrease in income and social status, thus suggesting more general vulnerability. However, some of the studies also show that the downward mobility is offset by a substantive upward mobility, particularly from casual labour status to regular wage salaried status (Mitra, 2006). In brief, the empirical evidences show high prevalence of job mobility in urban India, mainly among casual wage workers, self-employed and unprotected salaried workers. And a large proportion of job mobility is between casual wage workers and self-employed workers.

Concept, Methodology and Data

Concept

For a wage worker, job mobility could mean change in job within his/ her enterprise or across enterprise, or across industry groups, or across occupational groups, or from informal to formal (vice versa), or from wage worker to self-employed worker, or from regular wage worker to casual wage labour (vice versa). For the self-employed, job change could be in four ways: change from self-employment to wage employment (formal or informal), change from self-employment across industry groups (agriculture to manufacturing or services), change from self-employment across occupational groups and change from self-employment to home-based worker. We have used this broad definition of job mobility wherein a worker has changed either his/ her enterprise/employer, industry, occupation or status of employment during his/her working career.

Methodology

Mobility has been measured in several ways in the literature, the simplest being the labour mobility index, which is defined as the average job changes per worker per year. Although the inverse of mobility index gives the average duration of job held by workers (Acharya & Jose, 1991; Papola & Subramanian, 1975), we have calculated the mobility index based on the information on the number of job changes by a worker since his/her first employment. As we have detailed information of job history about the first and current employment of workers, we analyse mobility across different categories such as employment status, industrial groups and occupational groups by using the aforementioned broad concept of job mobility.

First, we provide some descriptive statistics on the proportion of workers who changed jobs during their work career and the patterns of job mobility among workers. We then analyse the determinants of job mobility (JM) among workers. To do this, we employ the following simple Logit model for the population in the 18–60 years age group.

$$JM_i = \alpha_0 + \beta_1(E_i) + \beta_2(H_i) + \varepsilon_i \qquad (1)$$

The dependent variable in the model JM indicates whether a worker changed jobs during his work career and is a binary variable, taking the value '1' if the worker has changed jobs, '0' otherwise. E refers to the number of employment characteristics of each worker (such as age, experience, sex, education levels, membership of social networks, employment status categories, industry categories and occupational categories), and H refers to the household characteristics of the worker (caste, annual household income and migrant household).

Data and Variables

This chapter uses the urban household survey undertaken during 2014–2015 for the study in four cities, namely Delhi, Lucknow, Pune and Coimbatore. The survey provides information on the characteristics of all household members (including sex, age, caste, educational level, occupation and industry groups, etc.). The survey also contains a small module on the work history of currently employed persons, restricted only to their first and current work, which restricts us from undertaking any in-depth analysis of all jobs. This survey was not specifically designed to study labour mobility, but was part of a larger study on job search and hiring practices in the urban labour market. Despite such limitations, this chapter attempts to understand job mobility in the Indian context, especially across employment statuses, industries and occupations, with special reference to gender and social group of workers. We have also attempted to analyse the role as well as the source of job information and social networks on job mobility in the urban labour market.

The EUS data by NSSO also provides information on short duration job mobility (with a reference period of three years) among workers, which can be analysed across the characteristics of all the household members (including sex, age, caste, educational level, occupation and industry groups, household types, social and religious groups, state, region, etc.). This data show less than 0.5 per cent of the workers experiencing job mobility, and thus hardly captures a relatively longer period of job mobility.

Job Mobility in the Urban Labour Market

Intensity of Job Change among Employed Persons

Before analysing job mobility, it would be appropriate to first discuss briefly the job mobility index. This is generally seen as the change in employer. Such job change may not necessarily involve job mobility as per the framework discussed in the section (Related Literature) in this chapter. The intensity of job change also helps in understanding the opportunities for job mobility in the labour market. Reasons for job changes may be varied, and may result in upward mobility for some workers and downward mobility for others (Anderson, Haahr, Hansen, & Holm-Pedersen, 2008).

In our sample, there were 3,465 sample workers in the 18–45 years age group, and only 1,150 workers had changed their jobs. In other words, about one-third of the workers did change their jobs. About 19 per cent changed their jobs first time. Over 7 per cent had changed their jobs twice. Thus, there were very few workers who witnessed three or more job changes in their job histories (Table 5.1). The intensity of job change is comparatively higher among males, workers in the 30–45 years age group, OCs (OSGs or high castes), and in Delhi and Pune. Nearly 40 per cent of the OC workers changed their jobs as compared to about 27 per cent in the case of OBCs and 31 per cent for SCs. It also appears that the employment status does matter in job change as well. A highest 46 per cent of the workers in Delhi changed their jobs as compared to lowest 22 per cent in Lucknow and Coimbatore, showing relatively better employment opportunities in the national capital.

Table 5.1 *Intensity of Job Change among Employed Persons (Age 18–45 Years; %)*

	Number of Times Job Changed since First Job					
Variable	No Change	One	Two	Three	Four and More	Total
Gender						
Male	66.2	18.4	8.4	4.3	2.7	100
Female	68.3	20.5	6.2	2.5	2.6	100
Age Group						
18–29	67.1	20.3	7.0	3.9	1.7	100
30–45	62.9	21.5	8.6	3.1	4.0	100
Social Group						
STs	68.8	19.8	7.3	0.0	4.2	100
SCs	67.5	18.1	7.0	4.4	3.0	100
OBCs	73.2	16.3	6.2	2.2	2.1	100
OCs	60.4	22.3	9.9	4.7	2.6	100
Migration Status						
Migrant	65.5	18.7	8.5	4.7	2.6	100
Non-migrant	67.1	19.1	7.6	3.6	2.6	100
City						
Lucknow	77.5	15.2	4.7	1.7	1.0	100
Delhi/NCR	53.7	22.8	11.8	7.0	4.7	100
Pune	67.9	20.4	6.3	3.0	2.5	100
Coimbatore	79.1	11.9	6.7	1.5	0.8	100
Total	66.8	19.0	7.7	3.8	2.7	100
Total number of sample persons	2,315	660	268	130	92	3,465

Source: Primary field survey (2014–2015) for this study.

We have also calculated job mobility index, that is, average job changes per worker per year during his/her working career. It is 0.36 or an average duration of 2.8 years in each job (Table 5.2). City-wise, job mobility index is highest in Delhi and lowest in Lucknow. Similarly, it is the highest among STs and the lowest among OBCs. City effect is more pronounced in job mobility, suggesting comparatively better employment prospects in Delhi and Pune for workers belonging to all social groups.

Patterns of Job Mobility

Despite the overall low intensity of job change in the urban labour market, we would be more interested in analysing the pattern of job mobility of those workers who changed their jobs. The analysis is based

Table 5.2 *Index of Job Change (Per Worker Average Annual Job Change)*

Variable	Male	Female	Person	Total Sample Persons
City				
Lucknow	0.20	0.13	0.19	135
Delhi/NCR	0.43	0.40	0.42	501
Pune	0.35	0.34	0.35	211
Coimbatore	0.26	0.35	0.27	82
Social Group				
STs	0.56	0.42	0.53	21
SCs	0.34	0.42	0.35	322
OBCs	0.33	0.32	0.32	214
OCs	0.38	0.35	0.37	372
All	0.36	0.37	0.36	929
Total sample persons	749	180	929	

Source: Primary field survey (2014–2015).

on a sample of 971 employed persons for whom detailed job information for their first as well as current job is available. It is observed that
over 80 per cent of these workers experienced job mobility as defined
earlier, and the proportion was higher among men, OCs, graduates,
migrants and younger workers (Table 5.3). The remaining one-fifth of
the workers did change their employers but without any job mobility.
Our findings broadly conform to findings in the organised sector for

Table 5.3 *Job Mobility among Employed Persons during Their
First Job–Current Job (%)*

Sex	Zero Job Mobility	Job Mobility	Total	Number of Persons
Male	19.28	80.71	100	783
Female	21.81	78.19	100	188
Social Groups				
SCs	22.22	77.78	100	333
STs	28.57	71.43	100	21
OBCs	21.72	78.28	100	221
OCs	16.16	83.83	100	396
Age Groups				
18–29	18.86	81.14	100	546
30–45	19.10	80.90	100	377
46–60	35.42	64.58	100	48
Education Groups				
Up to high school	21.71	78.29	100	152
Higher secondary	22.27	77.72	100	229
Graduate	17.26	82.74	100	446
Postgraduate and above	21.53	78.47	100	144
City				
Coimbatore	14.63	85.36	100	82
Delhi/NCR	17.36	82.64	100	530

Sex	Zero Job Mobility	Job Mobility	Total	Number of Persons
Lucknow	31.21	68.80	100	141
Pune	20.18	79.82	100	218
Migration				
Migrants	16.06	83.95	100	411
Non-migrants	22.5	77.50	100	560
Total	19.77	80.22	100	971

Source: Primary field survey (2014–2015).

all of India; wherein highly qualified as well as older employees exhibit lesser inclination towards mobility and mobility among young employees in the 25–34 years age group is quite high (Ma Foi Randstad, 2011). Our survey results also broadly conform to the earlier findings on job mobility, that is, every job change is significantly linked with job mobility as a large majority of employed persons witness change in terms of either the type of employment, sector of employment or occupation. This has been more among younger and migrant workers (see Acharya & Jose, 1991; Mitra, 2006; Pais, 2006; Papola & Subramanian 1975).

Change in Job Status

Now let us examine job mobility in the sense of change in job status during the first and current job (Table 5.4a). It is shown that almost half of the workers whose first job status was self-employed moved to regular salaried jobs, 16 per cent to contractual jobs and 30 per cent remained self-employed. About 4.5 per cent of the self-employed workers joined the rank of casual workers from their first to current job. Understandably, change in job status was least among regular salaried persons, indicating its high preference over other forms of employment. However, about one-tenth among them moved each to contractual jobs and self-employment. Among the contractual

Table 5.4a *Change in Job Status between First and Current Job of Employed Persons (%)*

First Job Status	Current Job Status						
	Self-employed	Regular Salaried	Contractual	Casual	Total	No. of Persons	Col%
Self-employed	29.5	50.0	15.9	4.5	100	44	4.6
Regular salaried	9.9	77.2	11.4	1.5	100	615	64.3
Contractual	9.8	27.8	60.8	1.6	100	245	25.6
Casual	11.3	26.4	17.0	45.3	100	53	5.5
Total	10.9	60.5	24.6	4.1	100	957	100.0

Source: Primary field survey (2014–2015).
Note: The correlation coefficient between first and current job statuses at 0.398 is significant at 0.01 level of significance.

workers, a majority (61%) did not witness change in their job status, around 28 per cent moved to regular salaried status and around 10 per cent became self-employed. Finally, among the casual workers, change in job status was substantive as over one-fourth among them moved to regular jobs, 17 per cent to contractual jobs and 11 per cent became self-employed since their first jobs. Such mixed patterns in the changes in job status-related mobility are largely directed towards regular employment. However, a significant number of those in regular employment tended to join the ranks of self-employed and contractual workers. Due to this, the proportion of regular workers declined by about four percentage between first and current employments. The corresponding shift has been in the favour of self-employment. This shows a general deterioration in the job status from the viewpoint of employment security in the urban labour market. Such deterioration in the quality of employment in recent years has been criticised, particularly in the context of higher economic growth's inability to create such jobs (Goldar & Suresh, 2017).

Caste-wise, there has been the highest 8 percentage points deterioration in the quality of employment among OBCs as they moved

Table 5.4b *Change in Job Status between First and Current Job of Employed Persons (%)*

Employment Status	SCs		OBCs		OCs	
	First Job	Current Job	First Job	Current Job	First Job	Current Job
Self-employed	5.1	10.3	5.9	12.3	3.4	10.9
Regular salaried	56.2	54.1	66.7	59.4	69.9	66.8
Contractual	31.7	29.9	21.0	25.6	23.3	19.7
Casual	6.9	5.7	6.4	2.7	3.4	2.6
Total	100.0	100.0	100.0	100.0	100.0	100.0
Observation	331		219		386	

Source: Primary field survey (2014–2015).

from regular salaried jobs as their first job to contractual and self-employed jobs. Unlike OBCs, job status mobility among SCs and other social groups (OCs) tended to be lower, mainly in the favour of self-employed jobs (Table 5.4b).

Mobility across Industries

Table 5.5 presents the data on change in the industry of work during first and current jobs. It has been the highest in the transport sector with almost 80 per cent workers shifted to other industries during their switch from first to current job. It has been the lowest 47 per cent in the service sector. In manufacturing, construction and retail trade, nearly half of the workers did not change their industry of employment between their first and current job (Table 5.5). A good majority of workers who joined their first jobs in Information and Communications Technology (ICT) and service sectors did not change their industry group. However, a substantive share of those working in ICT in their first job moved to the service sector. Overall, job mobility has been directed mostly to service sector, followed by ICT, manufacturing, retail trade and education. This pattern in mobility of workers across various industry groups is a reflection of macro

Table 5.5 Change in Job across Industries during First Job—Current Job (%)

First Job		Current Job								
	Manufacturing	Construction	Retail	Transport	ICT	Education	Service	Total	No. of persons
Manufacturing	51.94	1.55	13.95	2.33	6.20	0.78	23.26	100	129
Construction	25.00	47.50	5.00	2.50	5.00	2.50	12.50	100	40
Retail	10.62	2.65	48.67	5.31	7.96	2.65	22.12	100	113
Transport	8.70	4.35	13.04	21.74	13.04	4.35	34.78	100	23
ICT	5.03	2.52	4.40	0.63	61.64	4.40	21.38	100	159
Education	3.66	0.00	6.10	0.00	2.44	57.32	30.49	100	82
Service	7.83	3.04	9.57	2.17	7.39	6.52	63.48	100	230
Total	15.46	4.64	14.43	2.71	17.91	9.66	35.18	100	776

Source: Primary field survey (2014–2015).

Note: The correlation coefficient between first and current industry of employment at 0.443 is significant at 0.01 level of significance.

trend in the employment growth in urban areas mostly in the favour of service sector during the post-reform period (IHD & ISLE, 2014).

Occupational Mobility

Table 5.6 throws light on the occupational mobility, that is, if there has been a change in occupations of the employed persons along with their shift from first to current job. The lowest occupational mobility is observed in the case of workers in professional occupations (NCO 2) as three-fourths had the same occupation with their job change. This is obvious as occupations under the broad NCO 2 head belong to higher positions in occupational hierarchies and generally fetch higher mean earnings for workers employed therein. The highest occupational

Table 5.6 *Occupational Mobility*

First Job (NCO 1-Digit)	Current Occupation (NCO 1-Digit)									No. of Persons
	1	2	3	4	5	7	8	9	Total	
1	62.5	5.0	15.0	10.0	7.5	0.0	0.0	0.0	100	40
2	8.9	73.9	10.2	2.5	3.2	1.3	0.0	0.0	100	157
3	9.0	8.7	58.5	6.5	12.3	2.5	2.2	0.4	100	277
4	6.2	10.3	31.5	28.1	13.7	5.5	2.1	2.7	100	146
5	2.3	4.1	18.7	4.7	55.0	4.7	7.6	2.9	100	171
7	3.3	1.1	6.5	2.2	12.0	64.1	5.4	4.3	100	92
8	0.0	3.3	6.7	10.0	26.7	3.3	46.7	3.3	100	30
9	0.0	0.0	7.5	5.7	15.1	9.4	11.3	50.9	100	53
Total	8.2	17.1	28.3	8.5	18.9	9.3	4.9	4.4	100	971

Source: Primary field survey (2014–2015).

Notes: NCO 1-digit: 1. Legislators, senior officials and managers, 2. Professionals, 3. Technicians and associate professionals, 4. Clerks, 5. Service and sales workers, 7. Craft and related works, 8. Plant and machine operators and assemblers, 9. Elementary occupations; We have not included skilled agriculture and fishery works (NCO) due to a very small number (5 workers only); The correlation coefficient between first and current occupation of employment at 0.692 is significant at 0.01 level of significance.

mobility is observed in the case of those workers who are in clerical occupations (NCO 4) in their first job. Over one-third among
them moved to technicians and associated professional occupations
(NCO 3), while another 16 per cent moved to top two occupational
groups—a case of upward occupational mobility. Similar pattern is
seen for those who started their working career in sales and service
occupations. Those in craft and related occupations in their first job
also witnessed a significant upward mobility with over one-fourth
among them moving to sales and service-related occupations (NCO 5).
Another 10 per cent moved to professional and technical occupations.
In all, about 45 per cent of the workers experienced occupational
mobility during their shift from first to current employment.

Upward and Downward Occupational Mobility

We have categorised occupational mobility into three categories,
namely (a) no mobility: no change in the occupational group of a
worker (b) upward mobility: when workers move from lower rung
occupations to higher rung occupations in the occupational hierarchies;
for example, elementary occupations to skilled occupations or from
clerical and sales and service occupations to managerial, professional
and technical occupations; (c) downward mobility occurs when workers move from higher end occupations to lower end occupations in
occupational hierarchies; for example, from managerial and professional occupations to sales and service or clerical occupations. Viewed
from this perspective, about 55 per cent of the workers have not
experienced occupational mobility between their first and current job.
For 17 per cent workers there has been upward occupational mobility, whereas for 27 per cent there has been downward occupational
mobility (Table 5.7). Most of the upward mobility is seen in the case
of those working in their first jobs in clerical, sales and service, machine
operators, and crafts-related occupations. The downward mobility has
been observed mainly in managerial, professional and technical-related
occupations, which has been replaced by upward mobility from other

Table 5.7 Occupational Mobility along with Job Mobility since the First Job (%)

Sex	No Mobility	Upward Mobility	Downward Mobility	Total	Number of Persons
Male	55.70	15.82	28.48	100	632
Female	54.42	25.17	20.41	100	147
Social Groups					
SCs	51.74	22.01	26.25	100	259
STs	46.67	6.67	46.67	100	15
OBCs	60.69	15.03	24.28	100	173
OCs	56.02	15.96	28.01	100	332
Age Groups (in Years)					
18–29	59.82	16.25	23.93	100	443
30–45	48.52	20.00	31.48	100	305
46–60	61.29	12.90	25.81	100	31
Education Groups					
Up to high school	56.30	19.33	24.37	100	119
Higher secondary	64.04	15.17	20.79	100	178
Graduates	51.49	19.24	29.27	100	369
Postgraduates and above	53.98	14.16	31.86	100	113
City-Wise					
Coimbatore	51.43	24.29	24.29	100	70
Delhi/NCR	50.57	18.31	31.12	100	437
Lucknow	50.00	20.41	29.59	100	98
Pune	72.41	11.49	16.09	100	174
Migration					
Migrants	57.10	17.97	24.93	100	434
Non-migrants	54.15	17.28	28.57	100	345
Total	55.46	17.59	26.96	100	779

Source: Primary field survey (2014–2015).

lower end occupations. Such downward mobility has been relatively more among males as compared to females.

The social background variables like caste are found to have significant impact on the occupational mobility (Harris, Kannan, & Rodgers, 1990; Khandker, 1992). We also observed the highest occupational mobility among SC/ST workers, followed by OCs and the lowest among OBCs. Downward occupational mobility was observed to be the highest among STs, followed by OCs and SCs. In brief, SCs had higher occupational mobility than OCs and that too upwardly. This could be credited to the improvement in their educational levels that enabled them to move up the occupational ladders in urban areas in the formal sector. Our finding is contrary to the findings of some earlier studies in the informal sector. For example, Breman (1996), in his study of Surat city in Gujarat, finds caste as a major hindrance in the occupational mobility of workers. Scholars have argued that the occupational mobility of SCs is restricted due to the embodied features of historical caste system in India (Narayana, 1985) and due to the job discrimination which is based on the caste of an individual (Madheswaran & Attewell, 2010; Thorat & Newman, 2010). However, Mitra (2006), in his study of Delhi slums, does not find any evidence of caste discrimination in the context of mobility. Mamgain's (2017) analysis of occupational diversification based on NSSO data also shows that although occupational dissimilarity, as shown by Duncan's DI, between STs and OCs, and SCs and OCs is high yet it tends to decline during the post-reform period. SCs have witnessed significant occupational mobility both in low-end and high-end occupations (Mamgain, 2017).

Education helps in occupational mobility. About half of the graduates and 46 per cent of the postgraduate workers changed occupations between their first and current jobs. Such job mobility was comparatively low among higher secondary and high school graduate workers—about 40 per cent changed their occupations. Higher job mobility among graduates and postgraduates, however, was largely downward mobility, indicating tightening of the job market and tough competition for high-end jobs.

Occupational mobility is marginally higher among migrant workers, reconfirming the earlier findings that migrant workers gradually move from informal and precarious jobs to formal sector jobs (Mitra, 2006). City-wise, the highest occupational mobility is observed among workers in Lucknow, closely followed by Delhi and Coimbatore. Surprisingly, occupational mobility is observed to be the lowest in Pune where only about 28 per cent of the workers changed their occupations. If we juxtapose the overall job mobility as calculated in Table 5.3, the lowest occupational mobility in Pune is partly due to the access to better quality of jobs/occupations to workers even as their first occupation in Pune. Since Pune is a hub of IT and automobile industries, many young workers find ample opportunities even in the same occupation across different industry groups. Contrary to this is the case of Lucknow city which has the lowest job mobility but at the same time very high occupational mobility. This indicates that the city has low employment opportunities and even those finding opportunities to change their jobs, have to change their occupation as well. In cities like Delhi, higher job mobility is also reflected in comparatively higher occupational mobility.

Voluntary or Involuntary Mobility

The nature of job mobility could either be voluntary or an involuntary one. Voluntary job mobility has lots of beneficial effects at the individual level, both in terms of economic and social effects, as compared to involuntary job mobility. We have added two reasons under this category—voluntarily quitting the job and no scope for growth. Involuntary mobility could be due to the low income from employment, closure of units, retrenchments, harassment and unsatisfactory work environment. We find involuntary mobility much higher (71%) than voluntary mobility. Low income is the single largest reason for mobility. The proportion of such workers is highest among STs, followed by OBCs. One of the severest forms of involuntary job mobility is due to the loss of job. About 12 per cent of the workers had to change their first job due to retrenchment or closure of units where they were employed. The proportion of such workers was almost double among men as compared to women, among those in the 46–60 years age group as compared to their younger counterparts, and those with the lower levels of education. OBCs and SCs were more affected by such job losses as compared to OCs (Table 5A.1a). These patterns also reflect the 2008 global financial crisis causing huge job losses in many of the export-led sectors, which were labour intensive. Sector-specific studies like in IT also show that most of the job losses in the aftermath of the 2008 financial crisis were of an involuntary nature, and many of the workers who lost their job moved to other jobs at low levels of earnings (Singh, 2011). The recent data of Labour Bureau also shows a sizeable reduction in employment opportunities in labour-intensive industries such as textiles, garments and food processing due to the global economic slowdown in recent years (MoLE, 2017).

Determinants of Job Mobility

A number of studies in urban areas have explored the factors that determine mobility by either looking at occupational mobility or income mobility (Mitra, 2006). We make a modest attempt to analyse the determinants of job mobility using the Logit model as described in the methodology section. As mentioned in the earlier section, about 80 per cent of the workers witnessed job mobility either in terms of change in their status of employment, occupation or industry of employment. How such job mobility is influenced by individual as well as group characteristics of workers is explained with the help of Logit regression in Table 5.8.

The odds of job mobility are more than three times higher for younger workers as compared to their older counterparts in the reference 45–60 years age group. The older cohort of workers comprises those who would have joined the labour market prior to the economic reforms of the early 1990s. In our sample, a majority of workers in the 18–45 years age group are those who would have joined the urban

Table 5.8 Determinants of Job Mobility among Employed Persons in Urban Labour Market

Job Mobility	Coefficient	Odds Ratio	Standard Error	Z	P >|Z|
Constant	−0.726	0.484	0.605	−1.20	0.230
Age group (18–29)	1.192	3.292	0.364	3.27	0.001
Age group (30–45)	1.254	3.504	0.365	3.44	0.001
Male	0.232	1.261	0.220	1.05	0.291
SC/ST	−0.293	0.746	0.207	−1.41	0.158
OBC	−0.318	0.728	0.233	−1.36	0.174
Hindu	0.241	1.272	0.234	1.03	0.304
Higher Secondary	−0.355	0.701	0.285	−1.25	0.212
Graduate	−0.164	0.848	0.290	−0.57	0.570
Postgraduate and above	−0.513	0.599	0.351	−1.46	0.144
Migrant	0.369	1.447	0.188	1.97	0.049
Coimbatore	0.960	2.611	0.387	2.48	0.013
Delhi/NCR	0.629	1.875	0.241	2.60	0.009
Pune	0.311	1.364	0.275	1.13	0.258
Social networks	−0.422	0.656	0.183	−2.30	0.021
Regular job (First)	0.516	1.675	0.185	2.79	0.005
Self-employed (First)	0.005	1.005	0.415	0.01	0.991
Occupation A (First)	0.792	2.208	0.356	2.23	0.026
Occupation B (First)	0.481	1.617	0.346	1.39	0.164
Occupation C(First)	0.892	2.439	0.390	2.29	0.022
Private/MNC (First)	−0.270	0.763	0.222	−1.22	0.224
Public (First)	−1.042	0.353	0.302	−3.45	0.001
Observations			971		
LR chi2(21)			74.82		
Pseudo R2			0.0775		

Source: Primary field survey (2014–2015).

Notes: Reference groups are female, 45–60 years age group, OCs, education up to high school, Lucknow, non-migrant workers, other than social network (mainly formal job search channels), contractual/casual wage employees, elementary occupation and informal enterprises; For grouping of occupation and social networks, see Tables 5A.2a and 5A.2b, respectively.

labour market in the early 2000s. The onset of the new economic reforms and their further deepening led to substantial deterioration in the quality of employment and resultant job mobility among workers. During this period, the share of contractual employment significantly increased at the cost of regular employment, resulting in the substantial reduction in tenurial security and social security of workers in the Indian labour market (IHD & ISLE, 2014). A higher job mobility in the 30–45 years age group as compared to 18–29 years age group again reconfirms our argument that those who joined the labour market during the early period of the economic reforms in the early 1990s, were mostly the ones who were affected more by job losses due to retrenchment or closure of units, resulting in their higher job mobility. This can also be seen in Table 5.9. It shows that a higher proportion of workers in the 30–45 years age group and 45–60 years age group were forced to leave their jobs due to economic restructuring.

Job mobility is generally higher among migrant workers as compared to non-migrant workers (Mitra, 2006). This is primarily due to their entry mainly in informal sector jobs and, thereafter, gradually moving into formal sector jobs (Mitra, 2006; Papola, 1981). Our results also show the odds of job mobility among migrant workers

Table 5.9 *Job Changes and (Last Month) Income of Employed Persons in Urban Labour Market*

Job Changes	Mean Income (₹)	Median Income (₹)	Observations
Zero	13,920	10,000	192
Once	14,812	11,000	437
Twice	16,270	13,000	172
Thrice or more	16,875	12,000	169
All	15,254	12,000	970

Source: Primary field survey (2014–2015).

being 45 per cent higher than non-migrant workers, by keeping other characteristics of workers constant.

Social networks, which largely comprise relatives and friends, tend to play an important role in job search, especially towards upward mobility. Our findings show that such dependence on social networks in urban labour market may be more for first-time entry and that too for lower level positions. As workers settle in the urban labour market, they get access to other formal channels of job search, which they could use for subsequent job changes. This is what exactly emerges from the probability coefficient and odds ratio. The negative coefficient sign shows that for job mobility, the odds of those using social network as job search method tend to decrease by 66 per cent as compared to the reference category of those workers who use other methods of job search. Our results also corroborate to other studies (Mitra, 2006; Munshi & Rosenzweig, 2005), which found that networks tend to reduce upward mobility of the workers though they do play a very important role for entry into the labour market.

Gender and social group also have implications for job mobility. The literature shows how female workers and workers belonging to SC/ST social groups are less likely to experience job mobility compared to other workers. This tendency has been found in other studies also (Harris, Kannan, & Rodgers, 1990). However, this relationship is not found statistically significant in our study, neither for gender nor for caste. This corroborates with the finding of Mitra (2006), who did not observe any caste differentials in job mobility in his study in Delhi. This also means that although gender and caste do matter in job mobility, they do not significantly influence the chances of job mobility. Similar is the case with educational levels and job mobility, wherein probability of job mobility tends to decrease among those with higher level of education as compared to the reference category of workers with high school education. This is again not found to be significant, thereby implying that job mobility has much more to do with variables such as age, the type of employment, the type of enterprise, the type of occupation and city of work. Education, gender and social belonging definitely have a significant bearing on entry into the urban labour market for the first time, but not significantly for job mobility.

The probability of job mobility is significantly higher among workers who entered into their first job as regular workers than the reference group of those who were either in contractual or casual workers in their first jobs. This finding has important implications for job mobility as it is generally believed that job mobility tends to be higher among contractual or casual wage workers, as they would be more willing to move to better jobs. However, this interpretation needs to be carefully looked in as 23 per cent of those in regular salaried jobs moved into contractual employment and self-employment; and from those in contractual employment in their first job, about 28 per cent moved into regular salaried employment. However, regular job status seems to be significantly important for job mobility and career progression in the urban labour market.

As regards the probability of job mobility across occupational groups, the odds ratio of job mobility are 2.4 times higher for those in occupational group C (skilled workers in NCOs 6, 7, and 8) as compared to those who were in elementary occupations (NCO 9) in their first jobs. Similarly, the probability of job mobility was 2.2 times higher among workers belonging to top three occupational groups (i.e., NCOs 1, 2 and 3; Table 5A.2b). As shown earlier, there has been both upward and downward occupational mobilities among workers. Among those workers, particularly belonging to NCO 3 (technicians and associated professionals), about 42 per cent changed their occupational group for job mobility. While around 18 per cent of such workers moved to higher occupational groups (NCO 1 and 2), about one-fourth witnessed downward occupational mobility, mainly going into sales and service occupations. In other words, the higher probability of job mobility among this category of workers is associated with their difficulty in entering into the same group of occupations (i.e., Group A). In brief, urban labour market significantly offers better chances for job mobility for skilled and technically trained persons. Those in clerical, and sales and service-related occupations do not witness significant job mobility in the labour market despite having reasonably higher educational levels (graduate and postgraduates). Job mobility is largely a phenomenon in smaller and informal enterprises. The odds of job mobility among those working in the public sector are understandably 35 per cent lower than those working in the informal sector, which is significant at 95 per cent level of confidence. This also means that those who join public sector employment largely tend to remain therein.

The city effect on job mobility is also in expected direction. The higher odds ratios for Coimbatore and Delhi with reference to Lucknow again show better employment opportunities and job mobility in the former two cities. In the case of Pune, the chances of job mobility are 36 per cent higher than Lucknow but not found to be statistically significant. In brief, due to the lack of employment opportunities in Lucknow, particularly in the private sector, there is limited scope for job mobility and career progression for a large proportion of workers.

Impact of Job Mobility on Income Levels

In this section, we present the relationship between job mobility and (last month) income of employed persons in our sample households. Income tends to increase significantly with every job change after controlling other attributes of workers such as age, education, occupation and location (Table 5.9). The mean monthly income increases from ₹13,920 to ₹16,875 when a worker changes his job three or more times. We however get a different picture with respect to the median income. The median income increases from ₹10,000 to ₹11,000 when a worker changes his or her job once, and then increases to ₹13,000 when worker changes his job twice, but the median income decreases from ₹12,000 for three times job change. This also means that moderate job changes in labour market are a positive feature, but beyond a certain point, say three or more than three times, may be a distress phenomenon or involuntary mobility.

Conclusion

We have used a broad concept of job mobility taking into consideration whether the worker has changed his/her job or not during his/
her work career and then analysed mobility across different categories
such as employment status, industrial groups and occupational groups.
Though a large majority of workers did not change their jobs, of those
who changed jobs nearly half could do so only once. Such intensity
of job change was relatively much better among men, OCs and in
metropolitan cities like Delhi.

Associated with the job change, the employment status of about
one-fourth of the regular salaried workers changed between their first
and current job. Such job mobility was substantively high among self-
employed, contractual workers and casual labour. A sizeable proportion
among them switched to regular salaried jobs, which at least ensured
tenurial security in the labour market.

Along with the job change, more than half of the workers remained
in the same occupation. Occupational mobility is highest among SC/
ST workers, followed by OCs and lowest among OBCs. Our finding
is contrary to the findings of some of the earlier studies. Occupational
mobility is marginally higher among migrant workers. Among sample
cities, occupational mobility is highest in Lucknow, closely followed by
Delhi and Coimbatore. However, there is inverse correlation between
occupational mobility and job change intensity in cities like Lucknow,
implying overall low prospects of job mobility. Involuntary mobility
dominates the job mobility scenario in urban labour market, which is
largely due to low income levels of workers. Retrenchment or closure
of units also compelled over one-tenth of the workers to change their
jobs. The proportion of such workers is almost double among men,
older workers and those with the lower levels of education. OBCs
and SCs were more affected by such job losses as compared to OCs.

Logit results show significantly high job mobility among younger
workers, migrant workers and those entering the urban labour market
as regular workers. Also, job mobility is significantly influenced by the

type of city. Gender, caste and educational levels do not significantly influence the chances of job mobility. Rather, job mobility has much more to do with variables such as age, the type of employment, the type of enterprise, the type of occupation and city of work. Education, gender and social belonging definitely have a significant bearing on entry into the urban labour market for the first time, but not significantly for job mobility. The impact of social networks on job mobility becomes insignificant over the years as workers settle in urban labour markets and gain access to other sources of job information.

Job mobility generally results in the increase in income. Moderate job changes in labour market are a positive feature, but beyond a certain point, frequent job mobility may be indicative of distress situation or involuntary mobility. In brief, limited job mobility in urban labour market may be both due to limited job opportunities in the market and partly associated with the availability of stable employment ensuring better income. However, such employment opportunities are very limited and sticking to one job may be largely due to few employment opportunities in the urban labour market. This aspect needs to be explored further.

Annexure 5A

Table 5A.1a Most Important Reason for Leaving First Job (%)

Sex	Quit voluntarily	No Scope for Growth	Low Income	Bad Environment	Harassment at Workplace	Forced to Leave	Other Reasons	Total	Observation
Male	17.75	10.46	39.94	4.12	2.22	13.31	12.20	100	631
Female	21.77	8.16	35.37	6.80	4.08	6.80	17.01	100	147
Social Groups									
SCs	22.48	5.04	40.31	6.59	2.71	12.79	10.08	100	258
STs	0.00	13.33	66.67	0.00	0.00	6.67	13.33	100	15
OBCs	13.29	12.14	43.93	1.16	4.05	16.18	9.25	100	173
OCs	18.98	12.65	34.34	5.12	1.81	9.64	17.47	100	332
Age Groups									
18–29	18.51	11.06	41.08	4.29	3.39	10.16	11.51	100	443
30–45	19.08	8.55	36.84	4.93	1.32	13.82	15.46	100	304
46–60	12.90	9.68	32.26	6.45	3.23	22.58	12.90	100	31
Education Groups									
Up to high school	19.33	0.84	42.86	6.72	0.84	19.33	10.08	100	119

Higher secondary	14.04	11.80	41.01	2.81	2.25	14.04	14.04	100	178
Graduate	19.29	12.23	37.77	5.16	3.80	9.51	12.23	100	368
Postgraduate and above	22.12	9.73	36.28	3.54	0.88	9.73	17.70	100	113
City									
Coimbatore	5.71	4.29	54.29	4.29	5.71	21.43	4.29	100	70
Delhi/NCR	19.91	7.55	38.44	5.72	2.52	9.84	16.02	100	437
Lucknow	39.18	6.19	29.90	2.06	3.09	10.31	9.28	100	97
Pune	8.62	20.69	39.66	3.45	1.15	14.94	11.49	100	174
Migration									
Migrants	16.57	12.79	37.50	3.49	2.03	12.21	15.41	100	344
Non-migrants	20.05	7.83	40.32	5.53	3.00	11.98	11.29	100	434
Total	18.51	10.03	39.07	4.63	2.57	12.08	13.11	100	778

Source: Primary field survey (2014–2015).

Table 5A.1b *Description of Variables Related to 'Important Reason for Leaving Work'*

Quit the job voluntarily	(1) Quit the job voluntarily
No scope for growth	(9) No scope for further promotion; (10) Insufficient use of skills and abilities in work
Low Income	(6) Income too low
Bad environment	(7) Unpleasant environment; (12) Health hazard; (13) Inconvenient location
Harassment at workplace	(8) Employer harassed; (11) Harassment by fellow workers
Forced to leave	(2) Laid off/Dismissed; (3) Unit closed; (4) Lack of work in the enterprise; (5) Lack of work in the area
Other reasons	(14) Transfer; (15) Household moved out; (16) Ill health; (17) Safety and security; (18) Others

Table 5A.2a *Variables Related to Job Search Methods*

Social networks	(1) Family connections; (2) Friends/Acquaintances; (3) Caste/Community contacts; (4) Co-villagers; and (5) Former migrants
Formal sources	(6) Employment exchange; (7) Advertisements in newspapers; (8) Web portals/Internet; (9) Company's notice board; (10) School/College; (14) Private placement agencies; (15) HR firms/Staffing companies; and (16) Campus placement
Directly approaching employers	(11) Directly approaching employers
Employee referral	(12) Employee referral
Other sources	(17) Contractor/Middleman; (18) Apprenticeship trainee (19) Worked earlier in the enterprise; and (20) Others

Note: Social networks mainly comprise family connections and friends/acquaintances.

Table 5A.2b Details of Occupation Groups in Terms of NCO-2004

Occupation Group	Detail of Occupation Group	NCO
Group A	Legislators, senior official and manager; professionals; and technician and associate professionals	1–3
Group B	Clerks; service workers, and shop and market sales workers	4–5
Group C	Skilled agriculture and fishery workers; craft and related workers; and machine operators and assemblers	6–8
Group D	Elementary occupations	9

CHAPTER 6

Wage Earnings and Inequality

Introduction

In a developing country like India, nearly half of the working population is categorised as wage income earners. In this sense, wage income is an important outcome of the functioning of the labour market and assumes fundamental importance for determining the living standards of wage earners and their families (ILO, 2018). Wage levels in the labour market can be determined by a combination of several characteristics of employment and wage workers, namely nature and type of employment, industry and occupation of employment, rural–urban location of employment, formal–informal employment, and workers' characteristics such as age, gender, socio-religious background, and education and skill levels. Equally important are government policies on wage, taxation and income distribution. The dualistic nature of the Indian economy and resultant segmentation in the labour market often lead to wage disparities, which have been examined in a number of studies in the recent past (ILO, 2018; Papola & Kannan, 2017). Most of the studies at different points of time, largely based on NSSO data on employment, show substantial wage gap between men and women and between regular and casual workers both within and between rural and urban areas (Karan & Sakthivel, 2008; Rustagi, 2005). Similarly, the wages of contract workers are significantly lower than regular workers in the organised segment of the Indian industry (Goldar & Suresh, 2017). These studies also show a gradual decline in the disparity in wage earnings of male and female workers largely due to the comparatively higher wage growth of female workers (Karan & Sakthivel, 2008). Such decline in gender wage gaps has been widespread as noticed across most percentiles of income groups including the 90th percentile (Bhattacharjee, Hnatkovska, & Lahiri, 2015). The gaps have narrowed most sharply for the youngest cohorts in the workforce, suggesting that measured gaps will decline even more sharply over the next two decades. Although the wage differences in rural and urban areas tended to reduce both among regular and casual workers from 1983 to 2004 (Sarkar & Mehta, 2010), such gap still remains substantial (Hnatkovska, Lahiri, & Paul, 2012). Wage differences also exist between public and private sectors, regular as well as casual employments, and between formal and informal sectors.

Wages also vary among workers belonging to various socio-religious groups (P. Duraisamy & Duraisamy, 2016). The growth in wages was comparatively higher among ST, SC and Muslim workers during 1993–1994 to 2004–2005 and later on about 3.9 per cent between 2004–2005 and 2011–2012 for all social groups except Muslims. However, such growth was not sufficient to reduce the raw wage gap between various social groups as compared to other social groups (OCs) or high castes, suggesting that the economic reforms of the 1990s benefitted the SCs and Muslims at less than the desired pace (P. Duraisamy & Duraisamy, 2016).

Differences in wage earnings are largely due to differences in endowments of workers such as education, experience, occupation and the sector of employment. However, these are also affected by the prevailing discrimination in labour market against women (Chakravarty & Mukherjee, 2014) and SC/ST workers (Madheswaran & Attewell, 2007), as a significant proportion of the wage gap is not explained by the productive characteristics (endowments) of workers. In the case of female wage workers, a significant proportion of the wage gap is not explained by the endowment effect and hence remains unexplained, which is often attributed to the discrimination against female workers in the Indian labour markets. Similarly, in the case of SC/ST workers, about 15 per cent of their wages are low as compared to OCs due to discrimination in urban labour market in India (Madheswaran & Attewell, 2007). The discrimination component was higher in the private sector than in the public sector, which tended to decline between 1993–1994 and 1999–2000 in both public and private sectors, but sharper in the public sector. More recently, Singhari and Madheswaran (2016) found discrimination causing 19.4 and 31.7 per cent lower wages for SCs in the public and private sectors, respectively, as compared to the equally qualified people belonging to what is usually called 'forward castes' (FCs) during the year 2011–2012. Field survey-based studies for urban areas also observe discrimination in job offers and wages, the degree of which is highest in operative jobs, in which contacts are more important for recruitment, compared to white-collar jobs in which recruitment involves formal methods (Banerjee & Knight, 1985). Chakravarty and Somanathan (2008) find significantly lower wage earnings of SC/ST graduates as compared to those belonging to FCs from IIM Ahmedabad, which are mainly due to the weaker (on average) academic performance of SC/ST candidates. Gender-based wage discrimination is not that prominent as is measured in the case of caste.

Wage earnings also differ among migrant and non-migrant workers. Some studies find low income of migrants as compared to non-migrant workers in labour market mainly due to their weak endowments, low reservation wage and discrimination (Banerjee & Knight, 1985; P. Duraisamy & Narasimhan, 1997). However, studies such as Margirier (2006) and Nanfosso and Akono (2009) found that migrant workers are more productive than non-migrants; hence, they tend to earn higher wages than non-migrants.

In brief, there has been a general trend of increase in income inequality including wage inequality in India, particularly after the economic reforms of the 1990s (Acharya & Marjit, 2000; Cain, Hasan, Magsombol, & Tandon, 2010). Increasing wage inequality has not been uniform across different types of employment as it tended to decrease among casual workers (Abraham, 2007; Sarkar & Mehta, 2010) but increased among regular workers (Dutta, 2005). The major causes for wage inequality are complex and varied. However, education and skill levels tend to explain major variation in wage inequality (Azam, 2012). There has been a rising public concern about increasing inequality as an aftermath of neoliberal policies, and posing a serious challenge to governments, politicians and civil society organisations for seeking solutions.

In this context, this chapter attempts to explore the existing earning/wage differentials and determinants thereof in the Indian urban labour market based on a sample survey of four cities, namely Lucknow, Delhi NCR, Pune and Coimbatore in the 18–65 years age group. The monthly salary/wages at current prices are converted into daily wages for further analysis of inequality. Section 'Average Wage Earnings and Inequality' discusses the descriptive results. The econometric methodology of measuring discrimination in labour market is elaborated in Section 'Measurement of Discrimination in Labour Market'. The empirical evidence on gender and caste-based discrimination in the urban labour market is analysed in Section 'Empirical Evidence on Wage Discrimination in Urban Labour Market'. Section 'Conclusion and Policy Implications' concludes the chapter and provides policy implications. This chapter is unique because for the first time, we are estimating earnings/wage differentials by sex, caste, religion and by migration status simultaneously for regular and contractual employments.

Average Wage Earnings and Inequality

Let us first explain the pattern of average wage earnings for male and female workers across three types of wage workers, separately for public and private sectors. First, mean wages are highest for regular salaried workers, followed by contractual workers, and are the lowest for casual wage workers. Second, mean wages are higher in the public sector, followed by the private organised sector, and least in the private unorganised sector. Average wage earnings of regular salaried males in the public sector are almost 40 per cent higher than their counterparts in the private organised sector. Such difference is marginal in the case of regular salaried female workers, thereby suggesting that most of the regular salaried females in the public sector are employed in low-end jobs. Lowest per worker wage earnings in the private unorganised sector have also been observed in earlier studies (ILO, 2018). Third, there is a significant gender gap in mean wages of regular workers in the public sector, whereas such gap is negligible in the private organised sector. Fourth, in the case of contractual workers, gender wage gap is favourable in the public sector, but women's earnings remain much less in the private sector. Similar pattern in gender wage gap is seen for casual wage labour in public and private sectors (Table 6.1). Interestingly, the mean wage earnings of males are lower than females in the private unorganised sector. Fifth, the higher values of standard deviation around mean earnings for regular and contractual jobs indicate a wide range of wage earnings and related inequality in wage income distribution. Such inequality is generally low in the case of those working in casual wage employment.

Similar to earlier findings, female–male wage gap is comparatively higher in the lower percentile group of income distribution and tends to disappear at upper and middle percentiles, but again increases at the top percentile (Figure 6.1). Such wage gap almost follows the similar pattern across the sample cities, except Pune, where relative gap in female–male wages is negligible across all percentiles of income distribution (Table 6A.1). This also shows the vulnerability of females to accept low-paid jobs due to sheer economic compulsions.

Social Group-Wise Earning Difference

Mean wage earnings are lowest for STs, followed by SCs and OBCs, and highest for OCs. As stated earlier, the average wage earnings are highest for regular salaried workers, followed by contractual wage

Table 6.1 *Average Daily Wage Earnings (₹) of Wage Workers by Gender, Job Status and the Type of Enterprise*

Type of Wage Employment	Male		Female		F/M Ratio
	Mean	Std Deviation	Mean	Std Deviation	
Public Sector					
Regular salaried worker	992.71	719.96	667.92	526.45	0.67
Contractual worker	591.43	448.54	786.10	456.13	1.33
Casual wage labourer	185.71	64.15	333.33	117.85	1.79
Total	873.60	679.74	704.98	503.85	0.81
Private Organised Sector					
Regular salaried worker	686.37	541.95	661.58	573.95	0.96
Contractual worker	642.20	888.03	522.37	414.75	0.81
Casual wage labourer	342.03	195.27	280.29	70.48	0.82
Total	660.66	620.30	622.24	542.83	0.94
Private Unorganised Sector					
Regular salaried worker	510.06	369.25	561.36	435.23	1.10
Contractual worker	396.76	279.47	465.78	374.85	1.17
Casual wage labourer	273.69	153.41	306.34	192.01	1.12
Total	432.44	325.64	504.36	404.71	1.17
Total					
Regular salaried worker	709.52	570.58	640.16	538.59	0.90
Contractual worker	568.48	707.82	572.23	431.73	1.01
Casual wage labourer	301.30	175.11	298.40	156.29	0.99
Total	647.80	597.81	606.36	506.53	0.94

Source: Primary field survey (2014–2015).

workers, and least for casual wage workers. Similarly, average wage earnings are highest for those working in the public sector as compared to the private sector. This broad pattern holds true for all social groups. The raw wage gap between STs/SCs and OCs is about 22 per cent and that among OBCs and OCs is nearly 10 per cent. There is no wage

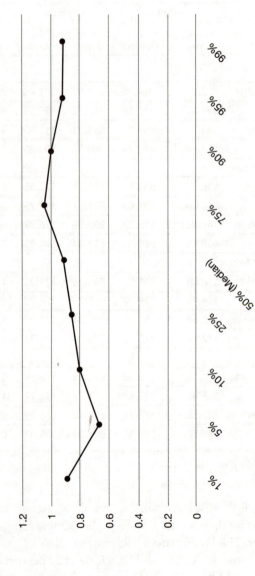

Figure 6.1 *Female/Male Wage Ratio*
Source: Primary field survey (2014–2015).

gap among SC and OC workers in regular jobs in the public sector, whereas such gap is more pronounced in the private organised sector. In the case of contractual wage workers, gap in mean wage earnings is observed between SCs and OCs, in both public and private organised sectors, but more pronounced in the latter sector. Similar is the wage gap between OBCs and OCs, particularly in contractual wage employment (Table 6.2). In brief, wages in the public sector are not only higher than the private sector, but they are also equally distributed with negligible wage gaps. This is due to transparent wage policies in the public sector employment, whereas the same may not be the case in the private sector and that too for contractual wage employment.

Apart from differing wage earnings of workers across social groups, there exists substantive wage inequality within a social group (Table 6.3). For example, the mean wage earnings of SC workers at bottom 25 percentile are more than four times lower than those at the top 10 percentile. Similar inequality is seen for OBC and OC workers in their respective social groups. Within group, wage inequality is more acute between the top 1 per cent and median percentile, but relatively highest among OBC (7 times), followed by OCs (6 times) and SC workers (5.1 times). Among STs, such inequality is comparatively lower.

Interestingly, the raw wage gap between SCs and OCs tends to widen at higher percentiles of income distribution. Such wage gap is also observed in the case of OBCs and OCs, but comparatively of lower magnitude across different percentile groups of income distribution, and that too without any clear pattern (Figure 6.2). Wage gap of STs/OCs tends to increase at higher income quintiles. In other words, STs, SCs and, to some extent, OBCs may be facing problem in access to higher paid jobs as compared to OCs, either due to their poor endowments or the prevailing discrimination in labour market, or a combination of both. This pattern in wage gaps is noticed across our sample cities except Coimbatore, where wage gap turns in the favour of SCs and OBCs over OCs (Table 6A.2). This could be due to the relatively better access to high-income jobs in Coimbatore, largely

Table 6.2 Social Group-Wise Mean Wage Earnings (₹) of Wage Workers by the Type of Enterprise

Type of Wage Employment	STs	SCs	OBCs	OCs	Raw Wage Gap Ratio STs/ OCs	SCs/ OCs	OBCs/ OCs
Public Sector							
Regular salaried worker	685.1	857.1	842.6	775.9	0.88	1.10	1.09
Contractual/piece-work/ad hoc worker	442.7	583.9	592.2	733.4	0.60	0.80	0.81
Casual wage labourer	–	232.3	357.1	252.4	0.00	0.92	1.42
Total	577.4	750.2	766.1	753.7	0.77	1.00	1.02
Private Organised Sector							
Regular salaried worker	584.9	546.9	709.1	777.3	0.75	0.70	0.91
Contractual/piece-work/ad hoc worker	532.3	559.5	536.7	754.3	0.71	0.74	0.71
Casual wage labourer	208.3	280.4	361.8	379.4	0.55	0.74	0.95
Total	555.6	534.8	666.5	755.4	0.74	0.71	0.88
Private Unorganised Sector							
Regular salaried worker	672.6	451.7	515.3	531.3	1.27	0.85	0.97
Contractual/piece-work/ad hoc worker	333.3	373.5	276.3	419.2	0.80	0.89	0.66
Casual wage labourer	352.0	275.7	259.0	292.0	1.21	0.94	0.89
Total	528.6	376.7	422.4	463.9	1.14	0.81	0.91
Total							
Regular salaried worker	623.4	608.0	706.1	748.4	0.83	0.81	0.94
Contractual/piece-work/ad hoc worker	471.8	530.2	502.1	686.4	0.69	0.77	0.73
Casual wage labourer	320.1	275.7	307.9	332.4	0.96	0.83	0.93
Total	552.5	557.8	644.3	712.2	0.78	0.78	0.90

Source: Primary field survey (2014–2015).

Table 6.3 Percentile-Wise Average Daily Wage Earnings (₹) of Workers by Their Social Groups

Percentiles/Mean (%)	ST	SC	OBC	OC
1	42.9	100.0	71.4	83.3
5	107.1	145.8	125.0	160.7
10	208.3	178.6	187.5	208.3
25	375.0	270.8	291.7	321.4
50	500.0	416.7	416.7	500.0
75	666.7	650.0	833.3	900.0
90	833.3	1250.0	1250.0	1428.6
95	1083.3	1500.0	1916.7	1875.0
99	2000.0	2142.9	2916.7	3000.0
Mean	552.5	557.8	644.3	712.2

Source: Primary field survey (2014–2015).

associated with social movements in southern states empowering SCs and OBCs over the years. Available research shows that wage gaps are largely due to differences in endowments and related access to jobs. However, a substantive wage gap still remains due to discrimination in labour market (Madheswaran & Attewell, 2007; P. Duraisamy & Duraisamy, 2016).

Earning Difference across Religious Groups

Average wage earnings also vary among workers belonging to different religious groups. We have divided our sample workers into three religious groups, that is, Hindus, Muslims and ORMs excluding Muslims. The average wage rate of Hindus and ORMs is almost same (₹639 and ₹637, respectively), which is higher than Muslims (₹602). Religion-wise, the average wage of regular and contract workers across public and private sectors follows the same pattern as mentioned earlier, that is, the highest for those in regular salaried jobs in the public sector,

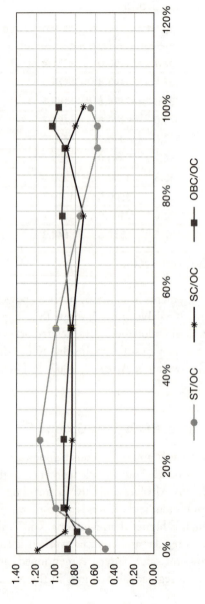

Figure 6.2 *Wage Gap Ratio between Social Groups (%)*
Source: Primary field survey (2014–2015).

followed by that in the private sector. The raw wage gap between Muslims and Hindus is comparatively much less than that observed in the case of SCs and OCs in regular salaried employment in both public and private sectors. The wage gap tends to be favourable to Muslims as compared to Hindus in contractual wage employment (Table 6A.3). Such wage gaps are not revealing across different percentile groups of income distribution, and hence not reported here. This also shows that wage inequality between Muslims and Hindus is not significant. The issue may be access to regular as well as contractual employment that Muslims generally face in the labour market (Mamgain, 2017; Thorat & Newman, 2007).

Within Group Wage Inequality

The mean wage gap presented previously simply shows the disparity in wage income between social groups. However, it does not reveal wage inequality among wage earners within their respective social or religious group, that is, intragroup inequality. For this, we have compared the relative wage of 90th by 10th percentile (Figure 6.3). The highest wage inequality is seen among females, followed by SCs and other religious minorities (ORMs), and the lowest among STs. For example, the average earning of a female worker at the top end is more than 7.5 times higher than that for the one at the lower end. In other words, both within group and between group, income inequality is a major distributional challenge in the country, which has several manifestations.

Education-Specific Wage Earnings

Educational achievements play an important role in determining wages in the labour market. Workers with higher levels of education generally face low barriers across different segments of the labour market, while those with lower levels of education face barriers to entry into different labour markets and have comparatively low wage income. Here the question arises: Does wage gap of workers belonging to various socio-religious groups decline with the improvement in their educational levels? Some important facts are worth mentioning. First, the average

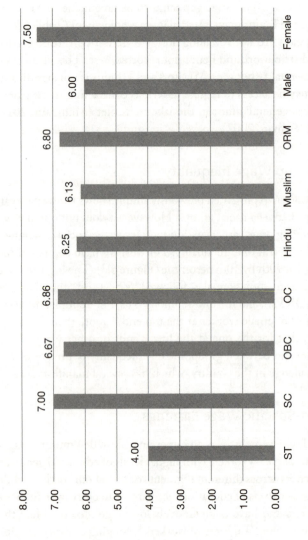

Figure 6.3 *Relative Wages of 90th by 10th Percentiles (within Group Wage Inequality)*
Source: Primary field survey (2014–2015).

wages of graduate workers are significantly higher than those with the middle-level education, irrespective of the nature of employment. However, the gap in wages of graduates and less educated workers is highest in the case of contractual wage employment. Second, male–female wage gap is pronounced among graduate workers employed in regular salaried jobs. Such gap is almost non-existent for workers with secondary and below education, and that too in the case of contractual employment. Third, wages of SC workers are substantially lower as compared to OC workers at each level of education, but the gap is more pronounced in contractual employment (Table 6.4). The wage gap between OBC and OC workers is insignificant in regular employment, whereas it is substantive for those with secondary and graduate (technical) education in contractual employment. Fourth, religion-wise no substantive wage gap is noticed except for Muslim workers with technical graduates (Table 6.5). Finally, in the casual labour market, the increment in earnings due to education is negligible, indicating

Table 6.4 *Average Daily Wage (₹) of Workers by the Levels of Education, Employment Status and Gender*

Educational Level	Male	Female	Person	F/M
	Regular			
Up to middle	573.12	642.41	605.97	1.12
High school and higher secondary	518.42	507.80	515.56	0.98
Graduate and above general	753.87	655.59	725.57	0.87
Graduate and above	1134.68	914.61	1078.52	0.81
Total	709.52	640.16	688.34	0.90
	Contractual			
Up to middle	297.61	363.90	327.81	1.22
Secondary and higher secondary	406.63	517.91	431.26	1.27
Graduate and above general	543.95	581.17	557.20	1.07
Graduate and above technical	1130.62	805.38	1019.74	0.71
Total	568.48	572.23	569.69	1.01

Source: Primary field survey (2014–2015).

Table 6.5 *Comparative Wage Ratios of Workers by Their Castes/Religion and the Levels of Education*

Educational Level	SCs/OCs	OBCs/OCs	Muslims/ Hindus	ORMs/ Hindus
Regular				
Up to middle	0.93	1.02	1.13	0.84
Secondary and higher secondary	0.89	1.00	0.92	0.84
Graduate and above general	0.88	0.97	0.96	1.03
Graduate and above technical	0.83	1.07	0.73	1.13
Total	0.81	0.94	0.90	0.97
Contractual				
Up to middle	0.84	0.92	1.12	1.85
Secondary and higher secondary	0.89	0.73	1.01	1.16
Graduate and above general	0.84	0.95	1.32	0.97
Graduate and above technical	0.76	0.60	0.82	0.91
Total	0.77	0.73	1.08	0.99

Source: Primary field survey (2014–2015).
Note: Calculated from Table 6A.2.

the limitations of casual wage work in awarding higher remuneration to workers with incremental education.

Occupation-Wise Wage Earnings

Understandably, average daily wage earning is the highest in the top-end occupation, that is, administrative and managerial officials (₹1,119). It is the lowest in elementary occupations, which is about 3.4 times lower than the top-end occupation (Table 6.6). This broad pattern is seen for workers irrespective of their gender and social belonging. However, some important features of disparities in occupation-wise wage earnings are worth the mention. First, the gender-wage gap is quite high in associate professional and clerical occupations, as women's wages are lower by approximately 18 and 14 per cent, respectively. Second, wages of SCs as compared to OCs

Table 6.6 *Average Daily Wages of Wage Workers by Gender and Occupation* (₹)

Occupation	Male	Female	Person
Administrative and managerial officials	1,142.59	1,054.97	1,118.90
Professionals	1,002.13	914.42	974.38
Technicians and associate professionals	657.73	539.72	610.06
Clerical jobs	559.23	478.59	529.80
Sales and services workers	422.22	422.36	422.26
Crafts and trade workers	437.32	480.12	446.05
Plant and machine operators	433.41	496.33	446.13
Other elementary occupations	337.58	299.60	327.61
Total	647.80	606.36	635.18

Source: Primary field survey (2014–2015).

are quite low in craft and trade occupations, followed by professional, and administrative and managerial occupations. The wage gap in the case of OBCs as compared to OCs is substantive in sales and service occupations, followed by professionals. Finally, Muslim to Hindu wage differentials is quite high in associate professional and elementary occupations. In clerical occupations, the wage gap is favourable to Muslims. The results are reported in Table 6.7. In brief, OCs are generally at an advantageous position in comparison to SCs and, to some extent, OBCs in their wage earnings. The explanations for such wage gaps are presented in the following section.

Measurement of Wage Inequality: Kernel Density Plots

The kernel density plot is a non-parametric measure of estimating wage inequality. The kernel density plots of wage distributions of different socio-religious groups of workers are depicted in Figures 6.4–6.7. We find that in the urban wage labour markets, the female wage distribution lies to the left of the male distribution, particularly at low wage levels. Also, the male wage distribution is skewed in comparison to

Table 6.7 Wage Ratio by Gender/Caste/Religion and Occupation for Wage Workers

Occupation	F/M	SCs/OCs	OBCs/OCs	Muslims/ Hindus	ORMs/ Hindus
Administrative and managerial officials	0.92	0.82	1.00	0.97	1.01
Professionals	0.91	0.72	0.86	0.90	0.81
Technicians and associate professionals	0.82	0.97	1.06	0.82	0.99
Clerical jobs	0.86	0.97	0.89	1.40	0.99
Sales and services workers	1.00	0.97	0.80	0.91	0.97
Crafts and trade workers	1.10	0.76	0.92	1.12	0.98
Plant and machine operators	1.15	1.00	1.09	0.94	1.29
Other elementary occupations	0.89	0.82	0.90	0.88	1.15
Total	0.94	0.78	0.90	0.94	1.00

Source: Primary field survey (2014–2015).
Note: Calculated from Table 6A.3.

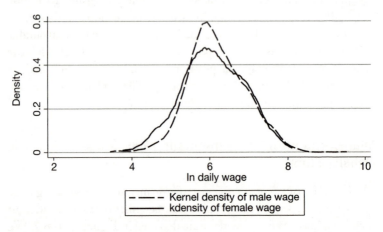

Figure 6.4 *Kernel Density of Log Daily Wage Workers by Gender*
Source: Own calculation based on Primary field survey (2014–2015).

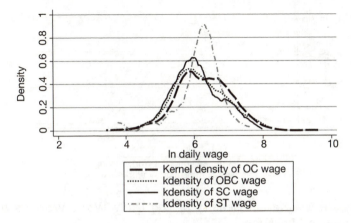

Figure 6.5 *Kernel Density of Log Daily Wage Workers by Social Groups*

Source: Primary field survey (2014–2015).

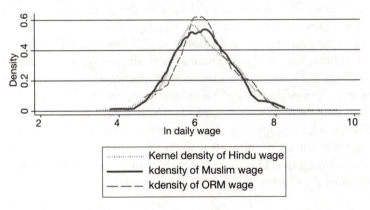

Figure 6.6 *Kernel Density of Log Daily Wage Workers by Religious Groups*

Source: Primary field survey (2014–2015).

females. This implies that at the lower end of the wage/earning distribution there exists a clear gender difference in earnings.

From the earning/wage distributions of workers by social groups, we find that the wage distribution of OC or FC workers lies right to

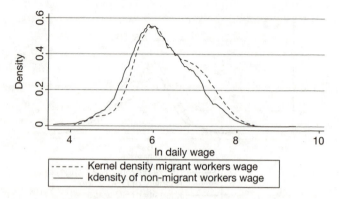

Figure 6.7 *Kernel Density of Log Daily Wage Workers by Status or Migration*

Source: Primary field survey (2014–2015).

the wage distribution of workers from all OCs. This shows higher earnings of OC workers in the labour market in comparison to all OCs. The wage distribution of STs is right to all OCs wage distribution at the lower tail of the distribution. This shows that STs belonging to lower income groups are in a better off position in comparison to all OCs. Moreover, the earning/wage distributions of workers by religious groups show that the wage distribution of Hindu workers lies right to the wage distribution of all OCs. But the difference in wage distribution by religious groups is marginal. Similarly, the earning/wage distribution of migrants workers lies right to the non-migrant wage distribution. This implies that the earnings of migrant workers are more than their non-migrants counterparts.

Measurement of Discrimination in Labour Market

As seen in the earlier sections, average wage earnings vary significantly across gender and social groups, and also by the characteristics of employment. The reasons for such variations are largely attributed to the attributes of workers such as their age, education, skills and experience (endowments). However, after controlling for such attributes, the unexplained wage gaps do exist in the labour market, which are generally attributed to the prevailing discrimination based on caste and gender of workers (Madheswaran & Attewell, 2007; P. Duraisamy & Duraisamy, 2016; Thorat & Newman, 2007). These components can be disentangled by decomposing the total wage gap using Blinder (1973) and Oaxaca (1973) method at the mean, and the Machado and Mata (2005) method at different points on the wage distribution. Both methods are based on the Mincerian wage equation which is elaborated in the following section.

In prior research, one finds different empirical approaches for studying discrimination in the labour market. The first approach predicts earnings from the characteristics of all workers including gender/ caste/religion dummy as a predictor (a single-equation technique). Unfortunately, this approach yields a biased result because it assumes a similar wage structure for the advantaged as well as disadvantaged groups. In other words, it constrains the values of coefficients on explanatory variables, such as education and experience, to be the same for both groups (Gunderson, 1989).[1]

The decomposition methods used to measure the extent of gender and caste discrimination in the labour market in India are explained as follows. While applying the decomposition methods, we have taken male/FCs as the advantaged group and female/SCs as the disadvantaged group. The mathematical logic of this decomposition is explained further. The notation used here stands for caste, and it can be replaced for gender.

For measuring caste discrimination, one finds three different empirical approaches in the available literature on the subject. The first predicts earnings from the characteristics of all workers while including caste as a predictor (a single-equation technique). Unfortunately, this approach yields a biased result, because it assumes that the wage structure is the same for both NSCs/OCs and SCs. We have employed

---

[1] This approach allows only change in intercept but not the slope. In order to overcome this problem, we estimate earnings function for each group separately.

the following decomposition methods to estimate the extent of discrimination against SC workers in the public and private sectors for regular and contractual employments, separately in the urban labour market in India.

Blinder–Oaxaca (1973) Decomposition Method

The Blinder–Oaxaca decomposition method enables one to separate the wage differential between SCs and OCs that can be explained by the differences in the characteristics and those that cannot be explained by the differences in the characteristics. It can be further applied within the framework of the semi-logarithmic earnings equations (Mincer, 1974) and estimated via ordinary least squares (OLS) such that

$$\ln \bar{Y}_{Nsc} = \sum \hat{\beta}_{Nsc} \bar{X}_{Nsc} + \varepsilon_{Nsc} \text{ (NSC wage equation)} \tag{1}$$

$$\ln \bar{Y}_{sc} = \sum \hat{\beta}_{sc} \bar{X}_{sc} + \varepsilon_{sc} \text{ (SC wage equation)} \tag{2}$$

where $\ln \bar{Y}$ denotes the geometric mean of earnings, $\bar{X}$ the vector of mean values of the regressors, $\hat{\beta}$ the vector of coefficients and ε is the error term. Within this framework, the gross differential G in logarithmic term is given by

$$\begin{aligned} \ln(G+1) = \ln(\bar{Y}_{Nsc} / \bar{Y}_{sc}) &= \ln \bar{Y}_{Nsc} - \ln \bar{Y}_{sc} \\ &= \sum \hat{\beta}_{Nsc} \bar{X}_{Nsc} - \sum \hat{\beta}_{sc} \bar{X}_{sc} \end{aligned} \tag{3}$$

The Oaxaca decomposition simply shows that Equation (3) can be expanded. In other words, the difference of the coefficients of the two earnings functions is taken as a priori evidence of discrimination. If, for the given endowment, SC individuals are paid according to the NSC wage structure in the absence of discrimination, then the hypothetical SC earnings function would be given as

$$\ln \bar{Y}_{sc} = \sum \hat{\beta}_{Nsc} \bar{X}_{sc} \tag{4}$$

Substituting Equation (4) into equation (3), we obtain

$$\ln \bar{Y}_{Nsc} - \ln \bar{Y}_{sc} = \sum \hat{\beta}_{Nsc}(\bar{X}_{Nsc} - \bar{X}_{sc}) + \sum \bar{X}_{sc}(\hat{\beta}_{Nsc} - \hat{\beta}_{sc}) \qquad (5)$$

Alternatively, the decomposition can also be done as

$$\ln \bar{Y}_{Nsc} - \ln \bar{Y}_{sc} = \sum \hat{\beta}_{sc}(\bar{X}_{Nsc} - \bar{X}_{sc}) + \sum \bar{X}_{Nsc}(\hat{\beta}_{Nsc} - \hat{\beta}_{sc}) \qquad (6)$$

In Equations (5) and (6), on the right-hand side (RHS), the first term can be interpreted as endowment differences. The second term in these equations has been regarded in the literature as the discrimination component. Studies use either of these alternative decomposition forms (Equation 5 or 6) based on their assumptions about the wage structure that would prevail in the absence of discrimination. This kind of problem is called the index number problem.

Cotton, Neumark and Oaxaca/Ransom Decomposition Method

To solve the index number problem, Cotton (1988), Neumark (1988) and Oaxaca and Ransom (1994) proposed an alternative decomposition. The true non-discriminatory wage would lie somewhere between the NSC and SC wage structure. The Cotton logarithmic wage differential is written as

$$\ln \bar{Y}_{Nsc} - \ln \bar{Y}_{sc} = \sum \beta^*(\bar{X}_{Nsc} - \bar{X}_{sc}) + \sum \bar{X}_{Nsc}(\hat{\beta}_{Nsc} - \beta^*) \\ + \sum \bar{X}_{sc}(\beta^* - \hat{\beta}_{sc}) \qquad (7)$$

The first term on the RHS of Equation (7) is skill differences between SC and NSC, while the second term represents the overpayment relatively to NSC due to favouritism, and the third term refers to the underpayment to SC due to discrimination. β^* is the reward structure that would have occurred in the absence of discrimination. The theory of discrimination provides some guidance in the choice of the non-discriminatory wage structure. In Cotton's (1988) decomposition, the assumption is operationalised by weighting the NSC and SC wage structures by respective proportions of NSC and SC in the labour force. The estimator β^* is defined as

$$\beta^* = P_{Nsc}\hat{\beta}_{Nsc} + P_{sc}\hat{\beta}_{sc} \tag{8}$$

Where P_{Nsc} and P_{sc} are the sample proportions of NSC and SC populations, and $\hat{\beta}_{Nsc}$ and $\hat{\beta}_{sc}$ are the NSC and SC pay structures, respectively. The non-discriminatory or pooled wage structure proposed by Neumark (1988), and Oaxaca and Ransom (1994) is written as follows:

$$\beta^* = \Omega\hat{\beta}_{Nsc} + (I - \Omega)\hat{\beta}_{sc} \tag{9}$$

Where I is the identity matrix, Ω is a weighting matrix, which is specified by

$$\Omega = (X'X)^{-1}(X'_{Nsc}X_{Nsc}) \tag{10}$$

Where X is the observation matrix for the pooled sample, X_{Nsc} is the observation matrix for the NSC sample. The interpretation of Ω as weighting matrix is readily seen by noting that

$$X'X = X'_{Nsc}X_{Nsc} + X'_{sc}X_{sc} \tag{11}$$

where X_{sc} is the observation matrix of the SC sample. Given $\hat{\beta}_{Nsc}$, $\hat{\beta}_{sc}$ and Equation (9), any assumption about β^* reduces to an assumption about Ω.

Expanded Decomposition: Combining Wage and Job Discrimination

The Oaxaca (1973), Cotton (1988) and Neumark (1988) methods do not distinguish between wage discrimination and job discrimination.

Earlier a separate model of occupational attainment was used by Brown, Moon, and Zoloth (1980) into their analysis of wage differentials. Banerjee and Knight (1985) use this decomposition by using a multinomial logit model to, estimate both wage and occupational discrimination for migrant labourers in India; they define 'occupational discrimination' as 'unequal pay for workers with same economic characteristics which results from their being employed in different jobs'. For our analysis we have combined elements from Oaxaca and Ransom (1994) and Brown, Moon and Zoloth (1980) to form a more detailed decomposition analysis of the occupational and wage discriminations (see detailed derivation in Madheswaran & Attewell [2007]). The expanded decomposition is given as follows:

$$
\begin{aligned}
\ln(G + 1) = &\sum_i \tilde{\beta}_{i\text{Nsc}} (\bar{X}_{i\text{Nsc}})(P_{i\text{Nsc}} - \hat{P}_{isc}) \; (\text{job explained}) \\
&+ \sum_i \tilde{\beta}_{i\text{Nsc}} (\bar{X}_{i\text{Nsc}})(\hat{P}_{isc} - P_{isc}) \; (\text{job discrimination}) \\
&+ \sum_i P_{isc} [\tilde{\beta}_i (\bar{X}_{i\text{Nsc}} - \bar{X}_{isc})] \; (\text{wage explained}) \\
&+ \sum_i P_{isc} [\bar{X}_{i\text{Nsc}} (\tilde{\beta}_{i\text{Nsc}} - \tilde{\beta}_i)] \\
&\qquad (\text{wage overpayment to NSC) wage} \\
&+ \sum_i P_{isc} [\bar{X}_{isc} (\tilde{\beta}_i^* - \tilde{\beta}_{isc})] \\
&\qquad (\text{wage underpayment to SC) discrimination}
\end{aligned}
\tag{12}
$$

Machado–Mata–Melly Decomposition Method

This method was initially developed by Machado and Mata (2005). It is an extension of the Blinder–Oaxaca decomposition method in the sense that instead of considering the difference at the mean of the wage distribution, it identifies the sources of wage gap at various quantiles of the wage distribution. The Machado–Mata decomposition is based on the estimation of marginal wage distributions consistent with a conditional distribution estimated by quantile regression. One can perform counterfactual exercises by comparing the marginal distributions implied by different distributions for the covariates. The counterfactual distributions (cf) are estimated as:

$$\left\{ \ln \tilde{Y}_i^{cf} = x_i^{sc} \hat{\beta}_{u_i}^{Nsc} \right\}_{i=1}^{n} \text{ and } \left\{ \ln \tilde{Y}_i^{cf} = x_i^{Nsc} \hat{\beta}_{u_i}^{sc} \right\}_{i=1}^{n}$$

The latest version of decomposition was developed by Melly (2006). The estimator of Melly decomposition will be numerically identical to the Machado–Mata decomposition if the number of simulation used in the Machado–Mata procedure goes to infinity. The mean square error in the Melly estimation is less than in the Machado–Mata estimation. The mean square errors of these two estimates converge only if the simulations in the Machado–Mata estimation become very large. The Melly estimator is also consistent and asymptotically normally distributed. For the θth quantile, the wage gap between NSCs and SCs can be decomposed into two components, as follows:

$$\hat{Q}_{Nsc}(\theta) - \hat{Q}_{sc}(\theta) = \underbrace{\left[\hat{Q}_{Nsc}(\theta) - \hat{Q}_{cf}(\theta) \right]}_{\text{Effects of characterstics}} + \underbrace{\left[\hat{Q}_{cf}(\theta) - \hat{Q}_{sc}(\theta) \right]}_{\text{Effects of coefficients}} \quad (13)$$

where $\hat{Q}_{Nsc}(\theta) - \hat{Q}_{sc}(\theta)$ is the wage gap estimated from the θth quantile of the unconditional log wage distribution for NSCs and SCs, respectively and $\hat{Q}_{cf}(\theta)$ is the estimated counterfactual unconditional quantile of the log wage distribution for SCs created using the coefficients of NSCs. It represents the wage distribution of SCs that would have prevailed if SCs had been endowed with their own characteristics but got paid like NSCs.

The first component on the RHS of Equation (13) is the contribution of the covariates to the difference between wage distributions of NSCs and SCs in the same θth regression quantile. It measures the wage differential due to the differences in endowment (or characteristics effect). The second component is known as the coefficients effect or discrimination component.

Empirical Evidence on Wage Discrimination in Urban Labour Market

Gender Discrimination

The Blinder–Oaxaca decomposition results of wage inequality, given in Table 6.8, indicate that the gender wage gap is largely attributable to discrimination in the labour market. The extent of gender wage gap is higher in the regular labour market, that is, 16 per cent.

We have further analysed gender wage gap using Reimer (1983; 1985), Cotton (1988), Neumark (1988) and Oaxaca and Ransom (1994) decomposition method. This is to find out the least objectionable approach of decomposition. Comparing the standard errors of each decomposition results given in Table 6.9, we find that Oaxaca and Ransom method has a smaller standard error and should probably be preferred. Another advantage of this method is that, we decompose the discrimination component further into two parts such as overpayment to males and underpayment to females. This form of the decomposition procedure yields more accurate estimates of the wage differential because it helps to model the true state of differential treatment by estimating the 'cost' to the group discriminated against as well as the 'benefits' accruing to the favoured group. Besides, the discrimination coefficient is reduced when we use this method.

Table 6.8 *Results of Oaxaca–Blinder Decomposition—Male versus Female (%)*

Components	Total Wage Workers	Regular Workers
Raw wage differentials	0.09	0.16
Explained (endowment)	−0.01	0.02
Unexplained (discrimination)	0.10	0.15
Endowment difference (%)	−10.97	10.40
Discrimination (%)	110.97	89.60

Table 6.9 *Reimers–Cotton–Neumark–Oaxaca and Ransom Approach—Male versus Female (Regular Workers in Labour Market)*

Components	Reimers/ Cotton (w = 0.5)	Neumark/ Oaxaca and Ransom (w = omega)	Oaxaca– Blinder Using Male Means as Weight (w = 1)	Oaxaca–Blinder Using Female Means as Weight (w = 0)
Raw wage differential		0.16 (0.036)		
Endowment difference (%)	−9.99 (0.020)	5.81 (0.019)	10.40 (0.021)	−30.37 (0.027)
Discrimination (%)	109.99 (0.034)	94.19 (0.030)	89.60 (0.035)	130.37 (0.038)
Overpayment to male (%)	65.18 (0.019)	28.76 (0.010)	—	—
Underpayment to female (%)	44.80 (0.017)	65.43 (0.022)	—	—

Source: Author's calculation.

Notes: Unexplained component: overpayment + underpayment component; figures in parentheses indicate standard errors.

The results of Oaxaca and Ransom decomposition method show that in the case of regular salaried worker in labour market, the gender wage gap attributable to endowment difference and discrimination is 5.81 per cent and 94.19 per cent, respectively. The male treatment advantage (benefit of being a male in the labour market) is 28.76 per cent. This is the difference in wages between what the males currently receive and what they would receive in the absence of discrimination. The treatment disadvantage (the cost of being female in the labour market) component for female is 65.43 per cent. This is the difference in the current female wage and wage they would receive if there was no discrimination. So, the magnitude of underpayment to female due to discrimination is higher than the overpayment to males due to nepotism.

Caste Discrimination

This section provides empirical evidence on caste discrimination in wages in the urban labour market in India. We have done separate analysis for the public and private sector workers as part of examining the effectiveness of reservation policy, which was confined only to the minuscule public sector and excluded the vast private sector. Our analysis focuses on regular and contractual workers, because the caste-based wage gap is found to be insignificant among casual workers.

Table 6.10 reports the estimates of the wage equations for OC/FC and SC workers working in regular and contractual mode of employments. The natural logarithm of real daily wage rate is used as the dependent variable, and age, level of education, gender, marital status, sector, city of employment and education of head of household are taken as explanatory variables. The age variable is taken as the proxy of experience. We have not taken other control variables such as the occupation and industry of employment, as these are sometimes not choice variables where barriers to mobility exist in segmented labour markets associated with caste and religion (Munshi & Rosenzweig, 2006). We find a significant positive impact of age and education variables on earnings both in regular and contractual wage employments. A positive sign of the coefficients of age variable and that negative for age square show that there is an increment in earnings with age, which tends to decline after the retirement age. It is to be noted that the age square variable is statistically significant only for SC workers in regular employment. As expected, for both SCs and OCs, the value of education coefficients is positive and tends to increase with higher levels of education. Interestingly, the values of education coefficients are comparatively higher for SCs than that of OCs, mostly at all the levels of education except for primary and higher secondary education. This is true for both regular and contractual wage employments. This also indicates higher impact of education on wage earnings of SCs as compared to OCs, and thus justifies the improvement of the educational levels of SCs and other marginal groups. It also indicates that within group, wage gap due to education is comparatively higher

Table 6.10 Estimates of Augmented Earnings Equation for SC and OC Workers in Urban Labour Market

Variables	Total Wage Workers				Regular Salaried Workers				Contractual Worker			
	SC		OC		SC		OC		SC		OC	
	Coeff	t-stats	Coeff	t-stats	Coeff	t-stats	Coeff	t-stats	Coeff	t-stats	Coeff	t-stats
	0.0600	4.29a	0.0300	1.86c	0.080	4.76a	0.0300	1.58	0.0300	1.22	0.080	1.93b
Age Square	−0.0005	−2.85a	−0.0002	−1.01	−0.001	−3.57a	−0.0002	−0.76	−0.0003	−0.70	−0.001	−1.63
Primary	0.2000	1.66c	0.3000	2.27b	0.350	2.21b	0.2000	1.37	0.1500	0.67	0.650	1.16
Middle	0.1800	1.72c	0.0400	0.36	0.250	1.87c	0.2000	1.51	0.2300	1.19	−0.120	−0.45
Secondary	0.1400	1.45	0.0500	0.56	0.180	1.46	0.0000	−0.03	0.3000	1.85c	0.360	1.31
Higher secondary	0.2400	2.48a	0.2500	2.45a	0.210	1.71c	0.2200	1.82c	0.4400	2.49a	0.360	1.36
Graduate and above (general)	0.4400	4.47a	0.3900	3.87a	0.460	3.74a	0.3900	3.12a	0.4600	2.63a	0.310	1.23
Graduate and above (technical)	0.8200	7.21a	0.8000	7.05a	0.750	5.08a	0.7600	5.71a	0.9900	5.09a	0.790	2.89a
Married	−0.1100	−2.31b	0.0700	1.43	−0.090	−1.64c	0.0800	1.31	−0.0400	−0.51	−0.050	−0.35
Delhi/NCR	0.0000	−0.02	0.0700	0.67	0.080	1.24	0.0300	0.24	0.1500	0.80	0.550	0.72
Pune	0.0900	1.64c	0.1300	1.31	0.210	3.28a	0.1400	1.12	0.0500	0.26	0.360	0.47
Lucknow	−0.3200	−5.75a	−0.2800	−2.26b	−0.160	−2.12b	−0.1800	−1.16	−0.4600	−2.74a	−0.110	−0.15

Public	0.2200	4.57a	0.0000	−0.01	0.270	4.24a	−0.0300	−0.43	0.0600	0.82	0.020 0.14
Head of household—secondary and higher secondary	0.1800	3.65a	0.0000	0.03	0.120	1.95b	−0.0800	−1.12	0.1100	1.10	0.050 0.32
Head of household—graduate and above	0.2800	5.09a	0.3100	4.31a	0.170	2.49a	0.2700	3.78a	0.2000	1.89c	0.180 1.07
Constant	4.2900	16.88a	4.9100	15.67a	3.960	12.8a	5.0000	13.24a	4.6600	8.81a	3.840 3.53a
R squared	0.3000		0.2200		0.280		0.2400		0.3900		0.250
Number of observation	1,112		1,103		711		801		304		242

Source: Author's calculation.

Notes: Dependent variable is the natural logarithm of daily wage. Coimbatore, private sector and unmarried status are reference categories. [a] denotes significant at 1 per cent level; [b] denotes significant at 5 per cent level, [c] denotes significant at 10 per cent level.

for SCs as compared to OCs. The implication is that such a gap can be reduced through improving the educational levels of SCs.

Gender variable is found to be significant for both SCs and OCs (FCs), but the value of male dummy coefficient is higher for SCs than OCs. This implies that gender wage gap is higher among SCs than that of FCs. Whether marital status has any influence on the wage earnings of workers? The pattern varies among SC and OC workers across regular and contractual wage employments. In contractual wage employment, marital status has a negative impact on wage earnings for both SC and OC workers, whereas opposite is true in the case of OC workers in regular employment. However, such coefficients are insignificant except in the case of SC regular employees, implying a mixed impact of marital status on wage earnings in labour market. This is contrary to the earlier findings, which find a positive and significant effect on earnings of FC workers but not for SCs (Singhari & Madheswaran, 2016).

The coefficient of public sector dummy is positive and significant for SCs, whereas it is negative yet insignificant for OCs in the case of regular employment. In the case of contractual employment, the value of the coefficient of public sector dummy is higher for SCs than OCs but not found significant. This implies that SCs are in a better-off position in regular employment in the public sector as compared to the private sector. Workers who are in regular job are getting better earnings than their counterparts, irrespective of social group.

Location of workers also impacts upon the wage earnings. Those working in Lucknow are disadvantaged as compared to the reference city Coimbatore, and other cities of Delhi and Pune, as their wages are significantly lower after controlling other variables. This is true for SC and OSG workers, but SCs are more disadvantaged in Lucknow as compared to OSG with reference to Coimbatore. Broadly speaking, city has significant impact on wage levels.

The educational level of head of household also determines the intergenerational mobility and earning levels of other members of households such as sons and daughters. We find a significant positive impact of graduate and above education of the head of households on the wage earnings of other members of such households working in regular or contractual wage employment.

Oaxaca–Blinder Decomposition Results

We have used Oaxaca–Blinder decomposition method to decompose the wage gap between OC and SC workers in regular and contractual wage employment, as well as in the public and private sectors, separately.

The wage difference between SC and OC regular workers is predominantly due to the endowment difference. However, about 15 per cent of the difference remains unexplained which is generally attributed to the discrimination in urban labour market (Table 6.11). The opposite is true in the case of SC and OC contractual wage workers as about 62 per cent of the wage gap is attributed to discrimination. The wage gap in the public sector is predominantly due to the difference in endowments of workers, whereas about 53 per cent of the wage difference in the private sector is due to the discrimination therein (Table 6.12). These findings are quite important from the perspective of equity in wage income distribution in urban labour market, particularly when there has been a rapid increase in the contractualisation of employment and worsening of quality of employment in India after the economic reforms of the early 1990s (Goldar & Suresh, 2017).

So far, we have analysed wage gap between forward castes (OCs) and SCs using mean-based decomposition method. Due to the limitation of mean-based analysis as discussed in the methodology section, we have used quantile regression decomposition method in order to decompose the caste-based wage gap at different quantiles of the wage distribution. From Figure 6.8, we find that in the wage labour market, the extent of caste-based wage gap as well as discrimination varies significantly across the quantiles of the wage distribution. The wage gap attributable to endowment difference is higher than that of the discrimination, irrespective of wage quantiles. The wage gap attributable to discrimination is higher at the top quantiles than at

Table 6.11 Results of Oaxaca–Blinder Decomposition—SC versus OC (%)

	Total Wage Workers	Regular Salaried Worker	Contractual Worker
Amount attributable:	−30.9	−64	100.5
—Due to endowments (E):	16.5	14.6	6.7
—Due to coefficients (C):	−47.4	−78.6	93.8
Shift coefficient (U):	50.9	81.2	−82.9
Raw differential (R) {E + C + U}:	20.1	17.2	17.5
Adjusted differential (D) {C + U}:	3.6	2.6	10.8
Endowments as % total (E/R):	82.3	85.0	38.1
Discrimination as % total (D/R):	17.7	15.0	61.9

Source: Author's calculation.

Note: A positive number indicates the advantage to OCs/FCs; a negative number indicates the advantage to SCs.

Table 6.12 Oaxaca–Blinder Decomposition Results for Public and Private Sectors—SCs versus OCs (Contractual Worker; %)

	Public Sector	Private Sector
Amount attributable:	358.3	−9.3
—Due to endowments (E):	33.7	6.0
—Due to coefficients (C):	324.6	−15.3
Shift coefficient (U):	−320.5	22.0
Raw differential (R) {E + C + U}:	37.8	12.7
Adjusted differential (D) {C + U}:	4.1	6.7
Endowments as % total (E/R):	89.2	47.3
Discrimination as % total (D/R):	10.8	52.7

Source: Author's calculation.

the bottom quantiles of the wage distribution. This gives indication of 'glass ceiling effect'[2] in the labour market.

Wage and Job Discrimination across Occupations: Simultaneous Estimation

We find that in the wage labour market, with the inclusion of occupation variable in the earnings equation, the final estimate of discrimination coefficient reduces substantially. This implies that the discrimination against SCs partially operates through occupational segregation. In this context, the expanded decomposition method is applied to integrate wage differential and occupational segregation into one framework. Using this method, we find that in the wage labour market, the extent of job discrimination against SCs is higher than wage discrimination in high-paid administrative, managerial and professional occupations. In clerical occupations also the extent of job

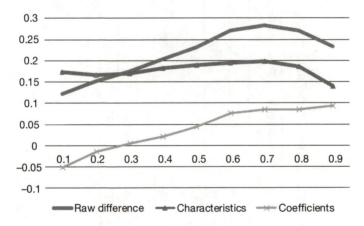

Figure 6.8 *Decomposition of Wage Gap between OC and SC Wage Workers across Wage Quantiles*

Source: Primary field survey (2014–2015).

[2] The 'glass ceiling effect' is said to occur if caste-based wage gaps increase throughout the wage distribution and accelerates in the upper tail (Albrecht et al., 2003).

Table 6.13 Full Decomposition of Gross Earnings Difference between SC and OC Workers

Occupational Group (NCO 1-Digit)	Observed Occupational Distribution		Predicted Occupational Distribution		Observed Difference	Explained Difference	Residual Difference
	P_{Nsc}	P_{sc}	$\hat{P}_{Nsc}$	$\hat{P}_{sc}$	$P_{Nsc} - P_{sc}$	$P_{Nsc} - \hat{P}_{sc}$	$\hat{P}_{sc} - P_{sc}$
	(1)	(2)	(3)	(4)	(5)	(6)	(7)
Administrative and professionals	0.602	0.443	0.602	0.542	0.159	0.060	0.099
Clerical	0.089	0.091	0.089	0.094	-0.001	-0.005	0.004
Service and sales	0.122	0.187	0.122	0.139	-0.065	-0.017	-0.048
Production	0.162	0.196	0.162	0.194	-0.034	-0.033	-0.001
Elementary	0.025	0.083	0.025	0.031	-0.058	-0.005	-0.053

	$G = \ln \bar{Y}_{Nsc}$ $-\ln \bar{Y}_{sc}$	$E = \beta_{Nsc}(\bar{x}_{Nsc}$ $-\bar{x}_{sc})$	$D = \bar{x}_{Nsc}(\hat{\beta}_{Nsc}$ $-\beta_{sc})$	$P_{sc} \times E(WE)$	$P_{sc} \times D(WD)$	$(P_{Nsc} - \hat{P}_{sc})$ $\times \ln \bar{Y}_{Nsc}(JE)$	$(\hat{P}_{sc} - P_{sc})$ $\times \ln \bar{Y}_{Nsc}(JD)$
	(8)	(9)	(10)	(11)	(12)	(13)	(14)
Administrative and professionals	0.112	0.084	0.028	0.037	0.012	0.386	0.634
Clerical	0.073	−0.029	0.102	−0.003	0.009	−0.030	0.023
Service and sales	0.040	0.048	−0.009	0.009	−0.002	−0.101	−0.286
Production	0.189	0.020	0.169	0.004	0.033	−0.198	−0.007
Elementary	0.192	−0.031	0.223	−0.003	0.019	−0.031	−0.307

Source: Computed from primary field survey data (2014–2015).

Notes: WE: Wage explained; WD: Wage discrimination; WD1: Wage overpayment to FC; WD2: Wage underpayment to SC; JE: Job explained; JD: Job discrimination; WD: (WD1+WD2); NSC: Non-scheduled castes; SC: Scheduled Castes.

discrimination is higher than wage discrimination (Table 6.13). This finding is consistent with Singhari and Madheswaran (2016) study. Access to such caveated occupations in labour market is significantly determined by the level as well as the quality of education apart from social networks; and SCs generally remain disadvantaged due to pre-labour market discrimination, which they experience in their access to quality education and skill training.

Conclusion and Policy Implications

This chapter examines wage earnings and inequality in the Indian urban labour market with exclusive reference to educated workers (higher secondary and above education) belonging to different socio-religious groups. Average wages of workers are highest in public enterprises, followed by the private organised sector and lowest in private informal enterprises. Similarly, average wages are higher in regular salaried employment, followed by contractual employment and are least in casual wage employment. Education and experience have significant positive relation with wage earnings. Although this broad pattern in wage earnings is observed in urban labour market, there exist significant inter as well as intragroup wage differentials for men and women, and also for SCs, STs, OBCs and OCs working in different occupations. The raw wage gap is higher between women and men at lower percentile groups of income distribution, whereas for SCs and OCs, it is higher at higher income percentiles of income distribution. Within group, wage inequality (the relative wage gap between 90th percentile and 10th percentile) is highest among women, followed by SCs, and ORMs, and least among STs. The Mincerian wage equation results show significant impact of education, experience, occupation and location on wage earnings. However, it has limitations in decomposing such wage gaps. For decomposing total wage gaps, we have used Blinder and Oaxaca decomposition method at mean, the Oaxaca and Ransom decomposition method and the Machado and Mata method at different points of wage distribution, which are based on the Mincerian wage equation.

We observe significant gender wage gap in regular employment in the public sector and contractual employment in the private sector. The gender wage gap is higher among SCs than OCs, clearly showing double disadvantage of being SC women in the urban labour market. The cost of being female in labour market is very high due to the discrimination in wages. The wage difference between SCs and OCs in regular salaried employment in the public sector is predominantly due to the endowment difference. Unlike this, about 53 per cent of the wage difference in the private sector is due to the discrimination. One of the important findings of the chapter is that only 38 per cent of the wage gap between SCs and forward castes (OCs) in the case of contractual wage workers could be explained with endowment factors, whereas over 60 per cent of the wage gap remains unexplained, thereby implying the underlying discrimination in contractual wage employment in urban labour market. Much of the wage disparities in urban labour market are attributed to the prevailing job discrimination which hinders equal access of employment opportunities, particularly in white-collar occupations, requiring social capital apart from education and experience. The results of quantile regression decomposition analysis show how the wage gap attributable to discrimination tends to be higher at the top quantiles than at the bottom quantiles of the wage distribution, indicating 'glass ceiling effect' in the labour market.

Our findings are quite important from the perspective of equity in wage income distribution in urban labour market, particularly when there has been a rapid increase in contractualisation of employment and worsening of quality of employment in India after the economic reforms of the early 1990s. The related policy imperatives are as follows: First, current measures aimed at improving the access to quality education and skill training of new entrants to labour force need significant upscaling for improving employability. Though education has significant impact on access to wage employment and wage earnings, the rising inequality in access to quality education and skill training is a major concern. This is particularly important for population belonging to SC, ST, and other socially backward communities who face discrimination in access to quality education and skill training, thereby reducing their chances of getting jobs with higher wages. Equally important would be to upscale current retraining of workers by both employers and government to enhance their skill sets and earning prospects. Special provisions should be made for higher education, responsive training, and multi-skilling of the tribal people and Dalits so that they are able to compete with the OCs for jobs.

Second, since wage discrimination is more pronounced in con-tractual wage employment, particularly in the private sector, public policy should aim at ensuring equal opportunities of work and equal remuneration for equal work, irrespective of any pre-conceived bias. For this, implementation of minimum wages by the private sector must be made effective. Third, discrimination in wage payments based on caste and gender of workers should be made illegal. Finally, employ-ers need to be sensitised on their social responsibility of diversifying their workplaces by hiring women and Dalits. Research has clearly demonstrated how social diversity is important in improving organi-sational productivity. Private enterprises need to be encouraged for imparting skill training to women, SCs, STs and other economically backward population groups under their corporate social responsibility for improving prospects of their employability and earnings.

Annexure 6A

Table 6A.1 City-Wise Daily Wage Earnings (₹) of Male and Female Wage Workers by Percentile Group

Percentiles/ Mean (%)	Lucknow			Delhi/NCR			Pune			Coimbatore			Total		
	Male	Female	F/M	Male	Female	F/M	Male	Female	F/M	Male	Female	F/M	Male	Female	F/M
1	62.5	50.0	0.80	100.0	75.0	0.75	83.3	83.3	1.00	125.0	83.3	0.67	83.3	75.0	0.90
5	125.0	62.5	0.50	214.3	108.3	0.51	166.7	125.0	0.75	208.3	125.0	0.60	166.7	112.5	0.67
10	156.3	104.2	0.67	270.8	125.0	0.46	208.3	200.0	0.96	237.6	166.7	0.70	208.3	166.7	0.80
25	208.3	166.7	0.80	350.0	250.0	0.71	321.4	291.7	0.91	300.0	208.3	0.69	291.7	250.0	0.86
50 (Median)	291.7	291.7	1.00	535.7	458.3	0.86	500.0	500.0	1.00	416.7	291.7	0.70	458.3	416.7	0.91
75	500.0	625.0	1.25	1,000.0	1,000.0	1.00	833.3	833.3	1.00	600.0	416.7	0.69	800.0	833.3	1.04
90	1,250.0	937.5	0.75	1,500.0	1,350.0	0.90	12,50.0	1,250.0	1.00	833.3	625.0	0.75	1,250.0	1,250.0	1.00
95	1,666.7	1,250.0	0.75	2,000.0	1,666.7	0.83	1,900.0	1,750.0	0.92	1,062.5	1,250.0	1.18	1,812.5	1,666.7	0.92
99	2,916.7	2,916.7	1.00	3,125.0	2,750.0	0.88	2,500.0	2,500.0	1.00	1,812.5	2,500.0	1.38	2,750.0	2,500.0	0.91
Mean	510.0	478.1	0.94	757.9	637.9	0.84	683.5	648.6	0.95	499.4	400.6	0.80	647.8	606.4	0.94

Source: Primary field survey data (2014–2015).

Table 6A.2 City-Wise Daily Earnings (₹) of Wage Workers by Social Group across Percentiles and Mean of the Wage Distribution

Percentiles/Mean (%)	Lucknow					Delhi/NCR			
	ST	SC	OBC	FC	ST	SC	OBC	FC
1	208.33	83.33	50.00	35.71	312.50	100.00	62.50	83.33
5	208.33	107.14	125.00	104.17	312.50	187.50	112.50	166.67
10	208.33	142.86	150.00	145.83	333.33	250.00	208.33	250.00
25	208.33	178.57	208.33	250.00	416.67	333.33	312.50	357.14
50	250.00	270.83	291.67	385.42	500.00	471.73	500.00	625.00
75	625.00	500.00	500.00	767.86	833.33	833.33	1,041.67	1,041.67
90	625.00	1,041.67	1,145.83	1,250.00	1,500.00	1,250.00	1,500.00	1,500.00
95	625.00	1,458.33	1,770.83	1,875.00	2,000.00	1,666.67	1,791.67	2,083.33
99	625.00	2,083.33	3,750.00	2,708.33	2,000.00	2,250.00	2,350.00	3,500.00
Mean	361.11	449.23	525.01	602.43	690.70	639.74	703.98	812.13

Percentiles/Mean (%)	Pune				Coimbatore			
	ST	SC	OBC	FC	ST	SC	OBC	FC
1	42.86	104.17	83.33	83.33	250.00	83.33	107.14	208.33
5	107.14	171.43	125.00	166.67	250.00	142.86	208.33	214.29
10	166.67	208.33	187.50	214.29	250.00	200.00	229.17	250.00
25	375.00	333.33	291.67	312.50	333.33	250.00	291.67	310.00
50	520.83	458.33	541.67	500.00	386.90	341.67	416.67	416.67
75	708.33	800.00	1041.67	833.33	416.67	500.00	600.00	500.00
90	833.33	1,250.00	1,666.67	1250.00	625.00	750.00	850.00	650.00
95	900.00	1,458.33	2,291.67	1,875.00	625.00	1,041.67	1,250.00	800.00
99	1,250.00	2,142.86	2,750.00	2,250.00	625.00	1,250.00	2,500.00	833.33
Mean	534.77	620.50	746.27	659.06	399.80	428.41	519.00	422.26

Source: Primary field survey data (2014–2015).

Table 6A.3 City-Wise Daily Earnings (₹) of Wage Workers by Religious Groups across Percentiles and Mean of the Wage Distribution

Percentiles/ Mean (%)	Lucknow			Delhi/NCR			Pune			Coimbatore			Total		
	Hindu	Muslim	ORM	Hindu	Muslim	ORM	Hindu	Muslim	ORM	Hindu	Muslim	ORM	Hindu	Muslim	ORM
1	53.57	50.00	416.67	83.33	62.50	229.17	83.33	166.67	104.17	91.67	125.00	145.83	83.33	83.33	104.17
5	107.14	125.00	416.67	178.57	125.00	250.00	125.00	196.43	125.00	178.57	178.57	187.50	142.86	145.83	125.00
10	145.83	145.83	416.67	250.00	166.67	333.33	208.33	250.00	196.21	208.33	208.33	208.33	200.00	187.50	196.21
25	196.43	208.33	416.67	333.33	312.50	437.50	321.43	291.67	321.43	291.67	250.00	250.00	291.67	285.71	321.43
50 (Median)	291.67	291.67	750.00	500.00	500.00	833.33	500.00	500.00	500.00	400.00	416.67	324.40	428.57	458.33	500.00
75	535.71	654.17	1,250.00	1,000.00	916.67	1,428.57	892.86	750.00	750.00	550.00	550.00	479.17	833.33	714.29	750.00
90	1,041.67	1,250.00	1,250.00	1,458.33	1,400.00	1,666.67	1,333.33	1,041.67	1,250.00	833.33	625.00	625.00	1,250.00	1,150.00	1,333.33
95	1,650.00	2,708.33	1,250.00	1,795.83	2,083.33	3,125.00	1,875.00	1,041.67	1,750.00	1,083.33	1,000.00	625.00	1,750.00	1,400.00	1,750.00
99	2,916.67	3,750.00	1,250.00	2,886.91	2,916.67	3,750.00	2,750.00	1,250.00	2,083.33	2,187.50	1,250.00	1,250.00	2,750.00	2,708.33	2,083.33
Mean	490.45	609.57	805.56	725.60	690.24	1,068.56	687.02	579.10	619.26	488.93	435.41	385.50	638.86	602.40	637.53

Source: Primary field survey data (2014–2015).

CHAPTER 7

Hiring Practices in Urban Labour Market

Introduction

Hiring or recruitment—an important demand side component of the labour market—has received renewed attention in recent years, especially post liberalisation. The economic reforms of the 1990s and the rapid penetration of ICT and financial services have brought about significant changes in the nature of employment opportunities as well as hiring practices of employers in India. An exponential increase in contractual and casual wage employments at the expense of regular wage employment even in public sector enterprises is a reflection of such changes (IHD & ISLE, 2014). Although employers are now able to hire and fire human resources depending on their requirements, at the same time they face a formidable challenge in finding competent human resources in spite of significant improvement in the educational levels of the Indian population (World Bank, 2011). More and more employers find themselves struggling in a situation where talent oversupply and low employability are leading to underemployment, on the one hand, and a supply deficit for the industry, on the other (FICCI, 2010; NASSCOM, 2014). Even as there is a fierce competition among employers to attract skilled personnel, SMEs are struggling with high attrition rates resulting in high volume of recruitments as well as hiring costs (Mamgain, 2018). This means a higher cost of signal to job seekers and to employers for recruitment and training.

In order to ensure efficiency, quality and profits, employers apply various methods of disseminating information for job hiring to get the best human resources at competitive costs. As a result, recruitment practices have undergone a sea change across various economic sectors/sub-sectors and geographical/administrative regions (Banerjee, 1984; Iversen, Sen, Verschoor, & Dubey, 2009; Mamgain, 2017; Papola, 2005). With the spread of IT, both employers and job seekers are increasingly using IT in their searches in the labour market. E-recruitment has emerged as a very popular mode for job postings, screening and selection by employers. The emergence of commercial job boards/portals (such as Naukri.com, DevNet, Monster and Babajob) for posting job advertisements are being used to bridge the information asymmetry gap between employers and prospective employees (Faberman & Kudlyak, 2016). Technology-supported social networks such as Facebook, LinkedIn and WhatsApp have also emerged as important sources of job information to active as well as passive job seekers. E-recruitment has enabled employers to get a larger pool of applications along with easier sorting and screening of job applications and contacting applicants, saving considerable time and costs. Keeping pace with the changing times, the National Employment Service was redesigned into NCS in 2015 (MoLE, 2017). The NCS portal facilitates registration of job seekers, employers, skill providers as well as career counsellors, and thus is distinct from other private sector job portals in that it provides job-matching services to job seekers and employers as well. In its new incarnation, NCS had registered 14.86 million employers and 39.14 million job seekers on its portal until 31 August 2017.

Private employment agencies such as RPO companies, private placement agencies, staffing companies and manpower consultants have emerged as new labour market intermediaries in a big way. These agencies not only provide recruitment services but also provide workers to perform project-specific jobs in the industry (Ernst & Young, 2012). Employers are increasingly looking to private manpower companies to provide them with workers without enrolling them as employees (third-party workers). Campus recruitments and job fairs are other channels of recruitment. Apart from these methods, social networks and employee referrals continue to remain a very common source of job information and recruitment (Mamgain, 2018; Munshi, 2003). It is argued that referral networks improve labour market efficiency by increasing access of information to both job seekers and employers (Dhillon, Iversen, & Torsvik, 2013). In India, most enterprises in the corporate sector have an employee referral policy, which takes care of about 15–20 per cent of job hiring at the entry- and middle-level positions (Mamgain, 2018). In short, the old methods of job information such as advertisements in newspapers, employment exchanges and displays outside enterprises have become things of the past. In this entire process, access to information by job seekers has become rather limited, particularly for lower-level jobs, where social networks including employee referrals act as a major mode of job information and selection, thereby reducing the likelihood of employment opportunities for those people or groups of people who are not members of such social networks.

Employers commonly argue that they practise highly competitive recruitment processes wherein they hire employees only on the basis of merit, and that factors such as caste, region, gender and class are irrelevant. The counter-argument is that the merit argument ignores the social and economic factors that produce 'meritorious' candidates in the first place, especially in a situation where a small proportion of socially and economically privileged groups continue to have their monopoly over the best educational institutions, and a large majority of others including the marginalised groups remain bereft of such advantage (Jodhka & Newman, 2010; Upadhya, 2007). Thus, the persistent under-representation of SCs/STs in private corporate sector jobs even in industrially developed states such as Tamil Nadu (CII, 2011) is not only due to their poor endowments such as education and skill sets but also partly due to the prevailing discrimination in the labour market (Madheswaran, 2017). A number of studies have confirmed the prevailing bias among employers for a callback of applicants with similar qualifications and experience yet belonging to various social, ethnic and religious groups (Thorat & Newman, 2010), and discrimination in screening and hiring processes (Banerjee, 1984; Desi, 1998). However, one of the major limitations of those studies is that they could hardly analyse the new forms of job information and related recruitment policies and practices in private enterprises and employers' preferences/prejudices while hiring employees. This chapter attempts to bridge that gap in the existing literature.

There is no recent comprehensive study in the Indian urban labour market for understanding the recruitment processes, workers' turnover and discriminatory practices in hiring. To fill this gap, we have conducted a pilot study of 45 enterprises selected from Pune, Delhi NCR and Coimbatore, and that too from IT/ITeS, automobile manufacturing, engineering, chemicals, textiles and hospitality industries. These industries witnessed a substantial growth in employment in the recent years. About four private employment services enterprises, which act as RPO and staffing companies, were also included in the sample.

We first begin with a brief analytical framework of the chapter with a focus on information asymmetries and related biases/prejudices leading to sub-optimal utilisation of resources in Section 'Understanding Recruitment Policies, Practices and Discrimination in Labour Market'. Section 'Recruitment, Retention and Social Diversity of Workforce' analyses the recruitment, retention and social diversity at workplace in private industry. In Section 'Understanding Recruitment Processes in the Context of Under-Representation of SCs/Muslims in Private Enterprises', recruitment policies and practices of job advertisement/ information in private enterprises are discussed. It also attempts to discern employers' bias and prejudices about certain groups of job seekers in the labour market and the resultant discriminatory practices in hiring processes. Section 'Difficulties Faced by Employers in Recruitment and Retention of Employees' briefly discusses the problems faced by employers in recruiting and retaining of their workforce. The concluding section provides major findings of the chapter.

Understanding Recruitment Policies, Practices and Discrimination in Labour Market

Theoretically, the hiring/recruitment decisions of any employer are guided by the requirement of human resource and its marginal productivity so as to maximise profit and minimise the search and recruitment costs. This requires perfect information at free cost to both employers and job seekers. But in the real world, the efficient functioning of labour and other markets is hampered by information asymmetries. Michael Spence's seminal 'signalling theory' is fundamentally concerned with reducing information asymmetry between two parties (Spence, 1973). In the context of labour market, Spence demonstrated how a job applicant might engage in behaviours to reduce information asymmetry that hampers the selection ability of prospective employers (Spence, 1973). For this, job seekers may go in for the costly route of signalling by opting for improving their education and skills. Thus, from an employer's perspective, a job seeker would like to match the information from personal characteristics—signals and indices are the terms used by Spence—to determine his assessment of an applicant's productive capacity, personality, interests, extracurricular activities, etc. According to Spence (1973), indices are immutably fixed attributes such as sex and race, whereas signals are alterable attributes like education, which is something that the individual can invest in. Employers trying to maximise the expected present value of profits make choices and engage in activities to affect the expected productivity of persons hired (Behrenz, 2001). Employers may therefore resort to invest on collecting more information about the prospective employee through different search channels to make the best choice, since one search channel may provide information about the background of applicants that differs from the information provided by another channel.

Akerlof (1976) argues that the employer's choice of search channels and the selection among applicants is made with a view to reduce the probability to hire 'lemons'–persons with bad job qualifications. The assumption regarding employers is that they try to maximise their profit by employing persons with a value of their expected marginal product that is higher than or equal to their expected total wage and other costs.

Screening mechanisms employed by employers include both objective and subjective sets of criteria such as educational qualifications, experience and testing aptitude. Due to incomplete information about job seekers for a given job vacancy, employers may use a variety of criteria for screening job applications to minimise risks and costs. This may also involve screening based on subjective criteria such as stereotypes of race, caste, ethnicity or gender (referred to as 'indices' by Spence, 1973), which employers consider to deliver less than the expected job performance or are more likely to create other problems in the firm. The most prominent neoclassical explanation for understanding the demand side screening of job applications and related exclusion/inclusion in hiring of workers by employers has been provided by Gary Becker (1971) in his economic model of 'employer taste'. This model explains that the discrimination exists because employers do not want to employ certain groups of workers and will only do so if these workers are paid lower wages than those paid to workers in general. It thus provides an explanation of wage discrimination—equally productive workers being paid different wages.

In contrast to taste-based theories of discrimination propounded by Becker (1971), statistical discrimination theories associated with Edmund Phelps (1972) and Arrow (1972) focus on the likelihood that information available to employers about the skill endowments of individual job applicants being relatively sketchy, while information about the average endowments of social groups being (or will be believed to be) relatively complete. The hiring and allocation of jobs and wages are often shaped by the perceived notion of productivity of a group of workers rather than the actual productivity. This may arise due to the past experience of employers of working with a given group of workers and incomplete information about the productivity of workers. Thus, in the presence of incomplete information, employers may screen candidates on the basis of perceived differences based on subjective stereotypes about job applicants such as caste, ethnicity and gender.

Even accounting for information asymmetries, the discriminatory process by employers can extend beyond access to information to the processes of selection in which, as mentioned earlier, attributes which have little relevance for the performance of the job but tend to favour candidates with better social and economic endowments (e.g., fluency with spoken English) are emphasised. This is explained by Sen's (2000) model of 'unfavourable exclusion' and 'unfavourable inclusion'. In the job market, some job seekers may be completely denied access to certain jobs based on their caste/identity (unfavourable exclusion), or some may be offered jobs but on differing terms and conditions (unfavourable inclusion). Job seekers may be discriminated during various processes of hiring by employers. The first and foremost process is the specification of job for which a worker is to be hired. Some employers may set job specifications in such a way which excludes certain groups of job seekers from applying for such jobs. One such example is the proficiency in English language which disables those who do not have the advantage of learning the same. Also, various hiring methods used by employers have inbuilt exclusionary/inclusionary features. For instance, when employers use employees' networks to hire workers, job seekers with no social networks automatically stand excluded from such opportunities. Further, at the time of interview, interviewers may deliberately ask such questions which hurt the sentiments of interviewee (Jodhka & Newman, 2010). Finally, a person can be offered job on different terms and conditions such as low salary and different employment contract (for more details, see Thorat & Newman, 2010).

There is no recent comprehensive study in the urban labour market for understanding the recruitment processes, workers' turnover and discriminatory practices in hiring. By using the above analytical framework, we now discuss the recruitment, retention and discriminatory practices in urban labour market based on our sample survey of private sector enterprises in the following sections.

Recruitment, Retention and Social Diversity of Workforce

The broad features of employment in sample enterprises are given in Table 7.1. Nearly half of the sample enterprises are small with less than 200 people. It needs to be remembered that there exist significant differences in the broad characteristics of employment, recruitment

Table 7.1 *Select Characteristics of Employment in Sample Enterprises by Their Size of Employment (%)*

Category of Workers	Size of Employment in Enterprises (No.)			
	Up to 200	*200–500*	*More than 500*	*Total*
Male	80.1	76.4	77.5	77.5
Female	19.9	23.6	22.5	22.5
Managerial workers	6.6	2.3	1.8	2.3
Supervisory workers	9.4	3.9	4.7	5.0
Other workers[a]	78.1	93.8	85.3	86.3
Contractual[b]	31.9	35.7	25.7	28.2
Casual	7.7	14.9	15.5	14.7
Total	100.0	100.0	100.0	100.0
No. of employees	1,772	3,906	14,231	19,909
% of sample firms	48.9	24.4	26.7	100

Source: Primary field survey (2014–2015).

Notes: Based on responses from 45 enterprises in Pune, Coimbatore and Delhi NCR; [a]Other workers also include contractual and casual workers. Hence, percentages may not add up to 100; [b]Contractual workers include those who are employed by companies and also those hired through private employment firms on a third-party contract basis.

and job turnovers across sample enterprises, which are camouflaged by aggregating enterprises. These enterprises are largely male dominated across all sizes of firms. About 28 per cent of the total workforces are working on contractual mode of employment. Much less than one-tenth of the workforce is working in managerial and supervisory jobs. This ratio is comparatively higher in small-size firms. Women, who constitute over one-fifth of the workforce, are proportionately under-represented in the sample enterprises, reflecting macro trend of their lower work participation in the urban labour market in India.

As a result of pro-liberal government policies, the nature and forms of employment have considerably changed as the industry has been increasingly switching over to the contractual mode of employment through third parties like private employment agencies. This has led to a significant leap in the share of contractual workers (Goldar & Suresh, 2017). A larger strategy of employers is to recruit only core human resources on a regular basis and provide them the benefits of job tenurial security, social security and relatively higher wages than those who are employed through private agencies. The strategy is to reduce the cost of labour and increase profits for further investment. This also has crucial implications for recruitment strategies and concerns about social diversity in the industry.

As is well known, recruitment is a major activity among enterprises. About 19 per cent of the existing strength of employees in the 45 sample enterprises was recruited during the last one year preceding the date of the survey. The ratio was much higher (30%) in smaller enterprises with an employment size of up to 200 people (Table 7.2). Recruitments were largely confined to core workers who constituted about 70 per cent of the total recruitments. The share of contractual and casual workers in total recruitments was 20 and 10 per cent, respectively. Larger enterprises often recruited higher proportion of core workers as compared to smaller enterprises. It merits mention here that a substantive number of workers are also hired on third-party contract basis from staffing companies/private placement agencies that do not form part of the recruitment process of the user organisation.

Table 7.2 *Employees Recruited over the Last One Year (%)*

Employment Size of Firm (No.)	Core	Contractual	Casual	Total	Total Recruited as % of Total Existing Strength	Total Existing Strength of Workforce (Nos)
Up to 200	56.8	29.8	13.3	100	29.7	1,772
200–500	59.2	31.9	8.9	100	23.7	3,906
More than 500	77.6	13.3	9.1	100	15.7	14,231
Total	70.0	20.4	9.6	100	18.5	19,909

Source: Primary field survey (2014–2015).
Note: Based on sample survey of 45 enterprises.

Table 7.3 *Percentage of Workers Who Left Their Job during Last Year*

Employment Size of Firm (No.)	Core	Contractual	Casual	Total
Up to 200	21.6	30.7	54.4	27.0
200–500	19.0	8.5	24.1	16.0
More than 500	12.2	5.3	25.9	12.5
Total	14.2	8.7	26.8	14.5

Source: Primary field survey (2014–2015).

The high ratio of recruitment in enterprises is closely associated with the higher rate of attrition. About 14 per cent of the workers quit their jobs during the reference period of one year. The attrition rate in smaller enterprises was as high as 27 per cent which is more than double than in larger enterprises (Table 7.3). Such high turnover of employees in smaller enterprises is attributed to several factors such as low salaries, low chances of upward mobility and job-related social security benefits. Surprisingly, a high turnover was also observed among core employees who were on the regular payrolls of the sample enterprises. Such high attrition of core workers is also indicative of the tough competition in the industry to attract the best talent (NASSCOM, 2014). According to the Small Industries Association, Coimbatore, 'in small-scale industries (SSIs), the attrition rate is as high as 50 per cent. They just join SSIs and after training join big industries. SSIs have become a training platform for big industries, for which SSIs should be compensated by big industries and government' (Field notes).

In similar vein, Pune-based Dalit Indian Chambers of Commerce and Industry (DICCI), claims, 'micro, small and medium enterprises (MSMEs) are becoming gateways of skill development for big companies in India'. Thus, we note that the burden of recruitment and retention of their workforce is comparatively more on smaller enterprises.

In response to a question about the social and religious backgrounds of the workforce recruited during the past year, most of the sample enterprises declined to disclose the caste/religion group of their employees in the first stance. They argued that there was no system or practice of maintaining personal records of their employees in terms of social or religious groups. At the time of interview, a 'personal details' form has to be filled up by applicants before the interview. The form, however, does not contain any column about the social group of the applicants, although there is a column seeking information on their religious category and gender. Following a great deal of persuasion, the researchers managed to elicit information about the approximate number of SC and Muslim candidates recruited during the reference one year by going through their recruitment lists. It was difficult to obtain information about STs, hence not reported. Thus, we clarify here that such numbers of new recruitments by their social groups are only broad estimates. Nevertheless, the figures are quite interesting. Among a total of 2,575 core employees recruited during the year under study, the share of SCs was about 7.2 per cent and that of Muslims was 5.7 per cent (Table 7.4a). In large-size enterprises, the share of SCs and Muslims in new recruitments was slightly more than small-sized

Table 7.4a *Percentage Share of SCs/Muslims among Core Employees Recruited during Last One Year Preceding the Date of Survey, by the Size of Firms*

Employment Size of Firm (No.)	Core Employees Recruited during Last Year (No.)			As % of Total Core Employees Recruited during Last Year	
	Total	SCs	Muslims	%SCs	% Muslims
Up to 200	299	14	5	4.7	1.7
200–500	547	28	22	5.1	4.0
More than 500	1,729	144	121	8.3	7.0
Total	2,575	186	148	7.2	5.7

Source: Primary field survey (2014–2015).
Note: Based on the information from sample 45 enterprises.

enterprises. Their share was smaller in managerial positions (Table 7.4b). These results again reconfirm the earlier estimates of significant under-representation of these marginalised groups in private sector employment as compared to their respective shares in the total population of the country (CII, 2007; Mamgain, 2016).

Understanding Recruitment Processes in the Context of Under-Representation of SCs/Muslims in Private Enterprises

For understanding the under-representation of SCs and Muslims in private sector employment in India, we briefly discuss the methods of dissemination of job information, criteria for screening and selection of applicants, and related exclusionary processes as under.

Job Signalling—Method of Job Information

Like job seekers, employers also use a variety of methods to disseminate information about vacancies. These include advertisements

Table 7.4b Percentage Share of SCs/Muslims among Employees Recruited during Last One Year Preceding the Date of Survey, by the Level of Job Position

Level/Position	Core Employees Recruited during Last Year			As % of Core Employees Recruited during Last Year	
	Total	SC	Muslim	SC	Muslim
Managerial	732	36	16	4.9	2.2
Supervisory	873	64	41	7.3	4.7
Other	970	86	91	8.8	9.4
Total	2,575	186	148	7.2	5.7

Source: Primary field survey (2014–2015).
Note: Based on the information from 45 enterprises.

in newspapers, job portals, company websites, campus recruitment, approaching staffing companies, placement agencies, job fairs, employee referrals, word of mouth and labour contractors. The job signalling methods significantly differ with the size of firms, and the nature of products and services. For managerial and supervisory-level positions, common methods of recruitment information dissemination include popular e-job portals, social network sites, company websites, leading newspapers and HR consultant firms. A rapid growth in e-job portals in the recent years has helped employers attract a large number of job applicants, many of whom are not necessarily looking for a change in their current jobs but are open to the right opportunity. For other positions, employee referrals, notice boards, placement agencies, campus placements, job fairs and contractors are used by employers to search suitable candidates for their firms. About 70–84 per cent of the sample firms have been reported using job portals for vacancy posting for supervisory and managerial-level positions, respectively. Nearly half of the surveyed firms used job portals for junior-level positions too (Table 7.5). However, a large proportion of small firms advertised their vacancies in local newspapers and extensively used the social network in search of suitable workers.

Table 7.5 *Percentage of Firms Using Job Posting Method*

Job Posting Method	Core Employees			Contractual	Casual
	Managerial	Supervisory	Others		
Newspapers	32.0	41.3	43.3	46.7	0.0
Electronic media like job portals	83.6	69.7	47.8	24.4	0.0
Website of company	68.9	80.0	35.6	11.1	0.0
Notice board of company	8.9	64.4	100.0	11.1	77.8
Employee referrals	18.6	46.7	51.1	31.1	51.1
Approach to staffing/recruitment company (RPOs)	20.0	26.7	52.2	62.2	42.2
Approach to placement agencies	11.1	15.6	45.9	48.9	0.0
Job fairs	0.0	0.0	22.2	4.4	0.0
Approach to campus placements	28.9	35.6	24.4	15.6	0.0
Word of mouth	20.0	20.0	33.3	22.2	37.8
Contractor	0.0	0.0	28.9	28.9	46.7

Source: Primary field survey (2014–2015).

Note: Based on responses from 45 sample firms. These responses do not add to 100 due to multiple responses.

Most of the sample firms engaged private employment firms or RPO organisations for hiring employees as third party mostly for shop floor works. On the other hand, the big and reputed firms chose HR consultant firms to find suitable applicants at the senior and mid-level positions. Their task involved the preparation of job advertisement, job description, scrutinizing applications and training the workers. This helped the firms in reducing time and costs. In brief, firms were using more than one method of job postings to fill vacancies.

Job portals are not effective nowadays. We get a large number of applications, and their screening and sorting is a tedious and time-consuming process. Our company is dependent now more on recruitment consultant firms' services for recruiting managerial and supervisory staff.

—Delhi NCR MNC

The number of such private employment placement agencies as labour market intermediaries has grown significantly in India during the last three decades. These are also known by different names such as private placement agencies, staffing companies, HR consultants, and RPO firms. One set of agencies only helps firms in finding suitable human resources (called as placement agencies), while the other set of agencies provides human resources to firms on a contractual basis. There are also agencies which provide both types of services to firms in the labour market. Private placement agencies are using social media sites like LinkedIn to link active or passive job seekers to employers. They match the profiles of the job and job seekers, and invite job seekers to apply for such jobs. For this service, they charge a 'user fee' to both employers and job applicants. It is now being argued that private placement agencies would gradually lose their role as labour market intermediaries with the rapid expansion of social network sites such as LinkedIn and Facebook.

Employee referral is considered as one of the best and reliable sources of job information and recruitment by employers, as it has the highest conversion rate, offer rate and offer acceptance rate (Mani, 2012). It has been in practice in big as well as small firms (Table 7.5). Some firms even provide incentive for each successful referral to their employees. Some of the job seekers have been reported using this method of their job search, as mentioned in Chapter 4. This practice is quite prevalent in automobile companies and big IT firms, such as Cognizant, TCS, HCL, WIPRO and Infosys, as mentioned on their respective websites. Cognizant has 'Bring Another You' (BAY) employee referral programme involving referral incentives such as a vacation, a brand new car, or double the referral money for niche and hard-to-find skills. Cognizant's referral programme contributes to over 40 per cent of the company's annual hires. Similarly, TATA Consultancy has adapted a marketing/CRM model for its referral programme (i.e., the company offers a 24×7 referral help desk with a toll-free number). It instituted a 'rapid hire' process where resumes were collected at referral desks that provide 'on-the-spot' screening followed by preliminary evaluation and instant feedback. They also offer early bird and spot prizes as well as contests between business units to foster a competitive mindset around referrals. Infosys believes that employees can make a good referral decision, as they understand the aspirations of the candidate they refer as well as the requirements/culture of the company. During the financial year 2012, 56 per cent of the Infosys's lateral hires across the globe came through employee referrals. In India, 62 per cent of its lateral hires were employed through referral programmes. Wipro has branded its employee referral programme as 'Wiplinks'. Its employee referral contributes to 20–25 per cent of the overall hiring.

One of the Lucknow-based automobile firms covered in the pilot study disclosed that about 15–20 per cent of its workforce in white and blue-collar jobs is filled up through employee referrals. For this, a dedicated data bank of employee referrals is maintained at the internal website accessible only to internal employees for referrals. Employee referrals are viewed as time and cost saving strategy in the recruitment process. There are economic as well as social prestige incentives for employees who refer best applicants from among their social network to work in their firms. Also, the referred candidate would be willing to put in more work with dedication so as to improve the prestige of the person who referred him/her. Thus, social networks play a significant role in employee referrals. On the flip side, however, they reduce the opportunities for those who are not the members of such informal networks despite being better qualified and experienced.

Labour market intermediaries like campus placement cells of educational institutions have emerged as an important method of recruitment for getting fresh talent to the industry at entry-level positions. The demand as well as quality of education is increasingly being judged by the ability of educational institutions to make employment placements of their students. Most of the institutions, therefore, have career guidance and job search assistance cells, commonly known as 'placement cells'. These cells offer career guidance to students and help them to find jobs with suitable occupations and vocational opportunities. They also help students to develop hard as well as soft skills such as personality development skills, communication skills and interview skills. But such placement cells are mainly functional in the educational streams of management, engineering and law, which are more in demand in the labour market. In most other disciplines such as arts, commerce, science and humanities, such placement cells are very few and far between, mainly restricted to reputed universities and institutions.

Nowadays, many firms approach management and engineering educational institutions situated in second or third-tier cities with an aim to get cheaper human resources. Diploma and certificate-level technical and professional institutions such as polytechnics and industrial training institutes (ITI) are also being approached by industry for workmen-level positions. In recent years, apart from various corporate giants, start-ups and SMEs have also taken a step towards campus recruitments from some top institutes. A substantive proportion of our sample firms had approached campus placement cells for hiring students for their core workforce (Table 7.5). The importance of campus placement strategy can be seen in the following statement of the head (business fulfilment, HR & talent deployment) of Cyient Limited–a company providing engineering, manufacturing, geospatial, network and operations management services to global industry leaders:

Campus hiring efforts help us bring in young talent who infuse energy into our work. Their ability to adapt and learn quickly also helps us become more responsive to customers' changing requirements. The young minds provide a fertile ground for the experienced seniors to test and pursue new ideas but not compromising on quality of delivery attained through established engineering or work processes.

Criteria for Screening and Selection of Job Applicants

Screening and selection constitute the most tedious and time consuming activities in every recruitment process. With the use of different channels of job postings and related flow of information, the number of job applicants has increased manifold. However, the signals which job seekers send to employers may be inadequate to assess the applicants. Thus, some firms use the services of HR consultants for job advertisements and screening of applications. Some others use recruitment and placement agencies for screening and the first round of interviews of job applicants, and may get involved after receiving only four to five names for the final interview for managerial and supervisory positions. Employers also collect information from social sites for assessing the social behaviour of job applicants. Firms/recruiters use various criteria for screening and selection of job applicants. In our sample, HR managers were requested to rate on the Likert scale a set of 14 indicators related to education, experience, social background, communication and language skills as the criteria of screening and selection of job applicants. Accordingly, we calculated the mean, standard deviation, entropy and consensus ratios for each indicator by using the method of Tastle and Wierman (2007). The high values of the mean score and consensus ratio show the higher importance attached to a given variable/statement by the HR managers and employers (Tables 7.6a–7.6c).

Almost all HR managers and employers agreed that education, experience, skills and knowledge are important criteria while screening the job applications for interview and final selection as well. They also attached very high score to communication skills and fluency in English language, especially for managerial and supervisory-level positions. The values of high mean scores and consensus ratios are evidence of such preferences by employers/recruiters (Tables 7.6a–7.6c). An MNC firm in Delhi NCR and an auto firm in Pune explicitly agreed that for fresh applicants without any experience at entry-level positions in their firms, they carefully see educational background, family background and the attitude of the applicant. To assess the attitude, they search in him/her attributes of positivity towards work and life,

Table 7.6a *Criteria for Screening and Selection of Applicants: Managerial Jobs*

Variables	Mean	Standard Deviation	Entropy	Consensus Ratio
Education	4.71	0.87	0.53	0.80
Experience	4.58	0.89	0.73	0.78
Technical/job-related skills	4.49	0.90	0.80	0.78
Knowledge/aptitude	4.53	0.89	0.77	0.78
Psychometric tests	3.91	1.29	1.30	0.67
Social background	2.11	1.35	1.36	0.63
Religious background	1.47	0.92	0.82	0.77
Family background	3.47	1.46	1.51	0.58
Rural/urban background	1.84	1.21	1.22	0.68
Institution of education/ training from where applicant got education	3.84	1.36	1.41	0.62
Cultural capital	2.31	1.33	1.24	0.62
Communication skills	4.27	1.14	0.92	0.72
Referrals	3.29	1.42	1.26	0.60
Knowledge of local language	3.73	1.23	1.36	0.69
Knowledge of English language	4.24	1.00	0.89	0.77

Source: Primary field survey (2014–2015).
Note: Calculations based on responses from 45 sample enterprises.

frankness, focus, leadership capabilities and honesty. For experienced applicants, they attach more value to the nature and quality of experience, leadership qualities, team spirit and commitment of the job applicant.

A few respondents attached high value to the social and cultural backgrounds of the job applicants while screening applications and

Table 7.6b *Criteria for Screening and Selection of Applicants: Supervisory Jobs*

Variables	Mean	Standard Deviation	Entropy Index	Consensus Ratio
Education	4.51	0.76	0.84	0.82
Experience	4.51	0.90	0.78	0.78
Technical/job-related skills	4.53	0.94	0.84	0.77
Knowledge/aptitude	4.07	1.10	1.00	0.76
Psychometric tests	1.89	1.28	0.97	0.64
Social background	1.93	1.25	1.26	0.67
Religious background	1.44	0.84	0.85	0.80
Family background	3.91	1.28	1.37	0.67
Rural/Urban background	1.82	1.15	1.20	0.70
Institution of education/training from where applicant got education	3.60	1.25	1.49	0.67
Cultural capital	2.09	1.24	1.24	0.66
Communication skills	4.07	0.99	1.00	0.80
Referrals	3.36	1.38	1.19	0.62
Knowledge of local language	3.73	1.12	1.29	0.73
Knowledge of English language	3.82	1.01	1.18	0.77

Source: Primary field survey (2014–2015).
Note: Calculations based on responses from 45 sample enterprises.

at the time of interview. Such considerations are more pertinent for entry-level positions. However, when the respondents were asked to rank their consideration of applicants' family background, the mean rank value of above three indicates the importance they attach to it. This is quite in contrast to the low mean values of social and religious backgrounds of job applicants with higher consensus ratios, thereby implying that employers were more open to disclosing their preference for assessing family backgrounds of job applicants, but were cautious about disclosing their considerations on social and religious backgrounds as criteria in screening and selection.

Table 7.6c *Criterion for Screening and Selection of Applicants: Entry-Level Jobs*

Variables	Mean	Standard Deviation	Entropy Index	Consensus Ratio
Education	3.31	1.31	1.40	0.65
Experience	3.56	1.04	0.95	0.76
Technical/job-related skills	4.00	1.17	1.21	0.73
Knowledge/aptitude	2.76	1.26	1.53	0.66
Psychometric tests	1.16	0.37	0.43	0.93
Social background	1.82	1.15	1.22	0.70
Religious background	1.38	0.68	0.80	0.85
Family background	3.76	1.26	1.46	0.66
Rural/urban background	1.73	1.07	1.15	0.72
Institution of education/training from where applicant got education	2.91	1.46	1.60	0.59
Cultural capital	1.64	0.91	1.07	0.78
Communication skills	2.98	1.32	1.39	0.67
Referrals	3.91	1.26	1.37	0.68
Knowledge of local language	3.51	1.10	1.34	0.72
Knowledge of English language	2.27	1.25	1.42	0.66

Source: Primary field survey (2014–2015).
Note: Calculations based on responses from 45 sample enterprises.

Exclusionary Practices in Screening and Selection

We have seen how most of the sample firms attach high scores to applicants' attributes such as education, skills, subject knowledge, family background, communication skills, knowledge of English language and referrals in their screening process. For managerial and supervisory-level positions, the reputation of educational institution is also considered while screening applications. A large majority of employers believe that most of the job applicants have poor knowledge and skills, and a huge disconnect with the world of work. This is mainly due to their poor quality of education and training. As a result, employers face shortage of knowledge and skilled people for whom there is obviously a fierce competition in the labour market. Such concerns of poor employability have also been raised by industry forums such as Confederation of Indian Industry (CII), Federation of Indian Chambers of Commerce and Industry (FICCI), National Association of Software and Services Companies (NASSCOM), and also by researchers (World Bank, 2011). While these concerns of employers are genuine, an overemphasis on attributes such as family background, communication skills and English language proficiency even for jobs that do not require such attributes indicates their preconceived notions about how a job applicant should be. Apparently, employers were more open to disclosing their preferences for assessing family backgrounds of job applicants, but they were cautious about acknowledging their considerations regarding the social and religious backgrounds of job applicants. There also exist preconceived notions about the knowledge, skills and productivity of workers of a particular group, explaining the Edmund Phelps (1972) thesis of statistical discrimination, Michael Spence's (1973) argument of information asymmetries, and Amartya Sen's (2000) unfavourable exclusion.

Other attributes which form part of screening and selection process include assessing learning capacity, creativity, stability (job hopping not preferred), educational institute's image and honesty. In a nutshell, private industry claims to select job applicants purely on the basis of their merit.

Our discussions with the select HR managers/employers with respect to prevailing prejudices (about job applicants knowledge, capabilities and productivity), discrimination and resultant under representation of SCs/STs and Muslims in the private sector in India are also quite revealing. Most of them feel that due to poor education and skill base of SC/ST and Muslims, they were unable to offer jobs to applicants belonging to these groups. For improving the employability of SCs/STs and Muslims, they generally argue for more intensive skill training of such groups but for which employers were reluctant to invest in readily. Some employers feel that preferential treatment to SC/STs in recruitment may adversely affect the productivity of their organisations. We also observed a significant number of caste conscious employers, who used a different method of eliciting information on the caste background of a job applicant for screening and selection purposes. This may include reading from surname, demanding caste certificate, etc., for screening and selection processes of job applicants. In case of religious background, it is rather much easier for the employer to identify the job applicants for their recruitment decisions. The prospects of being recruited may be also jeopardised by the common belief of employers about religious practices of certain population groups. For example, employers generally are hesitant to recruit more number of Muslim workers in their firms as they fear that offering Namaz by such workers during working hours affects the workings of their firm. Some also expressed their fear that Muslim workers get quickly united and create problems for the employer.

Questions on family background are often asked by recruiters/ employers to every job applicant, but not necessarily on caste background. A hospitality firm in Pune and an MNC in Delhi NCR argue that persons belonging to relatively better family backgrounds have better education, exposure, confidence, risk-taking behaviour, leadership qualities and future outlook for self and employers.

> The hospitality industry believed that applicants from middle and upper middle class families have command over their communication skills, language skills, business skills and approach to business, and hence suitable for the industry. In contrast, another set of employers argue that family background of the job applicant is assessed to understand the applicant's attitude, need and commitment towards work. They believe that a person belonging to a lower income family generally would be willing to work hard and staying for long with the company unlike a person from a very rich family who would be trying for a job just to get some experience and then switching to other job.

Similar observations are also made in earlier research pertaining to IT industry. Upadhya (2007) argues how in the name of meritocracy a large number of job applicants are simply rejected due to the lack of soft skills in IT industry. In their correspondence study of IT industry in Delhi, Banerjee, Bertrand, Datta, Sugato and Mullianathan (2009) show how Dalit applicants get rejected due to a belief that they may lack soft skills that BPOs emphasise. Many of them may not be benefitting through the employee referrals due to their poor social networks.

In brief, it is clear that in an environment where screening of applications and selections are based on educational background, skills and signalling during interviews, poor education and skills training are generally cited for the high rate of rejection of job applications. In such a scenario, job applicants from poor educational backgrounds such as SCs and Muslims are more likely to get excluded. This partly explains the under-representation of SCs and Muslims in the private sector as many of them face pre-labour market discrimination due to their unequal and discriminatory access to education and skill development opportunities (Sabharwal, Thorat, & Diwakar, 2016). More importantly, we observed a clear form of preconceived notion among HR managers/employers about the abilities of job applicants belonging to certain groups such as SCs and Muslims. This often results in the discrimination of job applicants belonging to SC and Muslim communities in the urban labour market, irrespective of their similar or better attributes than that of applicants from other socio-religious groups.

Difficulties Faced by Employers in Recruitment and Retention of Employees

One of the major concerns of employers in private industry relates to poor employability of job applicants (FICCI, 2010; NASSCOM, 2011; World Bank, 2011). SMEs face comparatively more challenges of getting trained persons. Such concerns are expressed by our sample enterprises. Most of them said that they did face the challenge of getting suitable candidates due to the dearth of adequate skill training. Due to such general shortage of skilled job applicants, there is always a tough competition among firms to attract qualified and skilled persons even through poaching. It is reflected in the following statements:

> Small enterprises have become training workshops for large enterprises for which they need to be compensated by large enterprises and government as well.
>
> —A small industry association in Coimbatore

> Complete disconnect between university education and industry's needs. Rigidity in education system needs to change.
>
> —DICCI, Pune

Trade unionist as well as training experts, however, have a different perspective on the question of shortage of skilled persons, as is reflected in the following two statements:

> Companies are not willing to give any skill development training to the unemployed youth within the company and argue that they are unemployable. This argument is not valid as education and training institutions would only provide broader education and training, and not certainly company-specific training. This role has to be taken up seriously by the industry in its own interest.
>
> —Trade union leader, Pune

> Training is not seriously taken by employers, whereas they always cry for skill shortages. Employers must recognise the long-term impact of training on their productivity and profitability.
>
> —Training expert, Lucknow

More specifically, we have attempted to analyse the ranking of various types of difficulties faced by employers in Table 7.7. Knowledge and skill-specific difficulties are more pertinent with mean values ranging between 3.60 and 3.91 with fairly high degree of consensus ratio among respondents. Due to such shortages of knowledge and skilled persons, there is obviously a fierce competition in the labour market for such persons. Labour market regulations such as labour laws, trade

Table 7.7 Difficulties Faced by Employers in Recruitment of Employees

Type of Difficulty	Mean	Standard Deviation	Entropy Index	Consensus Ratio
Do not get the person as per job specifications	3.91	1.18	1.38	0.70
Subject knowledge of job aspirants is too weak	3.60	1.39	1.46	0.62
Little or no practical knowledge	3.82	1.19	1.41	0.69
Low skill training	3.71	1.29	1.40	0.66
Competition among companies to attract qualified applicants	3.58	1.45	1.46	0.58
Labour laws	1.93	1.12	1.29	0.73
Trade unions	1.58	0.89	1.00	0.78
Local area skill base is poor	2.31	1.47	1.43	0.58
Political interference	1.73	1.01	1.11	0.75
Locational disadvantage of company	1.62	1.05	1.01	0.74

Source: Primary field survey (2014–2015).

unions and political interference are no more difficulties as shown in low mean values (Table 7.7). Most of the respondents agreed that these institutions of labour market are very supportive and nowhere creating any hindrances relating to recruitment of workers either on regular or contractual basis. This finding is contrary to what is being propagated by the proponents of labour flexibility for business development.

Difficulties Faced in Retaining Workforce

As shown earlier in Table 7.3, private industry, particularly MSMEs, face a major challenge of high attrition rate of their workforce. The reasons for such high rate of attrition include career prospects, salary, and other monetary and non-monetary benefits, learning opportunities, work culture, distance from work, employees' voice in decision-making processes, etc. A glimpse of such concerns is reflected in the following statements by employers:

> Local labourers are mostly educated and not willing to work in SMEs. Most of the labour comes from Bihar and Odisha. They are hardworking and do not create any major problems. But they also leave the company frequently even for minor salary gains.
>
> —Small entrepreneur, Coimbatore

> Acquisition and retention of talent are major problems in SMEs.
>
> —DICCI, Pune

> Retention is a problem in the hotel industry. There is about 80 per cent job hopping in the hotel industry.
>
> —Hospitality industry, Lucknow

Enterprises argue that in the cut-throat competitive environment to attract experienced and skilled workers, it becomes difficult to afford higher salaries to workers. Such concerns are largely among the SMEs. Many enterprises are not willing to train their workers for a long period due to non-affordability of such training and also the fear of losing trained workers after training. This dilemma has always been the concern of MSMEs.

For avoiding labour shortages and minimising overall labour costs, employers favour the use of job-specific contractual workers, many times from staffing companies.

> Contractual labour is the necessity of firms. Company (staffing) ensures that such workers get the benefits of employees' provident fund (EPF), gratuity, bonus and paid leave. To ensure this, the user company makes an agreement with the contracting firm about facilities to be provided to contact workers and demands salary slip of each contact worker.
>
> —Chemical firm in Delhi NCR

There is a huge usage of contract labour in Pune industries. Most of the contract labour firms are controlled/managed by those who have had criminal cases against them. They are now white-collar politicians controlling labour supply to industry.

—Sr journalist, Pune

Labour contractors/agents supply hassle free labour to SMEs.

—Textile industry, Coimbatore.

Table 7.8 sheds light on such concerns of employers relating to retention of their employees. The major difficulties faced by employers are high turnover of workers for better career prospects and cut-throat competition among enterprises for attracting experienced and skilled workforce. The high mean values of 4.4 and 4.2, and consensus ratio of about 78 and 76 indicate a large majority of respondents

Table 7.8 Difficulties Faced by Employers in Retaining Employees

Type of Difficulty	Mean	Standard Deviation	Entropy Index	Consensus Ratio
Cannot afford to pay high salaries	3.73	0.99	1.11	0.78
Cannot afford to train workers for a long period	3.53	1.08	1.25	0.73
Worker looking for better opportunities	4.40	0.92	0.92	0.78
Cut-throat competition to attract workers within industries	4.16	1.04	1.09	0.76
Government interference/regulations	1.98	1.18	1.33	0.70
Indulgence of workers in trade union activities	1.64	0.96	1.08	0.76
Difficult to get workers loyal to company	3.04	1.26	1.45	0.65
Locational disadvantage of company	1.64	0.93	1.05	0.77

Source: Primary field survey (2014–2015).

acknowledging these two major problems in retaining their workforce. There was a mixed rating of difficulties pertaining to higher salaries, training and loyalty of workers with high order of consensus, showing these as difficulties of moderate order. The mean value of less than two with high consensus ratio for difficulties such as government regulations, trade unions and location disadvantages indicate that most of the respondents do not see these as a major problem in retaining their workforce.

Conclusion

Hiring or recruitment methods by employers have undergone significant changes in India with the advent and penetration of IT. However, these differ in various economic sectors/sub-sectors and geographical/administrative regions. Based on our analysis of job screening, selection practices and statements by recruiters/HR managers/employers in the private sector in this chapter, the following observations have been deduced:

Employers' recruitment policy is largely focused on retaining core human resource on a full-time basis, particularly at the senior management and supervisor level, and reducing the costs of human resources. For this, the policy is to hire manpower at lower levels on contractual basis either through staffing companies or by the employer himself on a contract of one to two years.

Enterprises, particularly small and medium, face high attrition rates and resultant higher magnitude of recruitment. This often affects employers' recruitment costs, productivity and competitiveness. Employers are highly concerned about the quality of the new hires for ensuring maximum productivity, competitiveness, cost reduction and profitability of their enterprises. Workers are simply seen as a resource without any concern for their tenurial, emotional and social security, dignity, and above all being humans. The growing use of contract labour and worsening employment conditions is a testimony of this trend.

We found the share of SCs and Muslims in new recruitments under the category of core employees significantly lower than their share in population. This also corroborates the earlier observation of proportionately low representation of SCs/STs and Muslims in private sector employment. Employers often desire workers with education and knowledge along with skills such as communication, language proficiency, self-esteem and team spirit, which have little relevance on the performance of the job, and tend to favour candidates with better social and economic endowments (e.g., fluency in spoken English). They argue that their recruitment processes are highly competitive and merit based, and factors such as caste, region, gender and class are irrelevant. But the merit argument ignores the social and economic factors that produce 'meritorious' candidates in the first place, especially the continuing monopoly of a small proportion of socially and economically privileged groups over the best educational institutions and a large majority of others including marginalised groups bereft of such advantage (Upadhya, 2007).

With preconceived notions among employers regarding the merit of job applicants with relatively poor education and skill training, and weak social networks, they are more likely of being left out in the screening stage of the recruitment process. Unfortunately, the chances of SC/ST and Muslim job applicants get adversely affected due to their perceived low levels of education and training. This is known as endowment effect which explains a large variation in their employment and earnings in the labour market (Madheswaran, 2014).

Employee referrals and social networks as a method of job information dissemination and thereafter preferences in recruitment by employers have reduced the chances of employment of those equally educated, skilled and experienced but not having access to such networks in the labour market. Job seekers such as SCs and Muslims with weak social networks find it difficult to gain entry into private sector jobs. This in itself questions the IT-enabled flow of job information, which remains asymmetric.

The stereotype views among employers about the capabilities of certain social groups such as SCs and Muslims are indicative of the existence of Phelps's (1972) 'statistical discrimination' or Becker's (1971) 'taste of discrimination' in the Indian private sector industry. The over emphasis on family background, communication and language skills even for jobs that do not require such skills, and employee referrals put many job applicants from poor and SC/Muslim backgrounds on the back foot. Under-representation of SCs/STs and other marginalised groups remains a challenge for social policy. Employers are least concerned about the social diversity of their workforce (Kundu, 2004). This perpetuates social stratification with far-reaching impact on social and economic inequalities (Castilla & Benard, 2010; Dobbin, Kalev, & Kelly, 2007; Kelly & Dobbin, 1998). Unlike the big multinational companies (MNCs) and Western corporate sector, Indian private sector employers including our sample employers have hardly any policies and programmes for promoting social diversity among their workforce and reducing social inequality in their enterprises. The lackadaisical approach to AAP and programmes by the private corporate sector bears testimony to the attitudes and social concerns of the industry to reduce the existing social and economic inequalities in the country. The Indian industry needs to acknowledge these facts and come forward to strengthen the social diversity of its workforce through AA in a big way as part of corporate social responsibility.

CHAPTER 8

Discrimination and Promoting Inclusive Employment Opportunities

Introduction

We have seen how the Indian economy suffers with the deficit of quality employment opportunities for its overwhelming majority of population. A fairly high economic growth in India, particularly during last three decades after the economic reforms, had less than the desired impact on the employment growth, which has not been sufficient to clear the backlog of unemployment along with additions to the labour force. More so, a rapid contractualisation of employment opportunities and depletion in social security of workers have made employment precarious and vulnerable to income fluctuations. It was expected that a rapid growth in urbanisation and consequent expansion of economic opportunities therein would accelerate employment opportunities to absorb maximum additions to the labour force in the country in a Lewisian framework of economic transformation. This was expected to be non-discriminatory wherein opportunities are accessible to everyone irrespective of their caste, ethnicity and religious background. The prevalent policies and programmes have achieved only limited success in shifting labour from the less remunerative agriculture sector to other sectors for ensuring decent employment. After over six decades of planned economic development, half the Indian workforce is still employed in agriculture. In this backdrop, the country is still grappling with the issues of rising unemployment and ever-increasing disenchantment among the youth. An overwhelming proportion of workers still derive their livelihoods from low-income activities in the unorganised sector and have no access to the benefits of social security (see Kannan, 2014; NCEUS, 2009). This is because a large proportion of the job opportunities arising in the public sector and large private enterprises are contractual and informal in nature, which do not offer any social security benefits.

Similarly, the firms operating in the informal economy are often small and face barriers to growth, which prevent them from offering high-quality goods and services. And with the opening up of the Indian economy, the informal sector has also been acting as a default sector for workers who lose their jobs, thereby further depressing decent working standards, which would not occur if alternative employment opportunities were available in the formal economy. In a nutshell, informal sector firms lack the capacity to generate sufficient profits for rewarding innovation and risk-taking, two essential ingredients for achieving long-term economic success. The globalisation process has also added new sources of external shocks, leading to increasing informality of employment and rising vulnerability among the workforce.

The access to decent employment opportunities, particularly in the private sector, is limited as SCs/STs as compared to OCs continue to be disproportionately dependent more on casual wage employment. Meanwhile, discrimination based on caste, ethnicity and religion in the labour, capital and various other markets continues to haunt the Indian society. This hampers the equal participation of the discriminated groups in the growth process and results in the loss of income opportunities. In this scenario, ensuring decent employment with the dignity of labour while instituting the appropriate institutional mechanisms for a large proportion of the Indian labour force still remains a major concern.

Although there is a rich body of the literature available on examining the role of employment policies and programmes in promoting employment opportunities (IHD & ISLE, 2014; NCEUS, 2009), a little is known about promoting inclusive opportunities, particularly in the context of private enterprises from the perspective of marginalised social groups. It is in this context that this chapter briefly discusses various forms of discrimination and exclusion that prevail in the labour market, and argues for developing 'equal opportunity policies'.

Nature, Forms and Magnitude of Discrimination

Information, Belief and Discrimination in Labour Market

Most of the studies show how lack of access to information to both job seekers and employers creates inefficient outcomes in the labour market (Stigler, 1962). Many a time such imperfect information creates segmentations and duality in labour markets (Papola, 1981, 2005). It is argued that due to imperfect information or belief, employers may discriminate job seekers belonging to a particular group or region (Arrow, 1972; Phelps, 1972). Beliefs can also reflect prejudices, for example, negative stereotypes of certain groups. Belief-based discrimination is a market-based explanation for discrimination, which does not require a taste for discrimination. Persistent discrimination reduces the confidence of victims and undermines their self-esteem, as they begin to believe themselves to be of low worth. This is termed as 'implicit discrimination' by Bertrand, Chugh and Mullainathan (2005). It can discourage the motivation of equipping oneself for advancement in educational and skill levels among the discriminated group. C. Jeffrey, R. Jeffery and P. Jeffery (2004) find how Muslims in Bijnor

(Uttar Pradesh) experienced discrimination in the job market, which discouraged them to invest further in the education of their children.

In Chapter 4, we have demonstrated how social networks and employee referrals have emerged as major sources of job information to job seekers in the urban labour market. Job seekers from lower-caste groups or marginalised groups employ social network as a job search method to a greater extent as compared to higher caste groups. Job seekers with a high level of education do not employ social network as job search method as intensively as compared to the job seekers with low level of education. More so, the outcome of job search depends significantly on the quality of networks. If the referral is a person in a high position, the likelihood of job realisation for the referred candidate is very high and it may fetch high income offer as well. Marginalised groups are generally characterised by the poor quality of social networks, thus creating differential labour market outcomes in terms of employment, wages and other benefits. Social networks are generally helpful in getting access to low-paid jobs and that too at the bottom of occupational hierarchies. Our results show how open access to job information is used by just about 22 per cent of job seekers, implying the limitations of free access to job information in the labour market despite the deep penetration of IT in recent years. Employers are still using social networks of workers to disseminate job information, mainly for low-end jobs. This is mainly to reduce the cost of recruitments and to control the new hire through his social contact. Thus, job seekers who are not part of such networks are less likely to get jobs. Some of our respondents expressed their concerns about the closed-door nature of job information for most of the job openings, particularly in the private sector. In other words, social networks also mean discriminating those who are not a member of those networks. Ironically, social networks based on caste and community linkages are gradually waning in their importance. They are being replaced by 'friendship networks' developed during education and professional life. Friendship networks are gaining importance in job search in the urban labour market. They may not be necessarily based on caste and community bonding. In a recent study of Tiruppur and Ludhiana apparel manufacturing industries, Uchikawa (2017) finds social networks functioning beyond caste and community. This is in contrast with earlier works which show how clusters of industries are divided on caste and social backgrounds of owners as well as workers (Banerjee & Munshi, 2004; Swaminathan & Jeyaranjan, 1999). Thus, we see that networks, which are exclusionary in their basic character, are being increasingly used as a substitute to job information flow.

We tried to understand the discrimination at workplace from those job seekers who are actively searching another job. They were asked the reasons for their job search. The prominent reason for job search among SCs/STs was their low income, whereas for other social groups (OCs), it was mainly for enhancing career prospects. The reasons for job search due to harassment and discrimination at workplace are not explicitly stated by women and SCs/STs. They may face discrimination at the entry level in the labour market, specifically in job search and selection. For this, we illustrate the experiences of job seekers during selection processes in the following section.

Discrimination on the Basis of 'Medium of Instruction'

Our survey results revealed that nearly one-fifth of the respondents faced difficulty in their written test/interview simply due to the medium of written test/interview. About 28 per cent of OBCs and 18 per cent of SCs faced this type of difficulty as compared to 14 per cent of OCs (Table 8A.1). A high preference for proficiency in English language by a vast majority of large-size enterprises also indicates how job applicants with poor English and communication skills are generally screened out from the final selection. Perhaps, due to this, English-medium schools are becoming popular and an essential requirement for the disadvantaged groups, especially girls, after the neoliberal policies of 1991 opened up diverse economic opportunities (Munshi & Rosenzweig, 2005). Ito (2009) and Chakravarty and Somanathan (2008) find that a large part of the unobserved component of discrimination pertains to the educational attainment of backward and disadvantaged groups rather than discrimination only on the basis of caste. This pre-labour market discrimination is primarily due to the deterioration in government school education over the years on which marginalised groups largely depend for their educational development. Due to the absence of any serious attempt to equalise school-level opportunities, the current policy of reservations at elite educational institutions remains insufficient to equalise career outcomes even for the minuscule number of SC/ST candidates who can benefit from them (Chakravarty & Somanathan, 2008).

Questions about Caste/Religion/Belief

A substantive number of job seekers feel that they were asked questions about their caste, religions and faith, which have no relation to the job for which they appeared for interview. Over one-tenth of OBCs and SCs faced this difficulty at the time of their interviews in private sector jobs as compared to 5 per cent by those from OCs. Similarly, a substantive number of job applicants belonging to OBCs and SCs narrated how they had been ridiculed for their knowledge and how interviewers had used demeaning language with them. Surprisingly, OBCs and STs were more forthright in answering such questions than SCs (Table 8A.1). This may be due to the fact that SCs were hesitant to reveal their experiences more openly. Such biases that emerge can be discerned clearly if one looks at the success rate in interviews. It has been the lowest for STs, followed by SCs and the highest for OCs, followed by OBCs (Table 8A.1). This could be largely due to the differing individual endowments but also partly due to the prejudices of employers about the abilities of marginalised groups and their weak social networks.

Discrimination in Wage Offers

An employer offering differential wages for a similar type of work to persons belonging to various social groups is also a form of discrimination. Yet another form of discrimination may be the offer of lower wages than that mentioned in the job advertisement. A highest 41 per cent of SCs who were selected for a job said that they were offered less wages than that mentioned in the advertisement. Next to SCs were OBC job seekers who reported lower wage offers by employers. The proportion of such respondents reporting lower salary offers than advertisements was comparatively low among OCs as 32 per cent among them said so (Table 8A.1). It emerged from the discussion that employers generally tend to offer lower salaries particularly to those applying for low-end jobs, where employers receive a large number of applicants. This makes applicants vulnerable to accept the offer even at lower salaries than mentioned in the advertisements or without a substantive hike over their current jobs. However, in critical skill areas, a worker is generally in a better position to negotiate with employers who in turn eventually agree to offer. Though there are industry-specific surveys of prevailing wages and salaries available with the job seekers as well employers, these generally act just as a guiding force but ultimately leave much to the discretion of employers.

Gender Discrimination

The share of women in salaried employment is proportionately very low. According to NSSO estimates, share of women in total regular employment stood at 19.6 per cent in 2011–2012. If we combine casual wage employment, their share was 26.2 per cent. In urban areas, the share of women in wage employment (including both regular and casual employment) was 19.5 per cent. As seen in chapter 6, women's share in the total employment in our sample firms was just 22.5 per cent. The main reasons for low representation of women in work-force is primarily related to their low work participation rates, which tended to decline over the years due to a variety of reasons. These include higher participation in education, withdrawal from work with improvement in family incomes, and persistence of social taboo and patriarchal influence on women, particularly in urban areas who are educated and well qualified but desist from joining the labour force (Rustagi, 2017).

Gender-based discrimination is cited as one of the reasons for such low proportion of women in salaried jobs in India. A study of biases at workplace by *The Economic Times* (2013) covering 800 companies across the top eight cities in India—New Delhi, Mumbai, Chennai, Kolkata, Bengaluru, Hyderabad, Pune and Ahmedabad, shows high incidence of discrimination against women in recruitment and at their places of work. It reveals how pregnant women or women with young children are at a relative disadvantage, both during the recruitment process as well as vying for opportunities at the workplace. Similarly, women are also discriminated based on their colour and looks. Surprisingly, the study claims that discrimination on the basis of caste and religion has become almost obsolete. It argues for a complete and clear policy on reservation with proper enforcement; else productivity will be adversely affected (TeamLease, 2016).

There are a number of studies which show women facing various forms of discrimination in their entry to the labour market and during their career progression. They are discriminated in their access to managerial positions more frequently despite being equally qualified as male applicants for such positions (Haefne, 1977; Terborg & Ilgen, 1975). Women also face discrimination in promotions as they are required to be more qualified than their male counterparts (Olson & Becker, 1983), thus were receiving fewer promotions than similarly or even less qualified males (Olson & Becker, 1983); consequently having less opportunity for their career advancement (Cox, 1994). Women also face barriers in their career progression due to their exclusion from informal networks (Gupta, Koshal, & Koshal, 1998) that are believed to be in male domains. The incidence of such politics becomes still higher in a diverse, multi-lingual, ethnic and caste-based Indian society. Women face discrimination in work allocations due to the persistence of stereotypes about their capabilities, resultantly adversely affecting their career prospects and getting crowded in low-paying jobs. They are seldom given challenging and risk-taking jobs during the allocation of jobs. Due to such prejudices and stereotypes, requisite credit is not given to women, which has had an adverse impact on their performance (Khandelwal, 2002).

Nonetheless, women are gradually breaking such stereotypes whenever they get the opportunity. With the improvement in their education, women are playing a significant role in the expansion of the Indian software industry, where they constitute 45 per cent of the high-tech workforce (Budhwar, Saini, & Bhatnagar, 2005). It is argued that by promoting diversity at workplace productivity also improves. There are examples of Pepsi and ICICI which have more than 60 per cent women employees and both companies are known to be doing quite well; these could be interesting examples to build on affirmative measures for promoting women employment (Woodard & Saini, 2006).

Dalit women face double disadvantage: the stereotype of being 'weak' and 'non-meritorious' spills into workplaces as well despite their entry into private companies purely on 'merit' basis. Christina Thomas Dhanaraj narrates how 'lunch table conversations that veer around caste invariably end up in debating the need for caste-based AA policies, which most often are seen as unnecessary by the majority'. There is always a fear of being branded as Dalit if someone argues in the favour of reservation or against the caste system. In all likelihood, this may result in hostility from colleagues, both male and female. But hiding doesn't always mask one's caste identity either. 'Given that it is commonplace, almost casual, to discuss one's caste background, caste markers such as religion, surnames and skin colour give it away fairly easily' (The Wire, March 2017). Dalit women lack social networking which is generally perceived as a successful strategy for career progression in the corporate sector. This means that caste affiliations could help non-Dalit women where gender fails, leaving Dalit women completely helpless even within 'merit-based' private companies (The Wire, March 2017).

The nature and magnitude of discrimination that women face in their employment is revealed more vividly in a survey of 500 working women across 10 cities by the Associated Chambers of Commerce and Industry of India (ASSOCHAM's) Social Development Foundation during 2016. It shows how about one-fourth of the women respondents wanted to quit their jobs primarily due to the gender bias together with harassment, inconvenient working hours and pay gap at their workplaces. About 30 per cent of the women respondents had experienced harassment at work, and were denied promotion and plum assignments. Most of the respondents said that their organisations did not have redressal mechanisms in place and as such do not comply with legal requirements to provide a safe workplace for women, and display a very casual approach to such issues (ASSOCHAM, 2016, as reported in *Economic Times* 7 March 2016).

In brief, the existence of discrimination of various forms is a reality in the labour market. This may be a complete denial of jobs to a certain group of job seekers based on stereotypes or generalisation of information about an individual or the whole group (statistical discrimination); inclusion but at differing terms and conditions of employment such as low wage offers for the same job, unequal treatment in career progression and harassment at work. We have argued that discrimination could be one of the possible explanations for low representation of SCs, STs, Muslims and women in the private sector in India apart from their relatively poor endowments such as education, skills, experience and quality of social networks. These disadvantaged groups also face discrimination in their access to quality education and skill training, which again adversely affect their labour market outcomes in terms of access to quality jobs and income.

Hiring Practices and Discrimination

The private sector's arguments of 'meritocracy' in their recruitment and retention policies may be somewhat justifiable by the proponents of free market economies. However, recent researches on diversity in workplaces clearly show how it promotes the private firms' productivity and competitiveness. These studies also show how majority of firms remain ignorant about the impact of diversity of human resources due to their preconceived beliefs about the abilities of certain groups of population like women, SCs, STs and Muslims (Woodard & Saini, 2006). Such beliefs act as hindrances in promoting workplace diversity and affect employment opportunities for women, SCs, STs and Muslims.

Along with information asymmetries, statistical discrimination has been found to be a major tool of screening and sorting job applications by employers. Employers' commonly argue that they practise highly competitive recruitment processes wherein they hire employees only on the basis of merit, and factors such as caste, region, gender and class are 'irrelevant'. But merit argument ignores social and economic factors that produce 'meritorious' candidates in the first place, thus continuing the monopoly of a small proportion of socially and economically privileged groups over the best educational institutions and a large majority of others including marginalised groups remaining bereft of such advantage (Deshpande, 2010; Upadhya, 2007). In fact, the discriminatory processes set in since the early stages of human capital formation, produce the so called 'quality human resources' mainly from better off sections of the society; while others including marginalised groups toiling for their livelihoods have no access to such quality education. It is also true that not all firms in the private sector deliberately practise caste (or any other kind of) discrimination in recruitment. Rather the worker profile required by industry like out-sourcing business makes it more difficult for people from non-urban and lower caste/class backgrounds to enter, because certain social and cultural attributes are thought to be necessary to work in a 'global' environment, which the latter group had no access to.

A number of correspondence studies have confirmed the prevailing bias among employers for a call back of applicants with similar qualifications and experience yet belonging to various social, ethnic and religious groups. For example, Bertrand and Mullainathan (2004) sent almost 5,000 fictitious resumes with randomly assigned black-or white-sounding names to more than 1,200 help-wanted ads in Boston and Chicago. *Ceteris paribus*, white-sounding names received about 50 per cent more call backs. In a similar study in India, Thorat and Newman (2010) show how SC and Muslim applicants, who are equally or better qualified than higher caste applicants, are less likely to pass through hiring screen among employers in the modern formal sector in India. Such caste and religious prejudices among employers seriously hamper employment opportunities for SCs and Muslims. The managers in the private organised sector bring to the hiring process a set of stereotypes that makes it difficult for very low caste applicants to succeed in the competition for position (Jodhka & Newman, 2010). However, there are mixed experiences of such discrimination. Banerjee, Bertrand, Datta and Mullianathan (2009) observed no significant difference in call back rates for IT sector software jobs among applicants from different social groups; whereas in call centre jobs, large and significant differences in call back rates were observed among upper castes and OBCs, and, to some extent, SCs and STs. Since call centre jobs require soft skills, a preconceived bias of employers about inadequate or lack of such skills among OBCs and SCs would have resulted in screening out of such applicants.

Similar to Indian experiences, the prevalence of discrimination in hiring by firms is also reported in the United Kingdom, the United States of America, South Asia and Ireland among others. In the United Kingdom, white-sounding names were twice as likely as others to be shortlisted for jobs. The then British Prime Minister called this a 'disgraceful' practice in the labour market and initiated a new programme of 'name blind recruitment plan' in which employers do not know applicants' names when they are selecting them for interviews (The Times of India, 2015). Some big companies such as the Hongkong and Shanghai Banking Corporation (HSBC), Deloitte, the British Broadcasting Corporation (BBC) and the National Health Service had signed up for this programme but details about its success are so far scanty.

In a study of job placements of 242 final-year students of IIM Ahmedabad, Chakravarty and Somanathan (2008) observed gaps in wage offers among SC/ST and NSC/ST students were a fifth and a third lower than those in the general category. 'This has not been associated with their caste but with poor academic backgrounds for which they are heavily penalized in the elite job market' (p. 50).

Our results of employers' preferences and arguments for their hiring purely on 'merit' basis discussed in Chapter 7 also show how employers harbour various kinds of prejudices about the abilities of the marginalised groups. We argue here that 'merit'-based selections may be the necessity of the private sector to remain competitive. However, employers' general beliefs about merit may create a form of statistical discrimination wherein a relatively less meritorious person from 'Other' or general group is selected at the cost of a meritorious person belonging to a 'discriminated' group. We have already shed some light on job information, screening processes, and the views of employers about giving preferential treatment in their selections to applicants belonging to marginalised communities and women towards improving social diversity in their enterprises in the previous chapter. We also argued that job applicants from poor family, rural background and first-generation learners face difficulty in the urban labour market as many of them lag behind in the screening and selection criteria, particularly when employers look seriously at their educational and family background, and soft skills. Many of them may not be befitting through the employee referrals due to their poor social networks. Here, we briefly discuss employers' views regarding workplace diversity and inclusion while creating employment opportunities in their enterprises.

Social Diversity, Reservation and Inclusion

As is seen in the previous chapter, private enterprises are least diversified in terms of their social composition of workforce. Most of the research, though limited, has interpreted social diversity with respect to gender balance at workplaces, and generally missed out the issues of under-representation of marginalised groups in the industry. On the question of promoting social diversity at workplaces through reservation of jobs in the private sector, almost all employers were opposed to such proposals (for a detailed debate on reservation in the private sector, see Thorat & Negi, 2007). Their fears are a typical example of their misplaced beliefs about the competencies of workers belonging to certain groups, as reflected in the following statements:

If reservation is made for private sector employment, the industry would not get trained and qualified persons. Why should industry suffer then? Let the government continue with its reservation policy for SCs/STs for promoting their employment.

—(Pharmaceutical Industry, Pune)

Reservation should be provided only in education—provide them quality education and enable them to face the competition in the job market. Create awareness among SCs/STs to seek/demand quality education. Reservation is only benefitting the better offs among SCs/STs.

—(Hotel, Delhi)

I am ready to provide employment opportunities to every group of job seekers. But my major concern is of getting skilled persons for my company. How reservation is going to solve this problem of the industry? I do not have resources to first train a person and then use his/her services.

—(Textiles industry, Coimbatore)

In brief, the trouble is that most corporate entities consider caste as a problem that the government should look at and resolve. However, a few, such as Lupin and Tata, do try and fix their hiring strategies to be more inclusive (Gupta, 2016).

HR Managers and Their Sensitivities for Workplace Diversity

In the recent years, workplace diversity has emerged as a core issue in management theories and practices in Western countries (Konrad, Prasad, & Pringle, 2006). Accordingly, diversity management (DM) is being recognised as one of the critical elements of business success in the strategic human resource management (HRM) literature (Saini, 2007). As a core strategy of DM, many MNCs have policies for promoting diversity of human resources in their organisations. Such practices are yet to percolate in the private industry in India. Though HR managers in India are well aware about the socio-cultural diversity of India, they are often less trained in understanding the processes and consequences of such diversities, which arise with a long history of exclusion and discrimination, thereby adversely impacting upon the overall well-being. As a result, they tend to become 'diversity neutral' and become over concerned about meritocracy, productivity and organisational development (Woodard & Saini, 2006). The Tata Group of companies also recognised low levels of sensitivity towards social diversity among their senior and middle-level management leaders (see website of Tata Group of Companies). This is also due to the fact that a large majority of employees in managerial positions in the private sector belong to general caste as observed in the previous chapter. In the case of employees too, workplace diversity is not valued by the general category employees as strongly as others. This also means that the general category employees did not value increasing hiring and retaining, increasing diversity or representation, and providing equal access of development opportunities to minority, disabled, and socially disadvantaged groups (Kundu, 2004). However, there are encouraging examples such as Tata group of companies, which periodically organises sensitisation programmes on diversity and inclusion for senior and middle-management leaders with an aim to promote social diversity in their workplaces (see website of Tata Group of Companies).

Affirmative Action Policy and Social Diversity at Workplaces

The Constitution of India confers certain basic rights on all citizens under 'the fundamental rights'. In the context of diversity issues, the relevant fundamental rights include—the right to equality (Article 14); prohibition of discrimination on grounds of religion, race, caste, sex or place of birth (Article 15); equality of opportunity in matters of public employment (Article 16); and abolition of untouchability (Article 17). Article 17 of the Constitution declares that untouchability in any and every form has been abolished, and cannot be practised in any part of the country. Despite such comprehensive constitutional guarantees, untouchability is still practised (Shah, Mander, Thorat, Deshpande,

& Bhaviskar, 2006), which is the worst category of unequal treatment to humans that one can think of. Unfortunately, the caste system is deeply embedded in the Indian society and it still coexists despite the fast pace of urbanisation, industrialisation and the spread of mass education; and constitutional commitment to egalitarian social order. The public or government sector has comprehensive policy of AA or positive discrimination by extending the reservation in public sector employment, education and representation in politics. Such measures have made a significant impact on the presence of SCs/STs and later OBCs in public sector employment and in their educational progression. However, the gradual decline of the public sector after globalisation has adversely affected employment opportunities, more so for SCs/STs and OBCs. The private sector has now become the major employment-generating sector, although its growth has been very slow.

The private corporate sector, particularly, argues against the reservation policy on the grounds that it follows fair methods of employment, and hence disregards the need of any anti-discrimination measures. The argument that there is no discrimination in recruitment in the private sector is largely contrary to the empirical evidences obtained from studies on the working of the Indian labour markets. There is considerable evidence to show that the private sector follows recruitment methods that are discriminatory and exclusionary, resulting in low representation of women, SCs, STs and Muslims therein (Madheswaran, 2017; Thorat & Newman, 2010). The arguments that reservation might lead to decline in productivity and efficiency do not stand statistical scrutiny (Deshpande & Weisskopf, 2014). Such an approach has generally created social and economic inequalities, as discussed earlier, in the job market, and needs to be addressed for achieving the goal of more inclusive development as outlined in the 12th Five Year Plan of Government of India and recently in the UN Sustainable Development Goals (UNSDG). To overcome such disadvantage in the labour market, there has been a demand for extending reservation in employment in private sector jobs. This, however, led to a flutter among academicians, social thinkers and practitioners (see Thorat & Negi, 2007), the outcome of which was an assurance to the prime minister in 2006 by the industry agreeing to implement AA for the marginalised groups. In 2007, CII, backed by ASSOCHAM and FICCI, came up with a formal AAP outlining 'AA agendas' to 'embed' SC/ST communities in four areas, namely, employment, employability, entrepreneurship and education (four Es). Some major corporate groups such as Tata, Mahindra & Mahindra, Infosys, Godrej, Hindustan Unilever Ltd, Shri Ram Fibres (SRF) Ltd spelt out their AA agendas in that policy document (CII, 2007).

There are few corporate houses such as the Tata group of companies who have put in place CEO-led AA committees to decide their AA strategy and oversee the implementation of the related programmes. For improving employability and entrepreneurship abilities of SC/ST communities, the Tata group is helping in creating and promoting access to quality education and technical skills, and competencies for members of these traditionally marginalised groups. Twenty-four Tata companies have spent close to ₹70 million on more than 13,000 scholarships for students from the marginalised communities. In addition, 25 companies have spent ₹7 million per annum on 140-plus scholarships, given in partnership with the Foundation for Academic Excellence and Access to meritorious poor students enrolled in professional colleges. Thirty-four Tata companies have active skill development programmes in which nearly 16,000 youth from SC/ST communities were trained in various trades in 2011–2012. Many Tata companies have development programmes to encourage vendor-entrepreneurs from the marginalised communities. The Group periodically organises sensitization programmes on diversity and inclusion for its officials and leaders in senior and middle-management level (see website of Tata Group of Companies).

Like-wise, ICICI Manipal, has set up a Probationary Officers Programme for underprivileged students, who are generally Dalits. The programme functions like a finishing school which prepares students with the necessary soft skills, including a good knowledge of spoken English, so that they join the Bank far more confidently and assimilate with fellow officers from more privileged backgrounds.

Due to its voluntary nature, there has been no major progress in the programmes of corporate houses as envisaged under AAP. Many corporate houses and other larger enterprises are taking developmental initiatives under 'corporate social responsibility' but not necessarily addressing the aforementioned four Es. In SMEs concerns, such policy initiatives are almost missing. Not a single of our sample firm in the small and medium segment had any knowledge of AAP. Researchers have shown that organisations that have gender diversity at all levels are more likely to succeed than those which do not (Gupte, 2003). The same holds true for social diversity in organisations.

There are encouraging international experiences of reduction of socio-economic inequality through legal protection against discrimination in the form of Equal Employment Opportunity Laws (EEOL). Such laws prohibit any private or public employer from discrimination of workers or persons based on group identities such as religion, gender, colour, ethnicity, national and social origin, and provide legal safeguards to the discriminated groups in the event of discrimination in employment, ownership in businesses and other spheres of economic activities. The EEOL (Executive Order 11246) in USA, Fair Employment Act in Northern Ireland, Black Economic Empowerment in South Africa and the New Economic Policy of Malaysia are some examples of positive discrimination. These policies, particularly in the case of Malaysia and South Africa, have been criticised for favouring a small section of those population groups for whom such policies were made, thereby creating inefficiency and inequality in the overall distributional systems (Economist, 2013).

The Indian experience of affirmative policies is much older than the other two major AA-practising economies, that is, the USA and Malaysia. However, these policies are limited to providing reservation in public sector employment, education and political representation. These polices have made a significant impact on the upward mobility of SCs/STs (Heyer & Jayal, 2009). As in India, in other countries too these policies have been criticised for their inadequacies and limited impact on the upliftment of the larger section of such marginalised groups. Irrespective of these limitations, the concerns in the present day context are decreasing employment opportunities in the public sector and increasing privatisation of higher and technical education. The increase in contractual jobs in the public sector has not only led to deterioration in the quality of employment but also impacted upon the opportunities for SCs/STs in such jobs, as there is no provision of reservation in contract jobs. Similarly, the deteriorating standard of public sector educational institutions, particularly at the school level, has had more adverse impact on marginalised groups, who are more dependent on those institutions. The government schools are facing a situation of segregation as they are attended mainly by the children from poorer sections of the society, largely comprising marginalised groups. These developments have seriously eroded the employment opportunities, and employability of the poor and marginalised sections of the Indian society. The private sector needs to take these factors into consideration and come forward in a big way in improving the fours Es of such groups, and contribute towards reducing social and economic inequalities to a significant extent. The larger questions and myths about positive discrimination policies creating inefficiency in the economic systems can only be neutralised with intensive sensitisation programmes on social diversity and inclusion by private as well as public sector enterprises for their middle and senior-level employees.

Today, the big challenge is how to persuade the private sector to embed social diversity in its employment process. Since the promised affirmative measures are still a distant cry from reality, there is a need to use the 'carrot' instead of 'stick' to promote diversity. Kundu (GoI-Ministry of Minority Affairs 2014) suggests that since 85 per cent of the private companies are dependent on the public sector for support such as land at concessional rates, export subsidies, contract from public companies, tax benefits and concessional finance, it should be made clear to these companies that if they violate a specified diversity index, those incentives will be reduced.

Policy Imperatives

India like many other countries is facing a major challenge of creating decent employment opportunities to a large segment of its labour force.

The declining employment elasticity of growth since the neoliberal economic reforms of 1991 put forth a bigger and more fundamental question in the growth–employment relationship. A large proportion of regular employment on offer fall short of quality, characterised as poor working conditions, low earnings and lack of social security, thereby making them vulnerable to income fluctuations and exploitation by employers. Average wage earnings of regular workers vary hugely across the public, private and informal sectors and also among social groups. Moreover access to limited decent employment opportunities is limited, resulting in rising income inequality in labour market (Mamgain & Tiwari, 2017). Therefore, the employment question is not only one of quantity but also of quality that will continue to be at the core of India's quest for a decent standard of living for its poor and vulnerable population, who still constitute a vast majority of the population. As a policy intervention, it is important to make growth process to create employment opportunities in a large number to address the problem of unemployment as well as underemployment.

The challenge, therefore, is to promote both general policies and group-specific policies to create remunerative employment opportunities at a faster pace, particularly for youths who are growingly becoming impatient with the political systems incapable of generating employment opportunities for them. With the faster rise in urban population, mainly associated with migration from rural areas, in the next two decades, urban areas will have to face the challenge of employment generation at a much higher pace. Therefore, employment generation should be made central to development strategy, as it is an important pillar for achieving inclusive development. This calls for measures to increase investment in the labour-intensive sectors, especially in the industrially backward and remote areas, which include measures for easy to do business, infrastructure development, safety, good governance, and sound corporate social responsibilities and ethical practices on the part of industry.

The major challenge is to formalise the huge informal sector through scaling up its technology, production, productivity and employment. The big industry can play a role of facilitator to graduate micro units into small, medium and large in a steady fashion, thereby creating a proactive path of industrial development in the country. The growing profit margins of big industries enabled by capital-intensive production processes, intensive marketing but disproportionate rewards to labour may not lead to healthy relations between capital and labour for a long time. The strategy should be to redistribute the benefits of growth by the industry through creating more jobs with social security to workers. This will accelerate effective demand for the goods and services, and create a virtuous cycle.

For group-specific policy for employment promotion, it is important to intensify policy initiatives to promote enterprise development, particularly among SCs/STs/Muslims in a big way under the current 'Make in India' programme. This would require more intensive implementation of 'mentorship programmes for SC/ST entrepreneurs' as promised under AAP by the private sector in 2006. The Public Procurement Policy of 2012 needs to be operationalised in a big way by affectively allocating and using the funds under SCSP and TSP along with access to general funds. So far, the experience of effective allocation of resources under SCSP and TSP is far less than satisfactory, and there are evidences of how these funds are diverted to other uses, not benefitting SCs/STs (NCDHR, 2016).

Public policy should aim at extending credit points similar to carbon points to the private sector for improving the diversity of their workforce by employing persons from SC/ST/Muslim communities, particularly at the supervisory and managerial-level regular positions. These credits can be used for tax and other kinds of exemptions by the government. However, this would require monitoring of workforce which the private industry may like to avoid.

Another major challenge is to improve the educational development of youths. An alarming aspect is the increasing deficit of quality education and skill training. The deterioration in the quality of public educational institutions at primary, secondary and higher educational levels have most adversely affected the SCs/STs who are most dependent on these institutions. The major challenge is to improve access to quality education to all and to SCs/STs in particular. Thus, public educational institutions, at both the school and higher levels need to be strengthened and made accountable for their quality and relevance. Private educational and training institutions also need to be monitored closely for the quality of teaching they offer, and their fee structures. The current measures of skill development under the National Skill Development Mission (NSDM) need to be pegged up in a big way in order to address the skill shortages being faced by the Indian industry. Equally important would be to undertake a critical assessment of skill development under NSDM in promoting employability and income of beneficiaries. There is a scanty literature on this issue to draw any meaningful policy lessons.

We must not forget that unlike in the past, today's youths including SCs are more informed and keen to be a part of the IT revolution. They are justifiably asserting their concerns for a decent and dignified life. Politicians and policymakers must, therefore, come forward in a big way to facilitate the overall development of youths in the country and to ensure decent employment opportunities for them.

Access to job information through free electronic portals is the need of the time when employers are competing to get quality human resources and job seekers do not have free access to job information in the labour market. The larger pool of information both to job seekers and employers would help in better job matching and reduction in the costs of job search and job hiring. This would require strengthening NCS of Government of India in its new form.

AAP aimed at promoting employment of SCs/STs could hardly make any impact towards improving the employment opportunities for SCs/STs due to its own limits. This again shows the general apathy towards promoting employability and employment opportunities for marginalised groups. Thus, the major challenge is how to persuade the private sector to promote social diversity in their employment. Since promised affirmative measures are still a far distant goal to become a reality, there have been suggestions for the use of 'carrot' instead of 'stick' to promote diversity. Since an overwhelming majority of private enterprises are benefitted from the government support in the form of various promotional measures such as land at concessional rates, export subsidies, contract from public companies, tax benefits and concessional finance, these enterprises can be made accountable for not adhering to the specified diversity index, otherwise such incentives will be reduced. In fact, the private sector should come forward in a big way in improving employment, employability, entrepreneurship, and education of women and marginalised groups for reducing social and economic inequalities to a significant extent. The larger questions and myths about positive discrimination policies creating inefficiency in the economic system can only be nullified with intensive sensitisation programmes by private as well as public sector enterprises for their middle and senior-level employees on the issues of social diversity and inclusionary policies. Part of the problem lies with the HR systems of the companies which are often less trained in understanding the utility and promoting social diversities, particularly in the Indian context where there exist a long history of exclusion and discrimination-led inequality. As a result, they tend to become 'diversity neutral' and become over concerned about meritocracy, productivity and organisational development. Many of the western MNCs have well-defined policies of promoting social diversities in their workplaces, but such efforts are yet to become reality in most of the private sector in India.

Last but not least, employment expansion should be undertaken under the 'decent work' framework, ensuring fair and equal opportunities to everyone, increased productivity of workers, better working conditions, fair wages, skill development and social security. This also calls for building a sound moral responsibility environment along with usual business environment by employers as well as workers to leap into the next stage of inclusive development. Equally important would be to strengthen the database at the disaggregated level for group-specific planning, monitoring and quality control.

Annexure 8A

Table 8A.1 *Recent Experiences of Selection Process/Interview by Job Seekers (%)*

Variable	STs	SCs	OBCs	OCs	Total	No. of Persons
Faced interview (No.)	53	523	440	646	1662	1,662
Difficulty faced with the medium of written test/Interview	14.6	18.5	28.1	14.4	19.4	1,272
Difficulty in answering subject-related questions	6.1	10.1	16.3	16.5	14.2	1,272
Difficulty in answering job-related questions	3.6	12.0	13.4	11.0	11.7	1,711
Unnecessarily asked number of questions about family background and less on subject knowledge	21.8	15.7	20.2	13.7	16.3	1,769
Intimidating questions were asked about my caste/Religion/ Belief which have no relation with the job	12.7	10.5	13.3	5.0	9.2	1,792
Ridiculed for my knowledge and training	7.3	9.1	11.2	5.9	8.4	1,791
Demeaning language used by interviewer(s)	5.5	8.2	11.2	3.2	7.0	1,791
Referral is very important to get job apart from knowledge and experience	64.5	80.8	72.4	59.6	70.0	1,789
Got selected	52.7	58.1	68.8	70.5	66.5	1,787
Got selected but was offered less salary than the mentioned	22.7	41.3	39.4	31.6	35.9	1,188

Source: Primary field survey (2014–2015).

References

Abraham, V. (2007). Growth and inequality of wages in India: Recent trends and patterns. *The Indian Journal of Labour Economics, 50*(4), 927–941.

———. (2012). Wages and earnings of marginalised social and religious group in India. *MPRA*. Retrieved from http://mpra.ub.uni-muenchen.de/37799

Acharya, R., & Marjit, S. (2000). Globalisation and inequality: An analytical perspective. *Economic & Political Weekly, 35*(39), 3503–3510.

Acharya. S., & Jose, A. V. (1991). *Employment and mobility: A study among workers of low-income households in Bombay City* (ILO-ARTEP Working Paper 252), New Delhi: ILO-ARTEP.

Aedo, C., Hentschel, J., Luque, J., & Moreno, M. (2013, June). *From occupations to embedded skills: A cross-country comparison* (Background Paper for the *World Development Report* 2013). The World Bank, Washington DC.

Agarwala, R. (2013). *Informal labour, formal politics and dignified discontent in India*. Cambridge: Cambridge University Press.

Akerl of, G. (1976, November). The economics of caste and of rat race and other woeful tales. *The Quarterly Journal of Economics, 90*(4), pp. 599–617.

———. (1980). A theory of social custom, of which unemployment may be one consequence. *The Quarterly Journal of Economics, 94*(4), 749–775.

———. (1984). *An economic theorist's book of tales*. Cambridge: Cambridge University Press.

Akerlof, G., & Kranton, R. E. (2010). *Identity economics: How our identities shape our work, wages and well-being*. Princeton, NJ: Princeton University Press.

Ambedkar, B. R. (1936). *Annihilation of caste*. Jalandhar: Bheema Patrika Publications (reprint).

———. (1987a). Philosophy of Hinduism. In V. Moon (Ed.), *Dr. Babasaheb Ambedkar: Writings and speeches* (vol. 3, pp. 1–94). Bombay: Education Department, Government of Maharashtra.

———. (1987b). The Hindu social order: Its essential features. In V. Moon (Ed.), *Dr. Babasaheb Ambedkar: Writings and speeches* (vol. 3, pp. 96–115). Bombay: Education Department, Government of Maharashtra.

Anderson, T., Haahr, H. J., Hansen, M. E., & Holm-Pedersen, M. (2008, April). *Job mobility in the European Union: Optimising its social and economic benefits*. Final report for the European Commission, DG for Employment, Social Affairs and Equal Opportunities, Danish Technological Institute.

Arrow, K. (1972). Models of job discrimination. In A. H. Pascall (Ed.), *Racial discrimination in economic life*. Lexington, MA: DC Heath Publishers.

Atkinson, A. B. (2015). *Inequality—what needs to be done?* Cambridge, MA: Harvard University Press.

Azam, M. (2012). Changes in wage structure in urban India, 1983–2004: A quantile regression decomposition. *World Development*, *40*(6), 1135–1150.

Banerjee, A., Bertrand, M., Datta, S., & Mullianathan, Sl. (2009). Labour market discrimination in Delhi: Evidence from a field experiment. *Journal of Comparative Economics*, *37*(1), 14–27.

Banerjee, A., & Munshi, K. (2004). How efficiently is capital allocated? Evidence from the knitted garment industry in Tirupur. *Review of Economic Studies*, *71*(1), 19–42.

Banerjee, B. (1983). Social networks in the migration process: Empirical evidence on chain migration in India. *The Journal of Developing Areas*, *17*(2), 185–196.

———. (1984). Information flow, expectations and job search: Rural-to-urban migration process in India. *Journal of Development Economics*, *15*(1–3).

Banerjee, B., & Knight, J. B. (1985). Caste discrimination in the Indian urban labour market. *Journal of Development Economics*, *17*(3), 277–307.

Bardhan, P. (1989). The new institutional economics and development theory: A brief critical analysis. *World Development*, *17*(9), 1389–1395.

Barnes, T. (2014). *Informal labour in urban India—three cities, three journeys*. London: Routledge.

Becker. G. S. (1957). *The economics of discrimination* (1st ed.). Chicago, IL: University of Chicago Press.

Becker. G. S. (1971). *The economics of discrimination* (2nd ed.). Chicago: University of Chicago Press.

Behrenz, L. (2001). Who gets the job and why? An explorative study of employers recruitment behaviour. *Journal of Applied Economics*, *4*(2), 255–275.

Bergmann, Barbara R. (1971). The effect on white incomes of discrimination on employment. *Journal of Political Economy*, *79*(2), 294–313.

Bertrand, M., Chugh, D. & Mullainathan, S. (2005). Implicit discrimination. *The American Economic Review*, *95*(2). Retrieved from: http://links.jstor.org/sici?sici=0002-8282%28200505%2995%3A2%3C94%3AID%3E2.0.CO%3B2-B

Bertrand, M. & Mullainathan, S. (2004). Are Emily and Greg more employable than Lakisha and Jamal? A field experiment on labor market discrimination. *The American Review*, *94*(4), 991–1013.

Bhalla, A., & Lapeyere, F. (1997). Social exclusion: Towards an analytical and operational framework. *Development and Change*, *28*(2), 413–434.

Bhardwaj, K. (1974). Notes on farm size and productivity. *Economic & Political Weekly*, *9*(13), A11–A24.

Bhattacharjee, Shampa; Hnatkovska, Viktoria and Lahiri, Amartya (2015). The Evolution of Gender Gaps in India, *India Policy Forum 2014–15,* Vol. 11, Brookings Institution and National Council of Applied Economic Research, New Delhi, SAGE publications.

———. (1994). *Accumulation, exchange and development.* New Delhi: SAGE Publications.

Bian, Y. (1997). Bringing strong ties back in: Indirect ties, network bridges and job searches in China. *American Social Review, 62*(3), 366–385.

Birdsall, N., & Sabot, R. (1991). *Unfair advantage: Labour market discrimination in developing countries.* Washington, DC: The World Bank.

Blau, D. M., & Philip, K. R. (1990). Job search outcomes for the employed and unemployed. *The Journal of Political Economy, 98*(3), 637–655.

Blau, F. D., & Hendricks, W. E. (1979). Occupational segregation by sex: Trends and prospects. *The Journal of Human Resources, 14*(2), 197–210.

Blinder, A. S. (1973). Wage discrimination: Reduced form and structural estimates. *The Journal of Human Resources, 8*(4), 436–455.

Borooah V., Sadana N., & Naik, A. (2013). *Caste, employment, and wages in India: How do employees from different social groups fare in India's labour market?* (IIDS Working Paper Series, vol. 7, no. 4). New Delhi: Indian Institute of Dalit Studies.

Breman, J. (2010). *Outcast labour in India: Circulation and informalisation of the workforce at the bottom of the economy.* New Delhi: Oxford University Press.

———. (2013). *At work in the informal economy of India: A perspective from the bottom up.* New Delhi: Oxford University Press.

Breman, J. C. (1996). *Footloose workers.* New Delhi: Oxford University Press.

Brewer, R. M., Conrad, C. A., & King, M. C. (2002). The complexities and potential of theorizing gender, caste, race, and class. *Feminist Economics, 8*(2), 3–18.

Brown, R. S., Moon, M., & Zoloth, B. S. (1980). Incorporating occupational attainment in studies of male/female earnings differentials. *The Journal of Human Resources, 15*(1), 3–28.

Budhwar, P., Debi, S., & Bhatnagar, J. (2005). Women in management in the new economic environment: The case of India. *Asia Pacific Business Review, 11*(2), 179–193.

Cain, J. S., Hasan, R., Magsombol R., & Tandon, A. (2010, March). Accounting for inequality in India: Evidence from household expenditures. *World Development, 38*(3), 282–297.

Campbell, D., & Ahmed, I. (2012, September). *The labour market in developing countries.* Bonn: IZA Institute of Labour Economics.

Carsten, B., Kumar, S., Wagner, P. D., Kroll, M., Kantakumar, L. N., Bharucha, E., … & Kraas, F. (2017). Growing 'smart'? Urbanization processes in the

Pune urban agglomeration. *Sustainability*, *9*, 2335. doi:10.3390/su9122335. Retrieved from http://www.mdpi.com/2071-1050/9/12/2335/pdf

Castilla, E. J., & Benard, S. (2010). The paradox of meritocracy in organisations. *Administrative Science Quarterly*, *55*(4), 543–576.

Census of India. (2011). *District Census Handbook*, Coimbatore, Tamil Nadu.

Chakravarty, S., & Mukherjee, S. (2014). Gender wage gap in the Indian labour market: Evidence from the NSS 66th round data. *The Indian Journal of Labour Economics*, *57*(2), 259–280.

Chakravarty, S., & Somanathan, E. (2008). Discrimination in an elite labour market? Job placements at IIM-Ahmedabad. *Economic & Political Weekly*, *43*(44), 45–50.

Chandra, A., Khanijo M. K., & Mamgain R. P. (2006). *National Employment Service: Perspectives on development*. New Delhi: International Labour Organization.

Chari, S. (2000). The agrarian origins of the knitwear industrial cluster in Tirupur, India. *World Development*, *28*(3), 579–599.

Chatterjee, U., Murgai, R., & Rama, M. (2015). *Job opportunities along the rural urban gradation and female labour force participation for women in India* (Policy Research Working Paper No. 7412). Washington, DC: The World Bank.

CII. (2007). *Affirmative action: Empowering society for a brighter tomorrow*. Author. Retrieved from http://cii.in/WebCMS/Upload/report-affirmative-action.pdf

CII. (2011). Caste census of India Inc.'s Human Resources, Confederation of Indian Industries, New Delhi (reported in The Financial Express by P. Viadyanathan Iyer, 20 January 2011).

Cotton, J. (1988). On the decomposition of wage differentials. *The Review of Economics and Statistics*, *70*(2), 236–243.

Cox, T. (1994). *Cultural diversity in organizations*. San Francisco: Berrett-Koehler Publishers.

Cramer, C. (2010, 16 November). *Unemployment and participation in violence* (*World Development Report 2011* Background Paper). London: School of Oriental and African Studies.

Dandekar, H. C., & Sawant, S. B. (1998). Housing needs in new suburbs of Indian metropolli: Case study of Kothrud, Pune. *Economic & Political Weekly*, *33*(46), 2919–2928.

Darrity, W. (1975). Economic theory and racial inequality. *Review of Black Political Economy*, *5*(3), 225–248 (Republished in Darrity, W., Jr. (Ed.). (1995). *Economics and discrimination*: *Volume I*. Aldershot: Edward Elgar Publishing).

Dasgupta, B., & Laishley, R. (1975). Migration from villages. *Economic & Political Weekly*, *10*(42), pp. 1652–1662.

Debroy, B., & Bhandari, L. (2009). *Gurgaon and Faridabad—An exercise in contrast* (CDDRL Working Papers No. 101). Stanford, CA: Center on Democracy, Development and the Rule of Law Freeman Spogli Institute for International Studies.

Deshpande, A. (2010). *The grammar of caste: Economic discrimination in contemporary India*. New Delhi: Oxford University Press.

Deshpande, A., & Weisskopf, T. E. (2014). Does affirmative action reduce productivity? A case study of the Indian Railways. *World Development, 64*, 169–180.

Deshpande, L. K. (1979). *The Bombay labour market*. Bombay: Department of Economics, University of Bombay.

Deshpande, L. K., & Deshpande, S. (1990). *Labour mobility in Bombay's manufacturing sector* (ILO-ARTEP Working Paper). New Delhi: ARTEP.

Deshpande, L. K. et al. (2001). *Labour flexibility in India*. New Delhi: Institute for Human Development.

Desi, A. S. (1998). Caste, class synergies and discrimination in India. *International Journal of Social Economics, 25*(6/7/8), 1030–1048.

Dhillon, A., Iversen, V., & Torsvik, G. (2013, June). Employee referral, social proximity and worker discipline: Theory and evidence from India (CESIFO Working Paper No. 4309, Category 4: Labour Markets). Bangalore: Centre for Economic Studies and Info Institute.

Diddee, J., & Gupta, S. (2003). *Pune: Queen of the Deccan*. Pune: Elephant Design.

Dobbin, F., Kalev, A., & Kelly, E. (2007). Diversity management in corporate America. *Contexts, 6*(4), 21–28.

Doeringer, P. B., & Piore, M. J. (1971). *Internal labor markets and manpower analysis*. London: M.E. Sharpe.

Dupont, V. (2000). Spatial and Demographie Growth of Delhi since 1947 and the Main Migration Flows. In Véronique Dupont, Emma Tarlo, Denis Vidal (Eds.), *Delhi: Urban Space and Human Destinies* (Eds. Véronique Dupont, Emma Tarlo, Denis Vidal). New Delhi: Manohar Publications.

Duraisamy, P., & Duraisamy, M. (2016). Social identity and wage discrimination in the Indian Labour Market. *Economic & Political Weekly, 70*(4), pp. 51–60.

Duraisamy, P., & Narasimhan, S. (1997). Wage differentials between migrants and non-migrants and discrimination in urban informal sector in India. *The Indian Journal of Labour Economics, 40*(2), 223–235.

Dutta, P. (2005, April–June). Accounting for wage inequality in India. *The Indian Journal of Labour Economics, 48*(2).

Ernst & Young. (2012). *Human resources solutions industry—stepping into next decade of growth*. New Delhi: Author.

Faberman, J., & Marianna, K. (2016, January). What does online job search tell us about the labour market? *Economic Perspectives, 40*(1), 1–15.

Fernandez, R. M., & Weinberg, N. (1997). Sifting and sorting: Personal contacts and hiring in retail banks. *American Sociological Review, 62*, 883–902.

FICCI. (2010). *The skill development landscape in India and implementing quality skills training*. New Delhi: Federation of Indian Chambers of Commerce and Industry.

Fields, G. S. (2011). Labor market analysis for developing countries. *Journal of Labour Economics*, *18*(S1), S16–S22.

Gang, I. N., Sen, K., & Yun, M. S. (2002). *Caste, ethnicity and poverty in rural India* (IZA Discussion Paper No. 629). Bonn: IZA Institute of Labor Economics.

———. (2012). *Is caste destiny? Occupational diversification among Dalits in India* (IZA DP No. 6295, Discussion Paper Series). Bonn: Institute for the Study of Labor.

Ghosh, J. (2017). Who works in India? The implications of defining work in the Indian statistical system. In K. P. Kannan, R. P. Mamgain, & P. Rustagi (Eds.), *Labour and development: Essays in honour of Prof. T. S. Papola*. New Delhi: Academic Foundation.

Gille, V. (2013). How to get a job in the public sector? The role of local politics and caste networks in affirmative action programs in India.

Gilles, M. (2006). Migration and wages for new entrants on labour market, *Revue d'économie politique*, *116*(5), 657–681.

GoI. (2006). *Social, economic and educational status of Muslim community of India*. New Delhi: Ministry of Minority Affairs.

GoI-Cabinet Secretariat. (2006). *Social, Economic and Educational Status of the Muslim Community of India—A Report* (Chairperson: Justice Rajindar Sachar), New Delhi.

GoI-Ministry of Minority Affairs. (2014). *Report of Post Sachar Evaluation Committee* (Chairperson: Amitabh Kundu), Government of India, New Delhi.

Goldar, B. N., & Suresh, R. (2017). Contract labour in organised manufacturing in India. In K. P. Kannan, R. P. Mamgain, & P. Rustagi (Eds.), *Labour and development: Essays in honour of Prof. T. S. Papola*. New Delhi: Academic Foundation.

GoUP-DES. (2016). *Lucknow Statistical Diary 2015*, Government of Uttar Pradesh, Directorate of Economics and Statistics, Lucknow.

Government of India-Ministry of Minority Affairs. (2014). *Report of post-Sachar Evaluation Committee*. New Delhi: Ministry of Minority Affairs (Chair: Amitabh Kundu).

Government of India-NCEUS. (2009, April). *The challenge of employment in India: An informal economy perspective* (Vols. I–II). New Delhi: NCEUS, Ministry of Micro, Small and Medium Enterprises.

Granovetter, M. (1974). *Getting a job: A study of contacts and careers*. Cambridge, MA: Harvard University Press.

———. (1995). *Getting a job: A study of contacts and careers*. Chicago, IL: University of Chicago Press.

Gunderson, M. (1989). Male–female wage differentials and policy responses. *Journal of Economic Literature*, *27*(1), 46–117.

Gupta, A., Koshal, M., & Koshal, R. J. (1998). Women managers in India: Challenges and opportunities. *Equal Opportunities International*, *17*(8), 14–18.

Gupte, L. (2003, 9 March). She likes to be on top. *The Times of India*, New Delhi edition, 10.

Haefner, J. E. (1977). Sources of discrimination among employees: A survey investigation. *Journal of Applied Psychology* (3), 265–270.

Harris, J., Kannan, K. P., & Rodgers, G. (1990). Urban labour market structure and job access in India: A study of Coimbatore (Research Series 92). Thiruvananthapuram and Geneva: Centre for Development Studies and International Institute for Labour Studies.

Harris, J. R., & Sabot, R. H. (1982). Urban unemployment LDCs: Towards a more general search model. In R. H. Sabot (Ed.), *Migration and the labour market in developing countries*. Boulder, CO: Westview Press.

Hart, K. (1973). Informal income opportunities and urban employment in Ghana. *The Journal of Modern African Studies*, *11*(1), 61–89.

Heyer, J., & Jayal, N. G. (2009). *The challenge of positive discrimination in India* (CRISE Working Paper No. 55). Centre for Research on Inequality, Human Security and Ethnicity, University of Oxford, Oxford, UK.

Hirway, I. (2014, December). *Unpaid work and the economy: Linkages and their implications*. Presidential Address at the 56th Annual Conference of the Indian Society of Labour Economics, Ranchi.

Hnatkovska, V., Lahiri, A., & Paul, S. B. (2012). Castes and labour mobility. *American Economic Journal: Applied Economics*, *4*(2), 274–307.

Holmström, M. (1984). *Industry and inequality—the social anthropology of Indian labour*. Cambridge: Cambridge University Press.

Holzer, H. J. (1987). Job search by employed and unemployed youth. *Industrial and Labor Relations Review*, *40*(4), 601–611.

IHD (Institute for Human Development) & ISLE (Indian Society of Labour Economics). (2014). *India: Labour and employment report 2014—workers in the era of globalisation*. New Delhi: Academic Foundation.

ILO. (2014). *World of work report 2014—developing with jobs*. Geneva: International Labour Organisation.

ILO. (2018). *India wage report—wage policies for decent work and inclusive growth*. New Delhi: International Labour Organization Decent Work Team for South Asia and Country Office for India.

Institute for Human Development (IHD). (2013). *Delhi Human Development Report: Improving Lives, Promoting Inclusion*. New Delhi: Academic Foundation.

Ito, T. (2009). Caste discrimination and transaction costs in the labour market: Evidence from rural north India. *Journal of Development Economics*, *88*(2), 292–300.

Iversen, V., & Raghavendra, P. S. (2006). What the signboard hides? Food, caste and employability in small south Indian eating places. *Contributions to Indian Sociology*, *40*(3), pp. 311–341.

Iversen, V., Sen, K., Verschoor, A., & Dubey, A. (2009). Job recruitment networks and migration to cities in India. *The Journal of Development Studies, 45*(4), 522–543.

Jefferys, M., & Moss, W. (1954). *Mobility in the labour market-employment changes in Battersea and Dagenham.* Oxon: Routledge.

Jeffrey, C., Jeffery, R., & Jeffery, P. (2004). Degrees without freedom: The impact of formal education on Dalit young men in north India. *Development and Change, 35*(5), 963.

Jodhka, S., & Newman, K. S. (2010). In the name of globalisation: Meritocracy, productivity and hidden language of caste. In S. Thorat & K. Newman (Eds.), *Blocked by caste: Economic discrimination in modern India* (pp. 52–87). New Delhi: Oxford University Press.

Kannan, K. P. (2012). How inclusive is inclusive growth in India? *The Indian Journal of Labour Economics, 55*(1).

———. (2014). *Interrogating inclusive growth: Poverty and inequality in India.* New Delhi: Routledge.

Kannappan, S. (1977). *Studies of urban labor market behavior in developing areas.* Geneva: International Institute of Labor Studies.

———. (1985). Urban employment and the labor market in developing nations. *Economic Development and Cultural Change, 33*(4), 699–730.

Kapur, D., Prasad, C. B., Pritchett, L., & Shyam, B. (2010, 28 August). Rethinking inequality: Dalits in Uttar Pradesh in the market reform era. *Economic & Political Weekly, 45*(35), 39–49.

Karan, A. K., & Sakthivel, S. (2008). *Trends in wages and earnings in India: Increasing wage differentials in a segmented labour market.* New Delhi: ILO Sub-regional Office for South Asia.

Kelly, E., & Dobbin, F. (1998). How affirmative action became diversity management. *American Behavioral Scientist, 41*(7), 960–984.

Khandelwal, P. (2002, April–June). Gender stereotypes at work: Implications for organizations. *Indian Journal of Training and Development, 32*(2), 72–83.

Khandker, S. R. (1992). *Earnings, occupational choice, and mobility in segmented labor markets in India* (World Bank Discussion Papers No. 154, pp. 44). Washington, DC: World Bank.

Konrad, A., Prasad, P., & Pringle, J. (Eds.). (2006). *Handbook of workplace diversity.* Thousand Oaks, CA: SAGE Publications.

Kundu, S. C. (2004). HR diversity: A study of employees' perceptions in Indian organizations. *Asia Pacific Management Review, 9*(1), 39–59.

Lal, D. (1984). *Hindu equilibrium: Cultural stability and economic stagnation* (vol. I). Oxford: Clarendon Press.

Lambert, R. D. (1963). *Workers, factories, and social change in India.* Princeton, NJ: Princeton University Press.

Lewis, A. (1954). Economic development with unlimited supplies of labour. *The Manchester School of Economic and Social Studies, 22*(2), 139–191.

Lucas, R. E. B. (2015). Internal migration in developing economies: An overview (KNOMOD Working Paper No. 6). Global Knowledge Partnership on Migration and Development, Washington DC.

Machado, J. A. F., & Mata, J. (2005). Counterfactual decomposition of changes in wage distributions using quantile regression. *Journal of Applied Econometrics, 20*(4), 445–465.

Madheswaran, S. (2017). Is affirmative action policy for private sector necessary? In K. P. Kannan, R. P. Mamgain, & P. Rustagi (Eds.), *Labour and development: Essays in honour of Prof. T. S. Papola*. New Delhi: Academic Foundation.

Madheswaran, S., & Attewell, P. (2007). Caste discrimination in the Indian urban labour market: Evidence from the National Sample Survey. *Economic & Political Weekly, 42*(41), 4146–4153.

————. (2010). Wage and job discrimination in Indian urban labour market. In S. Thorat & K. Newman (Eds.), *Blocked by caste: Economic discrimination in modern India*. New Delhi: Oxford University Press.

Ma Foi Randstad. (2011). *Ma Foi Randstad work monitor 2011*. Chennai: Author.

Mamgain, R. P. (2004). *Employment, migration and livelihoods in the hill economy of Uttaranchal* (PhD Thesis). Centre for the Study of Regional Development, Jawaharlal Nehru University, New Delhi.

————. (2017). Occupational diversification in India: Trends and determinants. In K. P. Kannan, R. P. Mamgain, & P. Rustagi (Eds.), *Labour and development: Essays in honour of Prof. T. S. Papola*. New Delhi: Academic Foundation.

————. (2018). New forms of recruitment processes and discrimination in urban labour market in India. *Journal of Social Inclusion Studies, 4*(1), 131–150.

Mamgain, R. P., & Tiwari, S. (2016). Youth in India: Challenges of employment and inclusion. *Journal of Social and Economic Development, 18*(1), 85–100. Springer.

————. (2017, September). Regular salaried employment opportunities in India: Nature, access and inclusiveness. *The Indian Journal of Labour Economics, 60*(3), 415–436.

Mani, Vijay (2011). The effectiveness of employee referral as a recruitment, *International Journal of Management Sciences and Business Research, 1*(11), 11–25.

Marsden P., & Gorman, E. H. (2001). Social networks, job changes and recruitment. In I. Berg & A. L. Kalleberg (Eds.), *Sourcebook of labour markets: Evolving structure and processes* (pp. 467–502). New York, NY: Kluwer Academic Publishers.

Mason, P. (1999). Male interracial wage differentials: Competing explanations. *Cambridge Journal of Economics, 23*(3), 261–299.

Mathur, A., & Mamgain, R. P. (2004). Human capital stocks, their level of utilisation and economic development in India. *The Indian Journal of Labour Economics, 47*(4).

Mazumdar, D. (1983). Segmented labor markets in LDCs. American Economic Review, 73(2), 254–259. (Reprinted in World Bank Reprint Series No. 267).

McKinsey Global Institute. (2010). *India's urban awakening: Building inclusive cities, sustaining economic growth*. McKinsey & Co. Retrieved from https://www.mckinsey.com/~/media/McKinsey/Featured%20Insights/Urbanization/Urban%20awakening%20in%20India/MGI_Indias_urban_awakening_full_report.ashx

McNabb, R., & Ryan, P. (1990). Segmented labour markets. In D. Sapsford & Z. Tzannatos (Eds.), *Current issues in labour economics*. Basingstoke: MacMillan.

Melly, B. (2006). *Estimation of counterfactual distributions using quantile regression* (mimeo). St Gallen: Swiss Institute for International Economics and Applied Economic Research (SIAW), University of St Gallen.

Mincer, J. (1974). *Schooling, experience, and earnings*. New York, NY: Columbia University Press.

Mitra, A. (2006). Labour market mobility of low income households. *Economic & Political Weekly, 41*(21), 2123–2130.

MoLE. (2017). *National career service, Ministry of Labour and Employment*. New Delhi: Government of India.

Montgomery, J. D. (1991). Social networks and labor market outcomes: Toward an economic analysis. *American Economic Review, 81*(5), 1408–1418.

Mortensen, D. (1986). Job search and labour market analysis. Elsevier.

Munshi, K. (2003). Networks in the modern economy: Mexican migrants in the US labour market. *The Quarterly Journal of Economics, 118*(2), 549–599.

Munshi, K., & Rosenzweig, M. R. (2005, July). Economic development and the decline of rural and urban community-based networks. *The Economics of Transition, 13*(3), 427–443.

———. (2006). Traditional institutions meet the modern world: Caste, gender and schooling choice in a globalizing economy. *American Economic Review, 96*(4), 1225–1252.

Murti, Ashutosh B. & Bino Paul G. D. (2016). Efficacy of social-network and firm's recruitment behaviour", *Indian Labour Journal*. Ministry of Labour and Employment, Government of India, January 2016, 57(1), 3–18.

Nanfosso, Roger T. & Christian, Zamo-Akono. (2009). Migration and wages differentials in urban Cameroon, *Research in Applied Economics, 1*(1) E1, 1–20, DOI: 10.5296/rae.v1i1.139

Narayana, D. (1985, November). *A note on occupational mobility, caste and job reservation* (pp. 15). Thiruvananthapuram: Centre for Development Studies.

NASSCOM. (2014). *Analysis of talent supply and demand employment requirements and skill gaps in the Indian IT-BPM Industry*. New Delhi: NASSCOM.

NCDHR. (2016). *Pre-Budget memorandum 2016–17*. New Delhi: National Campaign on Dalit Human Rights.

NCEUS (National Commission for Enterprises in the Unorganised Sector). (2007). *Report on conditions of work and promotion of livelihoods in the unorganised sector*. New Delhi: National Commission for Enterprises in the Unorganised Sector, Government of India.

————. (2009). *The challenge of employment in India: An informal economy perspective*. New Delhi: Academic Foundation.

Neumark, D. (1988). Employer's discriminatory behaviour and the estimation of wage discrimination. *The Journal of Human Resources, 23*(3), 279–295.

O'Connor, L. T. (2013). Ask and you shall receive: Social network contacts' provision of help during the job search. *Social Networks, 35*(4), 593–603.

Oaxaca, R. L. (1973). Male–female wage differentials in urban labour market. *International Economic Review, 14*(3), 693–709.

Oaxaca, R. L., & Ransom, M. R. (1994). On discrimination and the decomposition of wage differentials. *Journal of Econometrics, 61*(1), 5–21.

Oberai, A. S. (1987). *Migration, urbanisation and development*. New Delhi: ILO.

OECD. (2007). *Labour Markets in the BRICS (Brazil, Russia, India, China and South Africa)* (Working Paper on Employment, No. *DELSA/ELSA/WP 5*). Paris: Author.

Olson, C. A., & Becker, B. E. (1983). Sex discrimination in the promotion process. *Industrial and Labour Relations Review, 36*(4), 624–641.

Ostry, J. D., Loungani, P., & Furceri, D. (2016). Neoliberalism oversold? *Finance & Development, 53*(2), 38–41.

Pais, J. (2006, March). *Migration and labour mobility in the leather accessories manufacture in India: A study in the light of economic reforms.* Paper presented at International Young Scholars' Seminar Papers on eSocial Sciences, p. 30.

Panini, M. N. (1996). The political economy of caste. In M. N. Srinivas (Ed.), *Caste: Its twentieth Century Avatar.* New Delhi: Viking Publishing House.

Papola, T. S. (1981). *Urban informal sector in a developing economy.* New Delhi: Vikas Publications.

————. (1982). *Women workers in an urban labour market: A study of segregation and discrimination in employment in Lucknow (India)* (mimeo). Lucknow: Giri Institute of Development Studies.

————. (2005). Social exclusion and discrimination in hiring practices: The case of Indian private sector. In S. Thorat, Aryama, & P. Negi (Eds.), *Reservation and private sector: Quest for equal opportunity and growth.* Jaipur: Rawat Publications.

————. (2012). Social exclusion and discrimination in the labour market (ISID Working Paper No. 2012/04). New Delhi: Institute for Studies in Industrial Development.

Papola, T. S., & Kannan, K. P. (2017, October). Towards an India wage report (ILO Asia-Pacific Working Paper Series). New Delhi: DWT for South Asia and Country Office for India.

Papola, T. S., & Rodgers, G. (1992). *Labour institutions and economic development in India.* Geneva: International Institute for Labour Studies.

Papola, T. S., & Sahu, P. P. (2012). *Growth and structure of employment: Long-term and post-reform performance and emerging challenges* (ISID Occasional Paper Series, 2012/1). New Delhi: Institute for Studies in Industrial Development.

Papola, T. S., & Subramanian, K. K. (1975). *Wage structure and labour mobility in a local labour market.* Mumbai: Sardar Patel Institute of Economic and Social Research and Popular Prakashan.

Phelps, E. S. (1972). The statistical theory of racism and sexism. *American Economic Review, 62*(4), 659–661.

Piketty, Thomas. (2014). *Capital in the Twenty-First Century.* Cambridge, Massachusetts London, England: The Belknap Press of Harvard University Press.

Pissarides, C. A. (1985). Short-run equilibrium dynamics of unemployment, vacancies and real wages. *American Economic Review, 75*(4), 676–690.

Portes, A. (1998). Social capital: Its origins and applications in modern sociology. *Annual Review of Sociology, 24*, 1–24.

Ramesh, B. P. (2004, 31 January). Cyber coolies in BPOs. *Economic & Political Weekly, 39*(5), 492–497.

Randhawa, N. S. (1989). *Economic development, food security and poverty—the core adjustment*, mimeo. Rome: International Fund for Agricultural Development.

Rangarajan, C., Iyer, P., & Kaul S. (2011). Where is the missing labour force? *Economic & Political Weekly, 46*(39), pp. 68–72.

Rees, A. (1966, March). Information networks in labour markets. *American Economic Review, 56*(1/2), 559–566.

Reich, M., Gordon, D. M., & Edwards, R. C. (1973). Dual labour markets: A theory of labour market segmentation. *American Economic Review, 63*(2), 369–365.

Reimer, C. W. (1983). Labour market discrimination against Hispanic and Black men. *The Review of Economics and Statistics, 65*(4), 570–579.

———. (1985). A comparative analysis of the wages of Hispanic, Blacks and Non-Hispanic Whites. In G.J. Borjas and M. Tienda (Eds.), *Hispanics in the U.S. Economy*, New York: Academic Press.

Rodgers, G. (1986, May). Labour markets, labour processes and economic development. *Journal of Labor and Society, 11*(2).

Rodgers, G. (1993). The creation of employment in segmented labour markets: A general problem and its applications in India (Discussion Paper No. 54). Geneva: International Institute for Labour Studies.

Rudra, A. (1967). *Relative Rates of Growth: Agriculture and Industry.* Bombay: University of Bombay.

Rustagi, P. (2005). Understanding gender inequalities in wages and income in India. *The Indian Journal of Labour Economics, 48*(2), 319–334.

Rustagi, P. (2017). Gender dimensions of work and employment in India. In K. P. Kannan, R. P. Mamgain & Preet Rustagi (Eds.), *Labour and development: essays in honour of Prof. T.S. Papola.* New Delhi: Academic Foundation.

Ruwanpura, K. N. (2005). *Exploring the links of multi-discrimination: Considering Britain and India* (Discussion Paper DP/157/2005). Geneva: International Institute for Labour Studies.

Sabharwal, N. S., Thorat, S., Balasubrahmanyam, T., & Diwakar, D. G. (2016). *Diversity, academic performance and discrimination: A case of a high education institution* (IIDS Working Paper Series, vol. 7, no. 4). New Delhi: Indian Institute of Dalit Studies.

Saini, D. (2007). Manpower diversity for business success: Some emerging perspectives. *Manpower Journal, 42*, 2.

Sarkar, S., & Mehta, B. S. (2010). Income inequality in India: Pre-and post-reform period. *Economic & Political Weekly, 45*(37), 45–55.

Scoville, J. (1991). *Towards a formal model of a caste economy in status influences in third world labour markets: Caste, gender, custom.* New York, NY: De Gruyter.

———. (1996). Labour market underpinnings of a caste economy. *The American Journal of Economics and Sociology, 55*(4), 385–394.

Sen, A. K. (2000). *Social exclusion: Concept, application and scrutiny* (Social Development Paper No.1). Manila: Asian Development Bank, Manila.

Shah, G., Mander, H., Thorat, S., Deshpande, S., & Bhaviskar, A. (2006). *Untouchability in rural India.* New Delhi: SAGE Publications.

Sharma, A. N. (2008). *Access to employment in India: The case of public and private corporate sector jobs* (mimeo). Hyderabad: Centre for Economic and Social Studies.

Siddique, Z. (2008, September). *Caste-based discrimination: Evidence and policy* (Discussion Paper No. 3737). Bonn: IZA.

Singh, R. K. (2011). Effect of economic recession on employment in India—a critical analysis. *Gurukul Business Review, 7*(Spring), 97–106.

Singhari, S., & Madheswaran, S. (2016). *Social exclusion and caste discrimination in public and private sectors in India: A decomposition analysis* (Working Paper No. 361). Bengaluru: Institute for Social and Economic Change.

Sinha, B. N. (1972). *Industrial geography of India.* Calcutta: The World Press.

Spence, M. (1973). Job market signaling. *The Quarterly Journal of Economics, 87*(3), 355–374.

Spriggs, W., & Williams, R. M. (1996, May). A Logit decomposition analysis of occupational segregation: Results for the 1970s and 1980s. *Review of Economics and Statistics, 78*(2), 348–355.

Srivastava, R. S., & Naik, A. (2017). Growth and informality in the Indian economy. In K. P. Kannan, R. P. Mamgain, & P. Rustagi (Eds.) *Labour and development: Essays in honour of Prof. T. S. Papola.* New Delhi: Academic Foundation.

Stigler, G. J. (1961). The economics of information. *Journal of Political Economy, 69*(3), 213–225.

———. (1962), Information in the labor market. *Journal of Political Economy, 70*(5), 94–105.

Stiglitz, J. (1973). Approaches to the economics of discrimination. *The American Economic Review, 63*(2), 287–295 (Republished in Darrity, W., Jr. (Ed.).

(1995). *Economics and discrimination: Volume I.* Aldershot: Edward Elgar Publishing).

Suryanarayana, M. H., & Agrawal, A. (2013). *Human development in India: Cost of inequality.* Brazilia: IPC-UNDP.

Swaminathan, P., & Jeyaranjan, J. (1999). The knitwear cluster in Tirupur: An Indian industrial district in the making? In A. K. Bagchi (Ed.), *Economy and organization: Indian institutions under the neoliberal regime.* New Delhi: SAGE Publications.

Tastle, W. J., & Wierman, M. J. (2007). Consensus and dissension: A measure of ordinal dispersion. *International Journal of Approximate Reasoning, 45*(3), 531–545. Elsevier.

Taubman, P., & Wachter, M. L. (1986). Segmented labor markets. In O. Ashenfelter & R. Layard (Eds.), *Handbook of labor economics* (vol. 2, pp. 1183–1217). Elsevier, Amsterdam.

TeamLease. (2016). *Gender diversity in the Indian workplace.* Bangalore: Author. Retrieved from https://www.teamleasegroup.com/sites/default/files/resources/Gender%20Diversity%20Report.pdf

Terborg, J. R., & Ilgen, D. R. (1975). Theoretical approach to sex discrimination in traditionally masculine occupations. *Organizational Behaviour and Human Performance, 13*(3), 352–376.

The Economic Times. (2013). Workplace biases still rampant in India: Survey. *The Economic Times.* Retrieved from https://economictimes.indiatimes.com/jobs/workplace-biases-still-rampant-in-india-survey/articleshow/21619574.cms

The Economist. (2013, 27 April). Black economic empowerment has not worked well. Nor will it end soon.

The Economic Times. (2016). Many women want to quit jobs due to gender bias, odd hours: Assocham survey. Retrieved from https://m.economictimes.com/jobs/many-women-want-to-quit-jobs-due-to-gender-bias-odd-hours-assocham-survey/articleshow/51291343.cms

The Times of India. (2015, 27 October). UK for name-blind hiring to cut bias. *The Times of India,* Lucknow edition.

The Wire (2017). Dalit women in corporate India are being left behind. Retrieved from https://thewire.in/gender/dalit-wome-corporate-india

Thorat, S. K. (2007, 9–10 August). *Economic exclusion and poverty: Indian experience of remedies against exclusion.* Paper prepared for Policy Forum on Agricultural and Rural Development for Reducing Poverty and Hunger in Asia: In Pursuit of Inclusive and Sustainable Growth, IFPRI and ADB, Manila, Philippines.

Thorat, S., Aryama, & Negi, P. (2007). *Reservation in private sector: Quest for equal opportunity and growth.* New Delhi: Rawat Publications.

Thorat, S., & Newman, K. S. (2010). *Blocked by caste: Economic discrimination in modern India.* New Delhi: Oxford University Press.

Todaro, M. P. (1971). Income expectations, rural-urban migration and employment in Africa. *International Labour Review, 104*(5), 387–414.

Uchikawa, Shuji. (2017). Caste membership, business access, and social mobility among Indian apparel manufacturers, *52*(22).

Upadhya, C. (2007). Employment, exclusion and 'merit' in the Indian IT industry. *Economic & Political Weekly, 42*(20), 1863–1868.

Verick, S., & Chaudhary, R. (2017). The participation of women in the labour force in India and beyond. In K. P. Kannan, R. P. Mamgain, & P. Rustagi (Eds.), *Labour and development: Essays in honour of Prof. T. S. Papola*. New Delhi: Academic Foundation.

Williams, R. M. (1987). Capital, competition, and discrimination: A reconsideration of racial earnings inequality. *Review of Radical Political Economics, 19*(2), 1–15 (Republished in Darrity, W., Jr. (Ed.). (1995). *Economics and discrimination: Volume I.* Aldershot: Edward Elgar Publishing Limited).

Woodard, N., & Saini, D. S. (2006). Diversity management issues in USA anwd India: Some emerging perspectives. In P. Singh, J. Bhatnagar, & A. Bhandarker (Eds.), *Future of work: Mastering change*. New Delhi: Excel Books.

World Bank. (2011). *Poverty and social exclusion in India*. Washington, DC: Author.

———. (2011). Employability and Skill Set of Newly Graduated Engineers in India, Andreas Blom and Hiroshi Saeki, Policy Research Working Paper 5640, The World Bank South Asia Region Education Team, New Delhi.

Index

About the Author

Rajendra P. Mamgain is a development economist having three decades of research experience. He has a doctoral degree in economics from Jawaharlal Nehru University, New Delhi, and he specialises in the areas of labour, employment, migration, skill development, human poverty, inclusive development and impact evaluation of government programmes. He has expertise in undertaking large field-based research in his areas of interest. With 25 research studies to his credit, he has authored/co-authored 9 books and more than 65 research papers in various national and internationals journals of repute.

At present, he is Professor at Giri Institute of Development Studies, Lucknow, India. He is an Adjunct Professor in Doon University, and a Visiting Professor to Indian Institute of Dalit Studies (IIDS). Earlier, he was the director and professor of economics with IIDS, New Delhi. He has also been a senior academic consultant at the Indian Council of Social Science Research for a brief period. He has worked as a senior fellow in the Institute for Human Development and faculty at the Institute of Applied Manpower Research, New Delhi.

He is the Editor of *Journal of Social Inclusion Studies* and Associate Editor, *Indian Economic Journal*, both being published by SAGE. As the Managing Editor of the *Indian Journal of Labour Economics* for 25 years, he has been instrumental in transforming the journal into a quality product with worldwide dissemination. He has been a consultant to various national and international organisations. He has been a member of various policy advisory bodies of reputed institutions in India and foreign countries.

His recent work on youth and the challenge of decent employment has been widely acclaimed by academia. He is actively engaged in research and policy advocacy, and has delivered more than 35 special lectures and keynote addresses in various seminars and workshops. He has also organised over 25 national and international seminars/workshops/conferences. He has travelled widely in India and abroad related to his research interests.